Roman Polanski

Roman Polanski

A Life in Exile

JULIA AIN-KRUPA

Modern Filmmakers
Vincent LoBrutto, Series Editor

PRAEGER
An Imprint of ABC-CLIO, LLC

A B C ☰ C L I O

Santa Barbara, California • Denver, Colorado • Oxford, England

Library of Congress Cataloging-in-Publication Data

Ain-Krupa, Julia.
    Roman Polanski : a life in exile / Julia Ain-Krupa.
        p. cm. — (Modern filmmakers)
    Includes filmography.
    Includes bibliographical references and index.
    ISBN 978-0-313-37780-8 (hardcopy : alk. paper) — ISBN 978-0-313-37781-5-5
(ebook)
1. Polanski, Roman. 2. Motion picture producers and directors—United States—
Biography. I. Title.
    PN1998.A3P5485 2010
    791.4302'33092—dc22   2009043870
    [B]

ISBN: 978-0-313-37780-8
EISBN: 978-0-313-37781-5

14 13 12 11 10   1 2 3 4 5

This book is also available on the World Wide Web as an eBook.
Visit www.abc-clio.com for details.

Praeger
An Imprint of ABC-CLIO, LLC

ABC-CLIO, LLC
130 Cremona Drive, P.O. Box 1911
Santa Barbara, California 93116-1911

This book is printed on acid-free paper

Manufactured in the United States of America

Copyright Acknowledgment

The author and publisher gratefully acknowledge permission to reprint excerpts
from the following source:

Roman Polanski. *Roman by Polanski*. New York: William Morrow, 1984. Copyright
© 1984 by Roman Polanski. Reprinted by permission of HarperCollins Publishers.

For Gienek

Contents

Series Foreword

The Modern Filmmakers series focuses on a diverse group of motion picture directors who collectively demonstrate how the filmmaking process has become *the* definitive art and craft of the twentieth century. As we advance into the twenty-first century, we begin to examine the impact these artists have had on this influential medium.

What is a modern filmmaker? The phrase connotes a motion picture maker who is *au courant*—they make movies currently. The choices in this series are also varied to reflect the enormous potential of the cinema. Some of the directors make action movies, some entertain, some are on the cutting edge, others are political, some make us think, some are fantasists. The motion picture directors in this collection will range from highly commercial, mega-budget blockbuster directors, to those who toil in the independent low-budget field.

Gus Van Sant, Tim Burton, Charlie Kaufman, and Terry Gilliam are here, and so are Clint Eastwood and Steven Spielberg—all for many and for various reasons, but primarily because their directing skills have transitioned from the twentieth century to the first decade of the twenty-first century. Eastwood and Spielberg worked during the sixties and seventies and have grown and matured as the medium transitioned from mechanical to digital. The younger directors here may not have experienced all of those cinematic epochs themselves, but, nonetheless, they remained concerned with the limits of filmmaking: Charlie Kaufman disintegrates personal and narrative boundaries in the course of his scripts, for example, while Tim Burton probes the limits of technology to find the most successful way of bringing his intensely visual fantasies and nightmares to life.

The Modern Filmmaker Series will celebrate modernity and postmodernism through each creator's vision, style of storytelling, and character presentation. The directors' personal beliefs and worldviews will be revealed through in-depth examinations of the art they have created, but

brief biographies will also be provided where they appear especially rele-
vant. These books are intended to open up new ways of thinking about
some of our favorite and most important artists and entertainers.

Vincent LoBrutto
Series Editor
Modern Filmmakers

Acknowledgments

I would like to thank many people for their support of this project. Vincent LoBrutto, my teacher and editor, without whom I never would have had this opportunity, and who has always been supportive and treated me with kid gloves. My dear friend Mara Hennessey, for it was through our conversations about exile that the concept for this book came together. Noa Ain, who has devoted countless hours to reviewing my work with a fine-toothed comb, and Andrew Seear and Marin Buschel, who have both been tremendously helpful in this process. Elysha Schneider, whose pure kindness, generosity, and support helped make this work possible. Olek Krupa, for his enthusiasm for this work. My early years spent in Poland and in the theater have impacted my life deeply, and I cannot write of Krakow without thinking of Olga, Franek, Krystyna, and everyone else at Teatr Stu. I cannot write of Polanski without thinking of Gienek Krupa—his wild humor, temper, imagination, and joie de vivre all echo in my appreciation of the life and films of Roman Polanski.

I would like to thank Adam Holender, who so generously shared with me his cinematographic expertise, his time and memories, and Everett Aison, who was also kind enough to tell me of his experience with Polanski. Annette Insdorf, who aside from being a wonderful professor, has guided me over the years, and Dr. David Sterritt, whose passion for film analysis is contagious. Richard Peña, for his insight into film noir and its contexts. Gene Stavis, Lukacz Jogalla, Tom Ruth, Julia Mishkin, Danusha Jarecka, and Fanny Soderback, all of whom have helped me with certain accuracies within the book. Daniel Harmon at Praeger, Peter London at Harper Collins, Ron at Photofest.

I would like to thank Dorothy Ain for her tireless support, and for considering my education to be one of her priorities in life. I would also like to acknowledge three women who have impacted my life—for my understanding of the artist's life, Leah Rhodes; for her sheer brilliance and friendship,

Elzbieta Czyzewska; and for being my loving grandmother, Elzbieta Krupa. Even though an ocean divides us, she has always been close by.

Given the solitude of writing this book, I am extremely grateful to those who helped draw me out of my bubble from time to time—in particular, Sofia, Ludmila, Tala, and Wendy. Thank you to Corinne, who saved me in a moment of panic. Finally, I would like to thank my beautiful students who over the past two years have enriched my life more than they will ever know.

Introduction

There is no lens that Polanski doesn't know. His way of seeing is both varied and profound. Drawing on his own unique experiences, he places the viewer inside a story in a way that no other filmmaker can. As his collaborator Ronald Harwood[1] has said, "He speaks five or six languages and I have always said that one of them is film."[2] He is the master jester, a chameleon who has moved from home to home and life to life, always working, always moving. Sometimes one thinks that he is running, but look from another angle and you will see that he is moving toward something. He is master of his own exile.

Polanski has been a fugitive ever since childhood. As a boy, both of his parents were taken in ghetto raids. He escaped through the ghetto wall, as he had learned to do many times before, moving from one world to the next. Traveling from one adopted family to another, he always found ways to survive, managing to retain his spirit despite tremendous upheaval and heartache. Though Polanski is small, he can fill the room with his energy, humor, and joie de vivre. This has always been the case. Fantasy was his food, his way to carry on. All he ever believed was that he would be the best.

Escaping into a world of desire and dreams, he watched films in search of who he wished to be. This celluloid provider of escape evolved into a salve for a broken heart, for here, in the theater of the imagination, everything was possible. Entranced by Carol Reed's[3] film *Odd Man Out*, the story of a wounded fugitive in search of shelter and salvation, Polanski found his idea of perfection. Under a haunting umbrella of snow falling with the sound of angels calling, Johnny, played by James Mason,[4] is transported from the care of one stranger to the next. In the process of his dying, there is always the sensation of a protective force, demonstrated in part by the woman who loves him, and who searches for him, killing herself so that they may die together. Identifying with this tale of one dark night, Polanski saw himself in the likeness of a lone figure traveling the streets in the snow, dependent on the kindness of strangers. This concept of a fugitive was one that Polanski could latch onto—a romantic figure who was tough yet gentle. There was a comfort in identifying with this idealized fugitive, and to this day, he often makes reference to the film.

Working as a director in the United States, Polanski has penetrated our concept of ourselves, and has wielded his knife to influence cinema with his outsider's eye. In fact, Polanski, along with Fritz Lang,[5] Otto Preminger,[6] Billy Wilder, and Douglas Sirk,[7] is among the "Hollywood" greats of foreign origin who have helped shape American cinema. In an interview with Antoine De Baecque and Thierry Jousse in *Cahiers du cinéma*[8] in 1992, Polanski spoke about the concept he called a "cinema of exile." He referred to Billy Wilder as a perfect example of an Eastern European filmmaker who made some of the greatest, most successful films of his time (*Double Indemnity* [1944], *Sabrina* [1954], *Some Like It Hot* [1959]), and was able to influence American cinema with his European sensibility. Polanski compares Wilder's in-film pranks to the bandage worn by Jack Nicholson in *Chinatown*. Such a device is conceived in an effort to push a character's misfortune toward a place in which meaninglessness coexists with the beauty of life, for the exile has distance and can often view character defects with great humor. These traits are evident in Wilder's films, and also in many of Polanski's, even if they remain a bit more disguised. To understand Polanski, one must comprehend that he is a man completely devoted to the magic of filmmaking.

In film, Polanski has found his voice, leading his audience down a dark, unwritten path. Together we see the truth. Together we understand things that until now have remained untold, for Polanski adds dimension to our experience. When he is at his best, his films become an investigation, an underwater excursion experienced above land. Polanski understands actors, and because he is himself a great actor, he directs by immersing himself in each part, pushing performers, yet never asking more than he would of himself. He is involved in every aspect of filmmaking, and has found satisfaction in the perfection of details. Being an artist and an exile, he has perpetually realized an imaginative life. Managing to retain a childlike curiosity, he has achieved the great feat of living on the edge of possibility.

In an interview in Paris with Charlie Rose,[9] Polanski said that he often has dreams in which he finds himself waking up in the wrong place, an example of his strong connection to his own exile. Though his exile may be deeply rooted, it is fantasy that has pushed him toward life and the art of filmmaking (the ultimate re-creation and fabrication). As a result of Polanski's exploration of fantasy and alienation, we have come to understand darkness, longing, and the great absurdity of life.

Poland: The Early Years

BOYHOOD

In 1933, Europe was suspended in the uncertainty that follows a major war. Germany had chosen to disobey many of the rules set up by the Versailles Treaty,[1] and throughout Europe power struggles ensued. As Adolf Hitler came to authority in January 1933, Benito Mussolini designed The Four Power Pact in order to rebalance power within Europe. One year later, in January 1934, Germany would sign the German-Polish Non-aggression Pact, guaranteeing 10 years free from armed conflict. In reestablishing Polish borders, the pact also softened them, thus creating an easier target. Five years later, Germany would invade Poland through its Western border.

It was in this political climate that Raymond (Roman) Polanski was born under the sign of the lion, in Paris, France, on August 18, 1933. His father, Ryszard (a Polish Jew who worked in plastics and who was an aspiring painter), had moved to France not long before (he was now Polanski, but had formerly been Liebling, another word for "darling"). He fell in love with and married a Russian Jewess named Bula Katz, who was divorced just as he, and had a daughter, Annette, from a previous marriage. Together they had Roman, making the family complete.

The first three years of Roman's life were spent in Paris. Still feeling like a stranger in his adopted hometown, Ryszard thought it best to bring his family back to Poland. It was at this same time that murmurings were beginning to surface of Germany's intentions for an Aryan-dominated Europe. Little did Ryszard know the consequences of his choice. Ryszard brought his family home to Krakow, where his mother and brothers lived, as did many of his friends. Krakow is situated in a valley, and many locals blame its dreamy sleepiness on the low air pressure associated with living between hilltops.

Krakow was a city in which Jews and Poles had lived side by side for centuries, and it was also the cultural capital of Poland. Resting along the Wistula River with numerous meandering cobblestone streets, one could never stray far without returning to the center. The entire city surrounded a beautiful medieval square with a boulevard of park space called Planty wrapped around it. There were plenty of ways to enjoy one's time there, including playing outside the sprawling Wawel Castle, or going to the gothic St. Mary's Church, where every hour on the hour one could hear a trumpeter playing the Hejnal, a traditional Polish song, trailing off midsong to commemorate a thirteenth-century trumpeter who was shot while blowing the signal of an attack.

Roman was diminutive as a child—so much so, that he was almost always mistaken for someone half his age, not coming into his own until well into his teens, when he became fixated on the idea of building up his body by lifting weights and exercising as much as possible. In fact, once he became an actor, Roman would be stuck in the role of a boy until well into his twenties. It must have been frustrating for this boy with a strong character and a vibrant sense of fantasy as well as individuality to be caught in the confines of an underdeveloped body.

Aside from being small for his age, as is recorded in his autobiography, *Roman by Polanski*, he had shoulder-length blond hair, which often caused him to be taken for a girl. Born in Paris, and given the name Raymond, a name that his parents believed to be the French version of the Polish "Roman," he was cursed in Krakow with the foreign-sounding "Remo," which was cause for mockery. He also had an accent, which made it difficult to pronounce the rolling "r" required by the Polish language. As time passed, Roman would assimilate, becoming a "normal" Polish boy, yet at such a young age he had tasted the bitterness of otherness, the aftertaste of which would return to him many times in his life. Despite these embarrassments, Roman's early childhood was mostly happy. This included holidays spent at Szczyrk, an idyllic mountain town with a scattering of perfect gingerbread houses, and days spent exploring Krakow and its movie theaters with older sister Annette, already an avid moviegoer, following his now notorious expulsion from kindergarten (he excitedly told a female classmate to "kiss his ass").

When distant murmurings of a German invasion began, Ryszard rented an apartment in Warsaw, but temporarily moved his family to his mother's home nestled in Kazimierz, the Jewish quarter of Krakow. Here they lived with Roman's grandmother, Maria, and two of his uncles, Bernard and Stefan. In his autobiography, Polanski recounts this time as strange yet interesting. Maria made a generous companion, and her kitchen was a treasure trove for Roman. One thing in particular, noted in his autobiography, was a bean growing in a glass jar. Roman watched in disbelief as it grew roots like antennae. This was an image that would crop up many years later in his film

Repulsion (1965). It was also a feeling—a fascination with something normal that transitions to become terrifying—that would remain with him.

Perhaps Roman's reaction was a portent of things to come, for daily life was becoming more and more unrecognizable. When the Germans invaded, Ryszard, concerned for his family's safety, thought it best to move them to Warsaw, which was further from the German border. How could Ryszard have known that he was sending them directly into the heart of the war? A torrent of bombs ensued, and Roman began to witness many horrors. Nights were spent in a basement bomb shelter, and days searching for food. Though there were still moments of childish fun to be had (ruins made great tunnels for games), now nothing would be the same.

Upon their return to Krakow, the family was moved into yet another building in the newly erected Jewish ghetto. Here apartments were inhabited by multiple families, and everyone was forced to wear white armbands embellished with the Star of David, even agnostics like the Polanskis. Years later, while making *The Pianist* (2002), Polanski would recall the difficulty and tedium of drawing the Jewish star.[2] He never could get it just right, yet would try often, as soon the star could be seen everywhere.

For a brief time Roman returned to school (Jews would soon be forbidden to attend). He went just long enough to discover a new fascination, the epidiascope, which was nothing less than magic. An opaque projector that used a system of mirrors and/or lenses, strong bulbs, and reflected light to display opaque and transparent materials, the epidiascope was a predecessor to the modern-day overhead projector. It became an obsession for him, a gateway into film, as he dreamed of understanding how it worked (it would make such an impact that he would discuss it years later in his interview with Charlie Rose). As for any child, there were day-to-day pleasures. No longer were there the endless afternoons by the river playing with his mother close by, but still there were family, his stamp collection, and new friends, for even at this early age Roman held friendship in high esteem.

Descent into ghetto life was subtle at first. In many ways life carried on as normal for a time, despite obvious changes in the environment. The dream of equal rights once offered by the Versailles Treaty now became no more than a memory, and the local administration, or Judenrat, was merely a Nazi puppet, helpless to protect the Jews. When the head of the Warsaw Judenrat, Adam Czerniakow, realized the extent of his error in carrying out German orders, he killed himself, sick with the truth of what he'd done. The encroaching loss experienced by living in the ghetto was such that one day schools would be closed, and the next fine possessions confiscated. Living in the ghetto meant being a second-class citizen, and though Jews had always faced turmoil, this was a new level of deprivation. Although the process of alienation was slow, the message was heard loud and clear: it had become very dangerous to be born a Jew.

Nothing was so horrible as the building of the ghetto wall. If to that point there was no clear understanding of the extent to which Jews were being cut off, this physically isolating symbol of alienation was a terror to behold. The ghetto wall meant separation from Krakow, from streetcars, from life. It erected a divide, and an enforcement of otherness. The wall said everything that the Germans did not—now you are dirty, second class; now we do not want you in our streets, in our sight for that matter. It is painful to imagine Roman's reaction as he watched the wall being built. What a horror for anyone, especially a child whose only right is to be free, to witness his world being closed in. It was a sensation that would remain with Polanski, one that would also appear in his films (a direct interpretation would appear in *The Pianist*). He would become a master of manipulating spaces on screen, daring to actually move walls to trick his viewer, terrifying his audience with both the vastness and the closeness of any given space. He came to intimately comprehend the necessity for freedom.

Life in the ghetto meant bearing witness to the dehumanization of Jews. It was not uncommon to see German soldiers slap someone for not walking in the gutter, or even shooting an innocent bystander for asking questions. Even though there was no context with which to understand the intentions of the German regime, things were quickly becoming clear that a chance for normalcy no longer existed.

It was impossible to experience such psychological confinement and fear without also suffering from physical symptoms. One needed a way out. In his autobiography, Polanski describes one spot in the wall where there was fencing and no brick, and this was where he found that he could slip out of the ghetto and return as if nothing had happened. The first time that he crossed over, he was impressed by the smooth, painted surface of the outside of the wall, in contrast with the primitive, ugly interior. He recalled this experience: "It was like walking through a mirror and emerging on the other side—entering a different world complete with streetcars and people leading normal lives." However intriguing the outside world now seemed, this freedom was tainted by the paranoia of being a Jew, and the possibility of being discovered was often not worth the risk. Yet it is important to note that as a small boy Roman took these risks, pushing the boundaries of his society's imposed limits, daring to experience more than what was indicated by the hand he was dealt.

Though one cannot deny Ryszard's misfortune in having made unlucky decisions in the past, he was a responsible man with the foresight to arrange for Roman's safety in the event of an emergency. Ryszard provided the Wilk family, who resided in town, with financial compensation for their risk (which was minimal in light of Roman's typically Polish, rather than Semitic, looks). It wasn't long before the warning of a raid on the ghetto brought Roman to the Wilks' apartment. His mother dropped him off (she was able to leave the ghetto, as she was working at Wawel, as a housekeeper for the

Germans), and when the raid was over it was Roman's father who came to pick him up, telling him that his mother had been taken away.

At the time that his mother was taken, people did not yet know about the camps, nor did they know what was to happen in them. Roman's mother would be among one of the first groups to be exterminated. She was pregnant at the time. Roman would not know of her fate until many years later, when someone made a passing remark. He would cling to the hope of her return, and even when relatives tried to tell him that she was gone, he would ignore them. He would develop a policy of not asking, so as not to get an answer, when it came to his mother's well-being. Yet at the time of her deportation, neither Roman nor his father knew what would happen to her. They would simply miss her, hoping that she was being taken care of and that she was okay.

More raids followed, along with other escapes. Roman did a stint working in a factory/orphanage with his dear and lovable housemate, Stefan, who was only four or five years old, and whose parents had been taken in a raid. During one raid in particular (recounted in the documentary *A Story of Survival: Behind the Scenes of "The Pianist"* [2003]), Roman was with Stefan when many Jews were at the Umschlagplatz, the square where Jews were rounded up prior to being taken away to the camps. There was a Polish soldier who was helping to organize the crowd, and Roman and Stefan made excuses about needing to get something from home. The Polish soldier let them go, and as they began to run, the soldier said quietly but sharply, "Don't run." This memory would be used to authenticate a scene in *The Pianist* over half a century later.[3]

The final raid that ultimately cleared out the ghetto came on March 13, 1943. Ryszard woke Roman before daybreak and brought him to the wall, where he used pliers to cut a hole in the barbed wire. It was here that he set Roman free.

Locked out of the Wilks' apartment, Roman walked the streets, completely at a loss. It was then that he witnessed his father, along with many others, being led out of Krakow by German soldiers. Onlookers gawked at the procession. Roman ran up to get close to him, but as soon as he did, he heard his father mumble the words, "Shove off," and he moved away.

In his autobiography, Roman says that he changed direction and never turned back (young victims of the Holocaust learned to look forward out of necessity). He was only nine years old and had already been an immigrant and an outcast. Now he was Roman Wilk, an imposter and a child of the war, a fugitive from the Nazis. From here on in, he would learn to make his own rules.

Suffering greatly from the separation from his parents, Roman found ways to entertain himself. Again he made new friends and learned to ride on the back of streetcars. He discovered a great painkiller in watching movies and went as often as he could. While he was living in the ghetto, his only chance to see a film was to peep through a hole in the fence and watch weekly screenings of anti-Semitic propaganda films as they were screened in Padgorze Square. Now Roman was a free agent and could watch films as he pleased. Though it was no compensation for family life, at least it was a chance for refuge. Movies became his fixation, a lingering dream of the epidiascope never far behind.

Soon after residing with the Wilks, Roman moved in with the Putek family. He was subsequently taken to Wysoka, in the country, where he lived with a simple farming family, the Buchalas. Mr. Buchala was a cobbler who rarely had work, and Mrs. Buchala was the salt of the earth, a woman who ran her household as well as their farm. The Buchalas had three children. The two older children were capable only of performing the simplest household chores, and their youngest son attended a local school.

Roman found his place within the Buchala home, though theirs was an unfamiliar, peasant way of life. Living in a small house without electricity, life was simple, based around survival. Roman helped Mrs. Buchala around the house, fed the animals, and made rope from hemp. He took their heifer out to pasture, and he discovered the great beauty and pleasure that nature had to provide. However kind the Buchalas were, taking Roman in and treating him as their own with little to no compensation, it was nature that supplied the joy and comfort that only family could provide. In nature he learned to feel encouraged and alive, and it was this gift that he would carry with him for the rest of his life.

Roman remained with the kindly Buchalas for a while, though as the war drew to a close and harder times arrived, it became clear that he had to return to Krakow, to see out the end of the war and begin a new life.

ADOLESCENCE

Unlike the majority, who soon become resigned to their lack of fulfillment, I never for a moment doubted that my dreams would come true.

—Roman Polanski

The Soviet invasion signaling the end of the war was cause for celebration. Never before had the presence of Russian soldiers in Poland been a reason to rejoice, nor would it ever be again. At the time of their arrival, however, the excitement was so great that many Russians were invited to join private celebrations. Poles were grateful and wanted to share what little food they had. After a long period of repression, Poles reveled in German powerlessness. As a result, the bodies of German soldiers were often violated on the street, and those who were found still alive were given treatment that would make them wish they weren't. Jewish or not, everyone had suffered and been changed by the war.

With this Russian presence also came Soviet ideals, and soon one tyranny was replaced with another. German films were switched to Russian ones, and audiences struggled to adjust to the sound of a new language. Although Roman was now nearing adolescence, he still looked like a boy of seven. With delicate features and a small frame he nevertheless carried himself courageously, wearing his extra-long pants tucked into his boots. Clothes were hard to come by, and many people resorted to wearing German uniforms that had been left behind. Necessity does not discriminate, as Roman was forced to learn early on. Here he was, still a child, with something of a young man's mind. Life had brought him a taste of manhood but not by his choice. He had no one on whom he could emotionally lean. These were experiences of life and death that could have made an old man out of a young boy, yet somehow Roman's character was feisty and resilient. He had seen horror upon horror, yet he still believed in possibilities. He was alive, after all, and who knew what the future could bring?

One of the greatest things about this postwar time was Roman's realization that he was no longer a fugitive. He could now walk the streets of Krakow free from the terror of being caught, and though he still suffered from the separation from his parents, he also found ways to enjoy himself.

Roman was able to maintain his anonymity until he ran into his uncle Stefan and once again became a child submitting to rules. Losing his freedom was not a welcome change if it did not come in the shape of his own parents, and Roman did not stay with Stefan and his wife, Maria, for long. He was sent to his other remaining uncle, David, who had been a Kapo[4] during the war and had not recovered his prewar personality. Though there was warmth in David's house, provided by his wife and the Horowitzes, whom Roman had known since before the war, life shared with a former Kapo was no treat.

In his autobiography Polanski recalls how he applied to the Boy Scouts in search of community. He still thought of himself as Roman Wilk, the Catholic (a persona adopted in earnest during the war), and he was surprised when a local organization denied him shoes with the excuse that they gave aid only to Jews. It was in the Boy Scouts that Roman discovered his joy of acting while performing a peasant's monologue before a campfire. The experience was a revelation, for now Roman knew that he had a chance to participate in the movies that he so adored. Not only was it important to watch as many movies as possible, but also to hold on to any objects conjuring their image. He accumulated programs and discarded pieces of film, such as one he obtained from *Snow White and the Seven Dwarfs* (1937). This was the time of Laurence Olivier's *Hamlet* (1948), Laurel and Hardy, and most importantly, Carol Reed's drama about a fugitive on the run, *Odd Man Out* (1947), which would make a tremendous impact on Roman.

Ryszard had returned to Krakow (he survived the Mauthausen camp in Austria and was subsequently cared for at an American base), and Roman was no longer an orphan. Still, for whatever reason, Ryszard was unable to remain close. He traveled in search of business opportunities and soon married Wanda, a svelte Catholic who enjoyed local café society, and was generally disliked within the family circle. Roman, who was in agreement with this sentiment, was subsequently placed in accommodations where he would live on his own. Ryszard continued to provide for Roman, helping him with his education (for Roman was basically illiterate, having never really attended school). Roman may have had his name back, but in many ways he remained on his own.

> I couldn't watch a bicycle race in Krakow without picturing myself as a future champion. I couldn't view a movie without seeing myself as the star or, better still, the director behind the camera.

> —Roman Polanski

As a result of his magical experience performing around the campfire, Roman knew what he wanted to do. Not long after that, he was given a job on a children's radio program, *The Merry Gang*, and subsequently he got a job in the Young Spectators' Theater. He became hooked on the theater, loving everything about it. Inside and out—anyway you looked at it the theater was a world of fantasy where people built stories based on dreams, and every night an audience came to applaud this revelation. Still a small boy, Roman investigated every nook and cranny, and soon he was known for his practical jokes backstage. He developed various tricks that involved feigning his own death.

It was around this time that he starred in the play *The Son of the Regiment*, where he worked alongside professional actors. The show even had a performance in a festival of Soviet plays in Warsaw, where Roman won a prize (which, as is noted in his autobiography, his director cleverly distributed among the cast so as not to "puff him up"). Performing in Warsaw also meant having his picture in the newspaper. Disconcerting is the image of small Roman in the arms of two soldiers, as seen in a still taken from the play. One sees his frailty and gets the feeling that even though he is being held by big, strong, men, he is in grave danger of falling through or floating away.

Roman also developed a love of cycling around this time. "Roman had a much better bicycle than I did," his longtime friend and cinematographer Adam Holender laughs. He still recalls with lighthearted envy the Simplex bicycle that Roman rode, and which boasted actual gears.

When Roman began racing, however, his bicycle was of comparatively poor quality, and it prohibited him from competing to his fullest capacity. It was at this time, with a big race coming up, that he met Janusz Dziuba, a young man who offered to sell him an excellent racing bicycle for a laughably low price. Roman was thrilled. In his autobiography Polanski recalls how he hocked his wheels to get the cash, and met Janusz at the agreed spot, the rendezvous arranged for June 30. Carrying an object covered in newspaper

Dziuba made Roman's friend wait outside as he led him into an old German bunker. They walked past piles of excrement and into a dark tunnel. When Roman asked him where the bicycle was, Dziuba hit him on the head with the newspaper. Inside the paper was a rock. Roman recalled only one blow, though he was hit multiple times. Stumbling outside after Dziuba, blood running down his face, Roman brushed away a woman who tried to help. She became hysterical when touched by his bloody hand.

For years to come Roman would be reminded of this sensation of the blood trailing down his face. It had imprinted itself onto his consciousness. In 1974 Roman would describe the memory to *Der Spiegel*: "When I woke up, I saw the blood running over my face and eyes. And ever since that day, whenever I'm standing under the shower, I feel the blood running over me." This image of blood permeating water would crop up in such films as *Two Men and a Wardrobe* (1958) and *Macbeth* (1971). Yet more frequent than this image would be the recurrence of a grotesque and gawking crowd. Whether it is the reality of one woman trying to help or many people, there is no cinematic image so Polanskian as the point-of-view perspective of a hovering and intrusive crowd, rendering the audience the victim. In varying guises and with different intentions, the recurring crowd would continue to horrify audiences, always dominating, suffocating the viewer into sharing the protagonist's alienation.

Despite all of his extracurricular activities, Roman had been attending the Krakow Mining Engineers' College since the age of 15. Much to his father's dismay, these traditional studies came to an end soon after he joined the local puppet theater, Teatr Groteska. Needing one more year of a classical education in order to enter the school of drama, he enrolled in Krakow's School of Fine Arts. In this environment Roman met new friends, gaining access to a world of art and literature. He cultivated his artistic abilities, which would continue to serve him as a filmmaker. Through the circle of curious, cultivated individuals at Krakow's School of Fine Arts, Roman began to discover a new and more fulfilling life. This would not last long, however, as Roman would be kicked out of school, along with his friend Tyszler, on the whim of his favorite teacher. Nearly defeated, he pulled himself together to complete his diploma at a school in Katowice.

Stalinism[5] was escalating its hold on the Polish population. Lenin[6] believed film to be a medium with great possibility for producing pure propaganda. This atmosphere was highly restrictive. To live in communist Poland was to place value on personal freedom, knowing that something so simple as a book or music of one's own choice was a reason for secrecy. This environment encouraged paranoid personalities, as well as a great love and appreciation of art. To Roman and his friends, art became the highest form of expression, and subsequently the peak of personal freedom. Discussions were held at a local bookstore, and at Piwnica Pod Baranami (the Sheep's Cellar), where they would sit for hours discussing politics and art. Piwnica Pod

Baranami was a political café, a cabaret that served as the center of student life. As Adam Holender says, "It was a place for students who were interested in art, who liked poetry or jazz—all the things that were not all that kosher." It was common knowledge that the only place where one could openly live these ideas was in the West. It was at this time that the idea of the West fixed itself in Roman's mind as a dream, and it was beginning to be apparent that Roman was someone who would try to leave no dream unrealized.

Jazz was the ultimate free form of this time. Not only did it come from the West, but it was also a mode of expression less frozen than any other. Jazz was being in the moment. Jazz was free expression, and in communist Poland it was the height of liberation. The fact that it was forbidden made it even more appealing.

The only radio station on which jazz could be heard was Voice of America, beamed from Munich, Germany. Every night it played two hours of jazz, yet in order to access the program, which was blocked, one had to use two hands to adjust various knobs. "It was like flying an airplane," Holender recalls. The show always started with a segment of Duke Ellington's song, "Take the 'A' Train," and was run by deejay Willie Canover, who worked for the American state department. He pronounced musicians' names very slowly, making sure that the listener understood. Of Canover, Holender says, "He was a deejay, and for everyone in my generation of Poles, he was possibly more important than the president of The United States. He was somebody who changed lives."

Three stories (1953) was a collection of three short exercises done as a diploma film by students from the Lodz film school. The premise revolved around a socialist propaganda story, and even though he had a small part, Roman was in heaven spending time with Lodz seniors. One of these was a young man named Andrzej Wajda, who would go on to become the hero of Polish cinema for his examination of ever-changing Polish life, and for films such as *Ashes and Diamonds* (1958) and *Kanal* (1957). At last Roman could see that not all was lost after being expelled from art school. More than in the theater or the poetry cafes, Roman felt that at last he had found himself and that from now on the film world would be home.

Too intimidated to apply to Lodz himself, Roman chose to apply to the Krakow Drama School as a stepping-stone to fulfilling his dreams. Sadly, even though all of his friends were accepted, Roman was not. It seemed that nobody wanted him. Various other schools rejected him, and the imminent threat of being drafted loomed. He concocted a scheme that involved smuggling himself onto a train in order to leave the country. With the help of two friends it almost worked, but the three returned home with an empty bottle and a story to tell.

Roman's world was on the verge of crumbling when he was given a part in Andrzej Wajda's first feature film. For Roman and his contemporaries, Wajda was a symbol of promise for the Polish film industry, which was a mock industry at that. A tribute to propaganda, the film business was government funded and storylines were constantly examined for deviations. Films were screened by officials, as were the screenplays upon which they were based, forcing directors to strictly adhere to the original script. Sweeping cuts and reshoots were not above the demands of the board.

In this atmosphere of censorship, conformity and mediocrity were the accepted form. This void left a blueprint for all the missing pieces. Polish youth longed to see films that spoke of the blood and guts that they, as children of war, knew to be true to life. They wished for films that would speak to *them*. It is no coincidence that Wajda's first film was titled *A Generation* (1955).

In his autobiography, Roman writes of how "Wajda, with the fire of youth and a painter's eye, set out to break the dreary official mold." Wajda got around the censors and the need to adhere to a simple, inoffensive script by using different camera techniques to tell the story. The result of this approach was raw, emotional filmmaking that inadvertently caused a stir in the cinematic community, ultimately creating a new style. Everyone on set could feel that they were participating in something new, and Roman spent all of his time soaking up the atmosphere and learning as much as he could from the way that Wajda worked. His part in *A Generation* soon followed with another role in *Magical Bicycle* (1955), which was scheduled to film in Lodz.

Thanks to his newfound good fortune and despite all his trouble and dread, Roman was not to be drafted after all. When he went to pick up his new identity card, it identified him as a student. At last destiny had offered him a gentler hand. A twist of fate had absolved him of his military duty and left Roman free to pursue his dreams.

LODZ

After a year of discovery, Roman Polanski was one of eight individuals out of hundreds of applicants to be accepted into the Lodz film school. His father rejoiced at this news. Polanski noted in his autobiography that, "For the first time in my life I hadn't let him down." The application process had been extremely arduous, taking place over the course of two weeks. There were written exams as well as numerous exercises. Adam Holender, who would attend the school four years later, recalls one test in which he was given a topic relating to an emotion, and after 15 minutes of working with actors, he was asked to present a scene based on that subject. Needless to say, being accepted into Lodz was a tremendous feat, and for Polanski, it was like winning a grand prize.

After he had slipped beneath the radar of the draft board, things began to improve. In his autobiography Polanski writes that through his new friend, art history student Wieslaw Zubrzycki, whom he had met at a local flea market, he was introduced to an entirely new crowd. At last Polanski was surrounded by like-minded people who were more concerned with art and freedom than they were the Stalinist regime. It was also through this group that he was introduced to sculpture student and champion skier, Kika Lelicinska, with whom he enjoyed his first great love affair. It was Kika who took Polanski sailing in Mazury, the lake district in the north of Poland, which would later become the backdrop for *Knife in the Water* (1962). These experiences had given him the courage to apply to Lodz and set the stage for his new life.

Attending Lodz during communist times was a privilege, for the prestige attached to filmmaking (earned through Lenin's stamp of approval) gave one quite an advantage in Poland. The excitement of Lodz's film community was palpable, and one felt lucky to be involved.

The film school was set up in a palazzo in the outlying industrial city of Lodz because Warsaw, having been decimated by the war, could not handle an entire film community. The town was filled with working factories, which only accentuated the gray tendencies of the Polish sky. Just as the entrance exam to the film school had been challenging, the curriculum was rigorous as well. Lodz took seriously the idea that it was training professionals, and its students were often given apprenticeships within the industry. There were a requisite number of films for each year, and equipment was made readily available so that one could work as much as one wished.

In spite of the postwar climate, Lodz had all the facilities a film school needed. There were screening rooms, cutting rooms, libraries, and even a bar. The most important and memorable aspect of daily life was the discourse exchanged on the steps outside the main screening room. It was there that ideas were discussed, and artistic battles waged. Adam Holender recalls the time that he and Polanski watched *Rashomon* (1950), and the argument that ensued with a fellow student when Polanski said that he had liked the film.

Students spent a good portion of their freshman year studying photography, perfecting their composition of the still image before moving onto motion pictures. They also devoted time to studying Marxist principles,[7] as well as the history of cinema. As Polanski wrote, "Films were our meat and our drink. We gorged ourselves on the great world classics, which were shown again and again, discussing, analyzing, and criticizing them *ad infinitum*." Such was the joy of devoting one's self to film. In fact, the only drawback to school life was mandatory military training. These exercises were run by the Defense Ministry, and they were a source of fear, as poor conduct meant being sent to the draft board.

One of the greatest privileges of attending Lodz was the opportunity to watch foreign films. Lodz became a stopover for films that would never achieve distribution in Poland. Students would have the opportunity to watch them, and then the films would be returned to their country of origin, having never been bought or approved by the censors. Although Lodz's upperclassmen were great fans of Soviet cinema and Italian neorealism, Polanski and his peers felt an affinity for films such as *Citizen Kane*.

Enthusiastic to stop taking photographs and at last make his first film, Polanski wrangled Bulgarian senior and cameraman Kola Todoroff to help him. Using Kola's color stock film, the two went off to Krakow to make *The Bicycle* (1955), which would recount Polanski's near-death experience with Janusz Dziuba. Making his first film turned out to be a great lesson, yet one with poor results. Recounting his memories of the night before the shoot, Polanski wrote that it was filled with "sleepless hours of bowel-churning terror." Even preparing storyboards with Kola and having his friend Adam Fiut act in the film could not calm his nerves. "Every shot was firmly imprinted on my mind, but I couldn't help inventing scenarios of failure," he wrote. As it turned out, the negative was accidentally sent to the Soviet Union for development, and only the first reel was ever returned. This was heartbreaking for Polanski, who dreamt of asserting his promise as a young director.

Although the first year at Lodz had been thrilling, the second was even more so. At last students were allotted stock footage and required to shoot exercises. His first film was one minute long and entitled *A Murder* (1957). It is a tense scene in which a man is stabbed to death, and the knife repeats the action over and over, while the camera remains steady so that one is granted no relief. The second film was *A Smile*. Two minutes long, *A Smile* (1957) is more varied in shots and in action. It depicts a man who peeks through the keyhole of a bathroom to watch a young woman as she bathes. When he returns later for another look, a man is there instead. *A Smile* is well done and quite humorous, a taste of the pleasures (and pitfalls) of voyeurism to come.

In the mid-1950s, following the death of Joseph Stalin in 1953, the socially inhibitive atmosphere of Poland began to soften. Wladyslaw Gomulka[8] became the new Polish Workers' Party secretary in 1956, and there was an influx of foreign literature and films. Passports were being allotted so that people could finally visit family outside of Poland. Polanski initiated the application process so that he could see his sister Annette, who had survived Auschwitz and was now living in Paris. It took him months to get necessary papers, and once he had them, he didn't want to let them go. Like a child with a toy he'd been dreaming to have, Polanski delighted in the possibility of traveling abroad. Remembering this time he wrote, "Even the vile-smelling glue under the cloth seemed redolent of freedom and adventure." The night before his departure he held a party for his friends. In the early morning he packed his bags and exited dramatically. As was typical of Polanski's flare, he said, "See you around. . . . Me, I'm off to Paris." It would be the best summer yet.

To finally touch the West was as fulfilling an experience as Polanski could have imagined. Seeing Annette, her new family, and the Paris of lights and color, "streets that seemed to be paved with gold," lifted Polanski to the prospect that perhaps at last he was discovering home. In his autobiography, he remarked that Paris with "its fountains and illuminations had all the magic, all the ethereal beauty, of the Christmas tree sparklers of my child-hood." The romantic dream was being realized.

It was a shock to experience the prosperity of French daily life in contrast with the Polish life that he knew. The simple fact of how many brands one had to choose from to buy a simple product was astonishing to Polanski, as it is to many émigrés stepping out of communism for the first time. In Polanski's autobiography he recalls carrying a map with him and walking everywhere, and how he found love with a visiting German student named Gesa. He went to see all of the Western films that had not come through Poland. It was the first time that he witnessed performances by the brilliant actors Marlon Brando and James Dean. He must have studied their work carefully, for when he returned to school, he would please his classmates with imitations of them both. He also had the chance to see Cannes[9] in full swing. He visited Wajda (who was there screening his film *Kanal*), had the good fortune of seeing Bergman's *The Seventh Seal* (1957), and even shared a taxi with Abel Gance (director of the extravagant silent film, *Napoléon* [1927]). Although Polanski's time in France had been a dream come true, he needed to return to school. The dream would have to wait.

Life at Lodz was becoming more and more exciting. Not only was there interesting work, but there was also Polanski's circle of friends, a progressive and intellectual group, some of whom would make a great impact on his life. There was Jerzy Kosinski, a Jewish social science graduate, who would later become the famous writer of "The Painted Bird" and "Being There," and would one day live in the United States. There was also Wojtek Frykowski, the son of a successful merchant, who was the only one of Roman's friends to have his own car. Frykowski was a tough yet loyal friend. A playboy of sorts and university-educated, he liked to spend his time with local ruffians and mix with the film school crowd. It was also at this time that Polanski befriended the great director Andrzej Munk, maker of *Man on the Tracks* (1957), and *Heroism* (1958). Munk was loved by everyone and was consid-ered to be the best Polish filmmaker of his time. A documentary teacher at Lodz, it was for Munk's class that Polanski made his next film.

Inspired by the habit of local gangs to crash parties and upset the proper environment of dances in the late 1950s, Polanski decided to play a trick of sorts. He would set up a lovely dance, shooting in a traditional manner, using establishing shots, and unbeknownst to the dancers, a crowd of ruffi-ans would break up the party and cause a ruckus. Only the crew and the ruf-fians would know the plan. This experiment would result in Polanski taking a lot of flak. He faced possible expulsion, and Munk dismissed the film as a distasteful prank.

Break Up the Dance (1957) was a bold experiment, as well as a practical joke taken too far. Some people were injured as a result of the project, and everyone was angry. This approach to filmmaking raised the question of how far one should go to achieve cinematic revolution. On the other hand, it is a film of some charm, conveying the innocence and pleasure of the dance, as well as the unsettling hunger of the ruffian intruders. Ultimately, it is an uncomfortable viewing experience, as the upbeat soundtrack is overtaken by moans of discomfort as the fight ensues. The final image is of a blackface papier-mâché doll, which was previously hanging above the crowd and now floats quietly along the river, a sweet song of innocence playing once again.

For his next film, Polanski returned to the world of fiction. Still wishing to push cinematic boundaries, he considered a surrealistic approach to human emotion.

"The short I aspired to make would have to be poetic and allegorical yet readily comprehensible," he later wrote. Filmed in the seaside town of Sopot, the shoot was set to take ten days, yet ended up running three weeks. It was here that Polanski discovered the difficulties of shooting on location. The interference of passersby created constant issues, not to mention the difficulty of carrying a heavy piece of furniture throughout nearly every scene. Perhaps this was where Polanski developed his aversion to location shoots.

These difficulties would prove worthwhile, for *Two Men and a Wardrobe* (1958) would establish Polanski's position as a promising young filmmaker, both in school and throughout the Polish film community. It earned him a bronze medal at the Brussels World's Fair (without first needing to go through the Ministry of Culture, no less), and became the first student short to be shown commercially in Poland.

Two Men and a Wardrobe initiated Polanski's collaboration with Krzysztof Komeda, the greatest jazz musician in Poland at that time. Formerly a doctor, Komeda had become very successful as a pianist and composer, but he had not yet attempted a film score. Intrigued by the possibility, Komeda created a soundtrack that adds greatly to the film.

Two Men and a Wardrobe is a film about two men, Kuba and Henryk, who emerge from the sea carrying a dresser. When they first reach the shore, they brush their teeth, dance together, and even do somersaults in the sand. They revel in the glory of being alive. They enter the city and try to board the tram, but they are rejected and pushed off. When they politely try to speak to a pretty young lady, she rejects them after seeing their massive wardrobe. It appears that the wardrobe is too much of a burden for any stranger to carry. They walk across a bridge. With the soundtrack paused, the men hum the song instead—using the punctuation of sound that Polanski felt to be most successful in a short film. Two other men, "friends" who laugh together while one picks the other's pocket behind his back, provide a stark contrast to Kuba and Henryk's relationship. The friends try to enter cafés and hotels, but the impediment of the wardrobe makes this social assimilation impossible. The burden of their innocence is heavy.

Next to enter is a group of hooligans (one of whom is played by Polanski himself), who kill a cat by throwing apples and then a large stone. When the tall blond gang member harasses a young woman and punches little Kuba, he hits him back. But Kuba is no match for the tall blond, who punches him and pushes him into the wardrobe, breaking the mirror, shattering any possibility for entering society. Now Henryk must defend his friend and take his turn to fight back. Yet in order to do so, he must close his eyes, so hesitant is he to engage in violence. He punches at the air, achieving nothing. Now it's Polanski's character's turn to beat up Henryk. In the scene following the fight, the two friends care for each other. Resting on a bridge they use a small tin to lift water from the river. Yet even when they relax against the wardrobe in a scrap yard, they are beaten and thrown out by a security guard.

The final sequence takes place after a young man is beaten to death with a rock. He lies helpless in a stream, while the murderer leaps away toward the forest. Meanwhile, the two men return to the beach, still carrying the wardrobe. They walk through dozens of sand towers built by a little blond boy who ignores them as they pass by. Even though they carry the heavy wardrobe, they are careful not to mess up a single tower. The boy's hopes live on as the men return to the sea. The last sound is of the waves crashing powerfully on the shore. The audience is left to quietly consider the sentiment of the film.

Heartbreaking, adorable, nostalgic, and cruel, *Two Men and a Wardrobe* has all of the absurdity and innocence that Polanski wished to portray. A lovely piece that stands on its own, the film also shows remarkable growth in Polanski's work up to this point. In his autobiography, Polanski notes that perhaps the film was conceived in part remembering his childhood friend Piotr Winowski, and all of the plans they had regarding his mother's piano— one of which was to move it into the street. Winowski had been Polanski's confidant after the war, and when he saw him again years later, he was a ravaged young man working in the mines. Winowski died soon after that meeting. Perhaps Polanski was thinking of Winowski, of their friendship, and also how easily hearts were bruised by the brutality of life, especially those who experienced communism and war. It was almost as if not to give away too much of his heart that he chose to play the bully in the ruffian scene. After all, one of the most important things to Polanski at this time in his life was the process of becoming a man.

Not long after Polanski completed *Two Men and a Wardrobe* he met the young and beautiful actress, Basia Kwiatkowska. Eighteen years old, Basia was from a small village, but her looks had a universal appeal. She had just starred in the film *Eva Wants To Sleep* (1958) and was already considered to be the Polish equivalent to gorgeous French film star Brigitte Bardot.[10] Although their friendship was platonic, Polanski was smitten from the start. As soon as the relationship was taken to a romantic level, he reveled not only in being with her but in being known as one half of a special couple. Being

"Basia and Romek" gave him the strength and the inspiration to make his diploma film, which of course would star Basia as the object of desire.

When Angels Fall (1959) is a heartbreaking account of the effects of war on one woman's life. Approaching the subject using vignettes and flashbacks, the viewer is made to understand the harshness of Polish existence at that time. The main character is a washroom attendant—an old woman with no teeth, a weathered, feeling face, and a babushka (kerchief) over her head. Every morning she walks the cobblestone streets to her decayed art deco washroom (built impeccably by Roman and his art director friend, Kazimierz Wisniak) beneath the street. She takes care to keep the bathroom clean, and then sits and waits all day as men relieve themselves. Through frosted glass panes she watches as people pass by overhead, recalling colorful memories (in contrast to the black-and-white present). We are privy to these memories, yet we are only given a taste of the troubles she has suffered. We watch as her younger self, played by Basia, looks dreamily out of another frosted window, only here, instead of finding promise in other people's lives, she is the promise. She is everything that is young and full, and as the film progresses, we watch how the world defiles that promise. She goes from being a young girl who makes love carelessly by a stream, to a mother whose son is violent in a way that she can't understand. She loses her son, and becomes an old lady who cleans rich people's houses. She is pushed away by a soldier to whom she only wishes to hand a package.

One of the most surprising and interesting aspects of this film is the moment in which the old woman, here convincingly played by Polanski, hobbles out into the street, trying to catch up with the soldiers. One must look once, and twice, to assure one's self that in fact it is Polanski, with all the seeking and twisted physicality of an old woman who has nearly been crushed by life. He/she tries so hard to catch up, to pass on a package to one of the soldiers, but is too small, too slow, and ultimately, cruelly, cast aside. This brings to mind the story of Polanski as a boy, running to catch up with his father as he was marched out of Krakow by the Gestapo. There, too, Polanski was small and didn't belong. There, too, he was cast aside. Polanski took on the role of the old lady because his actress had trouble with a trembling jaw, which was distracting to the viewer. But why did he choose to take her place here specifically? Perhaps he needed to install himself in this role of the tattered woman in part to prove his ability as an actor, yet also to show that he too had been hurt, revealing his own vulnerability.

Although at times the pieces don't fully come together, *When Angels Fall* is a more complete film than Roman's previous exercises. It has a definite structure and uses multiple locations to support grand ideas, particularly about the war. There is one scene in particular, not from the woman's memory but plucked from the atmosphere, in which a soldier finds an enemy combatant sitting alone behind a decrepit wall. When the enemy reaches into his inside jacket pocket, the soldier shoots him, only to later discover that he simply wanted to share with him his last two cigarettes. It is a devastating moment in which the truest horror of war is exposed.

When Angels Fall makes many sentimental gestures with regard to the past and the war, yet judging from his body of work, one cannot help but wonder, is this film truly Polanski? Were these sentiments that came from his heart, or were they an attempt at wrangling the emotions of a public who understood this message as it resonated with their own lives? This question is furthered by a certain disconnect within the film, which although very moving does not resonate as did *Two Men and a Wardrobe*. One might even argue that *Two Men and a Wardrobe* is as much a representation of the heartbreak of war as *When Angels Fall*, by virtue of its use of simple day-to-day experiences made more poignant by the surreal.

Yet regardless of these disparities, *When Angels Fall* remains a deeply moving film, rich with childish wonder, such as when a small brass angel chimes a bell to punctuate the beautiful music provided by Komeda, or when snow falls over a model of a Polish town. At the end of the film, an angel falls through the glass roof (unstable world) of her public toilet, and as snow falls into the old woman's space, all is redeemed.

Polanski's school films have an emotion and a sentimentality that are absent from most of his later work. His approach to making shorts was to represent an experience, and not try to fit an entire film into a few minutes. This was a wise decision, and the thoroughness of his approach is apparent in his short films. There was a feeling coming through that would later become obsolete, except when one looks deep down at the center of certain films. One cannot always feel the heart, but only sense a thread of longing.

A short exercise shot in the same year as *When Angels Fall*, was *Lampa* (1959), a film also commenting on the end of an era. Though Polanski was director, *Lampa* was the diploma film of his fellow classmate Krzysztof Romanowski (a cinematography student). *Lampa* has a style all its own and is unlike any of Polanski's previous films. The film addresses the loss of an old world—a doll maker's shop is burned to the ground once electricity is installed—using a dark atmosphere to convey this sinister deterioration. The haunting sounds of a humming boiler and of voiceless dolls travel along the electrical wires as they conspire to explode. Watching this film one imagines the inspiration that filmmaker David Lynch[11] and his contemporaries would gather from *Lampa*'s atmosphere. And though it is not the style that Polanski would continue to employ (in fact it is a film that he excludes from his autobiography), it still indicates his ability to convey a darkness to come.

Although Polanski would make a few more short films, his time at Lodz was drawing to a close. He never did write his thesis, noting in his autobiography that his idea for an index of French and Polish filmic terminology did not conform to the type of analytical essay that the school board wanted. He was soon hired by the highly regarded production company, Kamera, and was set to be Andrzej Munk's assistant on the film, *Cross-Eyed Luck*, also known as *Bad Luck* (1960), which Basia was starring in as well. As Polanski was conceiving of his first feature film about a couple's interaction with a stranger, which would take place on a small yacht in Mazury, he married Basia. The two set off for Paris, where she would become a star and where they would reside for the next two years.

Polanski's time in Paris would be rich with experience, but difficult in certain ways. Much of his energy was spent supporting Basia, who was busy working and who was photographed wherever they went. She made her first French film with director Robert Menegoz, and under Polanski's tutelage learned French at a heightened speed. Her second film was *Quelle Joie de Vivre* (1961), made with the director René Clément, who changed her name to Barbara Lass, and who had directed the successful film *Purple Noon* (1960). Polanski and Basia lived all over Paris, at times staying with friends such as the producer Pierre Roustang, who gave them a black poodle that they named Jules, or in their own apartment, which would increase in size as Basia became more established. Riding on anyone's, especially a woman's coattails was not Polanski's style, and he struggled to assert himself, pitching his new project, *Knife in the Water*, wherever he could.

Unable to get the funding for a feature, he found the means to make a short. Not having made a film since *When Angels Fall*, Polanski itched to shoot something. *The Fat and the Lean* (1961) was to be shot in a small studio in Paris and on location outside of town. The film would star Polanski as a young man who serves as a slave to an overweight and lazy master, who stands only when Polanski's character tries to run away. The master, played by Andrzej Katelbach, a nonactor who owned a plastic factory (and had once even hired Zbigniew Cybulski[12] to work on his assembly line), sits in his bursting wicker rocking chair, as Polanski's character dances and plays the flute. Polanski's character also plays the violin while tied to a goat, nearly fainting from exhaustion and deprivation. He fans Katelbach and shades him from the sun. He cooks for him, yet takes no food for himself. He leaps through the fields, dancing for him, gazes at the town in the distance, and though he repeatedly tries to run away, he never manages to escape. He enjoys his role of devotee. In the final sequence he attaches tulip buds to large, sturdy stems and scatters them through the fields as a gift to his master, as well as to enhance his own view of the town.

The Fat and the Lean is charming, spontaneous, tragic, and humorous all at once. Reminiscent of pieces by Charlie Chaplin and Buster Keaton, *The Fat and the Lean* plays with time and physicality. Punctuated by a soundtrack by Komeda, it is pure Polanski. He is the pied piper and the little drummer boy. And as Katelbach drums, he performs in his tattered clothes. He is the mistress of the house and master of the land, managing to be charming at every turn. The film would win a prize, and receive local distribution among film clubs in Paris. It also marked the end of another phase in Polanski's life.

Returning to Poland with Basia for Christmas, Polanski decided to make one last short. Privately funded by his friends Frykowski and Andrzej Kostenko, it would be the first independent film made in Poland since the war. They had to illegally obtain equipment and stock in order to make the project happen. Shot in Zakopane, a small mountain town, *Mammals* (1962) starred Michal Zolnierkiewicz, Henryk Kluba, and included an unbilled cameo by Frykowski as a sausage salesman. *Mammals* is about two friends riding through the snow on a small sled that is ultimately stolen by a sausage salesman. One friend pulls the other, who is lazily plucking a chicken, and when they switch places, the other begins to knit a scarf. They feign minor injuries until their physical ailments gain in magnitude. Zolnierkiewicz walks on crutches; Kluba becomes blind, and even pretends to be headless at one point. Frightened, Zolnierkiewicz runs away and the two begin to fight, rolling around in the snow. Kluba wraps his body in a white bandage, rendering himself invisible against the snowy backdrop. Enraged, Zolnierkiewicz attacks him, and as they fumble, their sled is stolen. The two are friends again, on equal ground at last. Pretty soon one friend is injured, and must be carried away on the other's back.

Mammals is pure comedy. An exercise that is simple in its content and pleasurable to watch. With a lighthearted soundtrack by Komeda, it is endearing without being sentimental. After completion of filming, Polanski left the dailies behind to be edited in secret (the print would later be produced along with *Knife in the Water*), and returned to Paris with Basia. As it turned out, this was to be a brief visit. At last the Polish Ministry of Culture had approved the revised script for *Knife in the Water*. Basia, who was now Barbara, flew to Rome where she was to make her second film in the Italian city. Leaving Jules behind with Katelbach, Polanski returned to Poland, prepared to make a feature film at last.

2

Knife in the Water (1962)

Making a feature film was an altogether new task, but Polanski was up to the challenge. In fact, it seemed as if his entire life had been leading to this point. The script had endured certain changes since its original inception (the result of collaborating with Jerzy Skolimowski), but the primary story remained the same. Like a classical Greek tragedy, the action was reduced to one 24-hour period, rather than taking place over the course of a few days.

The film was to be shot in Mazury, the lake district where Polanski had learned to sail with Kika Lelicinska years before. It would be produced by Kamera, and represented by Jerzy Bossak, Jozef Krakowski, and Stanislaw Zylewicz. Friends Kuba Goldberg and Andrzej Kostenko were hired as assistants. Jerzy Lipman (who had worked on *Three Stories* and taken Polanski under his wing) was to be cameraman, and Wojtek Frykowski, the lifeguard. Skolimowski,[1] Polanski's collaborator on the script, was also a good friend, a former boxer, and a poet.

Knife in the Water is the story of a trio—the relationship of a man and his wife as it is affected by a young hitchhiker's presence in their lives. The only professional actor hired for the film was Leon Niemczyk, who was set to play the husband, Andrzej. Jolanta Umecka, who was hired to play the young wife, Krystyna, was picked up at a public swimming pool, and Zygmunt Malanowicz, the hitchhiker, was a young acting student who specialized in the method.[2] Polanski had wanted to play the part of the hitchhiker himself, and one story claims that he had fought Bossak tooth and nail to get the part, going so far as waltz into his office naked to prove his sexual appeal, yet whatever the reason, he did not play the young man. Once the filming was over, however, Polanski would be dissatisfied with Malanowicz's performance, and would dub his voice in, thus ultimately playing the hitchhiker's part. He would also dub the voice of Krystyna, using a more seasoned

Knife in the Water. (Courtesy of Photofest)

actress, as he had been disappointed by Umecka's performance. Both of these choices would prove to be successful.

Shooting an entire film on one sailboat was an incredibly difficult task, as the weather proved to be an ever-changing variable. Though the actors and crew rented a massive houseboat in Mazury and enjoyed drinking and having fun most nights, the challenge of the piece was overwhelming at times. The constant movement of the clouds was an enemy to any attempt at continuity, yet as the end result proves, the masterful camerawork combined with the tense atmosphere make these subtleties irrelevant in the end. At the time of shooting, however, the mounting of lights, the framing of shots, everything was made more complex by the ever-changing environment of the lakes.

Knife in the Water is a combustion of youthful frustration, an examination of the male ego as it confronts itself, not belonging, yet wanting to assert itself as independent and strong. It is about desire, exploring the need to dominate and be free, and it does so with such perfection that one is taken in completely. Ideas become more and more transparent, until finally they need not be concealed. As the sailboat plunges farther out into the water, everything is revealed. The perfect embodiment of this idea is the original American poster for the film designed by Everett Aison, the sail ripped to shreds by a knife implying dominance and desire. One sail frames an image of the young man and Krystyna about to kiss. The bottom of the boat is shaped like a knife. Here every tension is displayed.

The movie opens with a darkened image. A man and woman are driving on a country road, their faces concealed by the reflection of trees passing over the windshield. The soundtrack is composed by Krzysztof Komeda, consisting of a mix of piano and tenor saxophone, a longing and nostalgia projected into the audience, the music emoting what the concealed faces cannot. As the couple is revealed, we feel Andrzej's hotheaded tension as his wife drives, for he even holds the wheel at one point, helping her to drive. They argue in silence, and soon stop the car so that he can drive. Having it his way, he begins to kiss her neck while driving, paying no attention to the road. A hitchhiker stands in the road, and however much the driver honks the horn, the man doesn't move. Nearly hitting him, he quickly loses his temper, and already we understand that this story will be a battle of will, if not wits.

The driver yells at his wife, passing his responsibility onto her, saying that if she had been driving she would have run him over. Condescending to her further, he comments that—even worse than running him over—she would have given him a ride. As it turns out, Andrzej is the one who gives the young man a ride, perhaps just to prove that he's not such a heartless guy after all. They chat as they drive, and Andrzej asks the hitchhiker why he plays his game of chicken. The answer is that "Life gets boring."

As it turns out, the couple will be sailing for a day. When they arrive at the lake the young man lingers, as if deciding whether or not to stay. The lake provides a visually stunning backdrop, and the moment they arrive, one can feel the tension between the three characters, sturdy as obelisks against an endless sky. The camera work is tight and wide at the same time. Employing the use of deep-focus photography, which requires wide-angle lenses and a lot of light in order to keep the foreground and background in focus, the vastness of the water becomes entangled with the claustrophobic atmosphere of the boat. There is no visual distinction between the two. This merging of near and far is appropriately disturbing to the viewer, who is subconsciously confused and thus immediately immersed in the action. We, the audience, wish to assert ourselves in order to survive the oppressive atmosphere.

The lake, vast as an ocean, creates an ideal setting for layered imagery. Reflections double reality, allowing for one truth that is defined, and another that is more complex and unstable. Truth becomes obscured, leaky, and watery, symbolic of the subconscious. The presence of water creates shaky ground.

As the two men stand on the dock preparing to push off, their standoff begins. The hitchhiker doesn't know how to sail. He says that he'd rather hike. This inadequacy gives Andrzej the upper hand. The young man curses often, yet always apologizes, embarrassed by his own misstep. Andrzej asks him to untie the rope that attaches the boat to the dock, and as they do, the camera floats away from the dock, capturing an image of the two men (from now until the end of the film, they will struggle to differentiate themselves as much as possible). After some conversation, Andrzej asks the young man to join them for the day. He says that he knew Andrzej would ask, that he's "a mind reader." The sunlight sparkles on the water, with Andrzej in the foreground in a glow outlining his face, while the hitchhiker stands in the background, hands in his pocket, ready for anything, yet also a bit timid. He may be clairvoyant, but he is also young, and his youth gives him the anxiety of inexperience. They climb aboard the boat. The jazz soundtrack and the movement of the water, the ropes, and the sail all create a feeling of excitement that is tangible to the audience. The boat is named "Christine," a pretentiously Western version of Krystyna, Andrzej's wife's name.

After a relaxing beginning to the day, the three sit to have a drink. From his rucksack the young man pulls some black radishes, which he offers as an accompaniment. It is a simple, earthy offering, one that asserts his difference as a young and perhaps innocent man. Krystyna is happy for the surprise, and Andrzej makes a comment about their nutritional value. Krystyna goes to cut them, and the hitchhiker pulls out a large knife. "Why do you carry that murderous thing?" she asks, continuing to use her own small version. "A knife comes in handy," he says, "Especially in the woods. You don't need one on the water," he says, "but cutting your way through the woods . . ." He begins to play a game. It is another game of chicken, only this one involves spreading his fingers over the surface of the boat, and running the knife back and forth between each of his fingers. The idea is to go faster and faster, hoping that he doesn't make a wrong move and accidentally stab himself.

"Sailing's easy," the hitchhiker says, turning back to face the others. Krystyna comments that he is "a real child," and Andrzej laughs and says, "You could cut yourself." This is a layered warning, for the knife represents everything that is daring and forceful, full of ego and youth. Andzrej begins to tell a story, a moral tale of sorts about a seaman he once knew who smashed a glass bottle, and overzealously took off his boots and began to dance. The young man looks off into the distance and yawns. Andrzej tells him that if he needs something to do he should gather the rope, but the youth would rather be at the helm. Andrzej smiles and lets him, expecting him to fail. When he is nearly whacked over by the sail, glasses crash onto the floor and Andrzej laughs, regaining his position. "It takes brains not brawn," he says, shaking his finger at the young man, who has turned away in frustration. We see them both from behind with Andrzej, who is older but still fit, in the foreground and the young hitchhiker in the back. The camera cuts to a close-up on Andrzej's face as he threatens, "If two men are on board, one's the skipper."

"Or the drill sergeant," the young man says, as he coils the rope, defeated. Now he takes his place in the foreground of the frame. He asks Andrzej if he was in the military, and Andrzej replies that he was a student instead. The young man asks him what he does for a living. When Andrzej doesn't answer, he sarcastically asks him if he's a gynecologist, privately wondering if he screws every woman, not just one. Ignoring the comment, Andrzej says that he writes for a sports paper, further emphasizing his impotence, as he only writes about activity.

The camera cuts to long reeds in the marshes, the frame pushing through, following the rope that is slung over both Andrzej and the young man's shoulders. It is a primitive, striking image of men half naked, in a tug of war with their pride. In reality they are pulling a boat through shallow waters, yet internally they are struggling with this test of manhood. There is a medium close-up of the young man's face. His expression is determined, as he leads the weighty procession. The rustling of the reeds in the wind is overpowering and scratchy, irritating the viewer to the point of sympathy for the tired men. "Christine" floats by casually, carrying Krystyna who appears relaxed as well.

Tired, the young man throws down the rope, arguing that he's "a hiker, not a coolie," and asks for his rucksack. Andrzej tells him he's a wimp, which doesn't seem to bother him. But when Krystyna offers to give him her place on the boat, saying she'll pull the rope, he is deeply insulted. He becomes jumpy and argues that he wasn't speaking to her (the way that he deals with women exposes his immaturity). He grabs the rope, and running down the marsh, yells for them both to get in the boat. Testing his manhood, Krystyna has given him the impetus to continue on his way. The high-energy jazz soundtrack starts up again, and Andrzej runs after him, offering to give him a hand. He refuses help, and it is a comic scene as the two argue in the distance, touching absurdity with their rope and sweaty torsos amid the placid landscape of Mazury. Finally, the young man concedes.

What follows is a reprieve from the frantic energy of the past two sequences. The music continues to play, only it too, has softened, perhaps with the dying down of the wind. Here we see a series of moving stills taken from above, in which each character happily enjoys his or her surroundings. Krystyna sits at the helm of the boat, posing in her bikini, her long shadow languid as water flows underneath. Andrzej lies on his stomach, legs outstretched, quietly reading a map. The young man lays on his back at the bow of the boat, feet crossed, arms out to his sides and eyes blissfully closed. The coiled rope is perfectly placed beneath his head, forming a halo of sorts, emphasizing his position as a Christ-like figure.

There is the feeling here that however powerful youth may be, it has an inherent struggle, and with its impermanence comes unfulfilled desire. The young man is being carried forth on the boat, led by his own masculinity into unconsciousness. The knife is the boat, and vice versa. They both symbolize a powerful assertion of will and desire: for the young man, all that is needed is a portable knife, whereas for the middle-aged professional who is losing steam, a large sailboat with a Western name will suffice. It takes the portable knife's place. The young man is being carried forth by a desire to prove himself. He lifts his legs in a pas de bourrée, as would a gymnast or a dancer, admiring his own strength.

The perspective switches from a bird's-eye view to an extreme low-angle shot, and we see what the young man sees, admiring the grandiosity of the sail as it bellows in the wind. He picks his index finger up in front of the sail, and like a child, squints one eye and then the other, creating an optical trick in which his finger appears to be moving from side to side. This moment underlines his openness and his curiosity, whereas for Andrzej, such innocence is merely a memory of the past.

When the young man asks Andrzej if his compass is used for cooking, Andrzej says that it would be of "no use for hiking." When the young man begins to whistle, Andrzej becomes irritated and tells him to stop. The young man climbs the mast to assert his individuality. Andrzej threatens to beat him up, and coming down the young man, who had been wearing only a bathing suit, puts on his pants once again. When moments later Krystyna sings, followed by Andrzej whistling, the young man smiles to himself and looking up at the sky comments that the cloud resembles a sheep. Andrzej flinches at first, assuming that the young man is speaking of him. The young man spits in the water. The wind has dropped, and they have stopped moving.

The young man ties a checkered napkin around his neck, creating a bib to cover his naked chest, as Krystyna prepares lunch. When he sees a clamp that Andrzej has made to hold the hot pot of soup, he laughs at him, mocking his invention. Angry, Andrzej turns to him, thrusting the soup pot into his hands. The soundtrack is of an unrelentingly high-pitched note, as the young man turns to Krystyna, like a little boy with his bib turning to his mother for approval, or at least for the impetus to carry on. He holds on to the pot, in spite of alarming pain, and when Krystyna cannot stand to watch anymore, she pulls it from him, dropping it to the floor. Defeated and ashamed, the young man shouts at Krystyna that she has "spilled the soup." It is the insecure reaction of a little boy. And, just like a boy, he turns his back on the others, and leaning against the mast while they eat their lunch, says that he wants to get off. Again we see the tortured image of youth and are reminded of the longing for freedom and the desire to prove (although here freedom cannot be found in the open landscape, for it is an internal need that can only be filled by internal satisfaction).

Andrzej makes the comment that "Sailing's for grown-ups," and Krystyna says that the young man should join them for lunch. Though she is not much older than he, she speaks to him like a mother who knows best. Desperate for movement, the young man finds an oar, and attempts to paddle ashore. As Andrzej changes course, the camera leaves the boat entirely, trailing behind in a rare moment of respite. The boat's reflection quivers in the water as Andrzej and Krystyna laugh at the young man struggling on the bow. We need this visual space in order to see the opposition of character that is taking place, and it is this distance that gives us a clear picture.

When the young man throws down his oar in anger, we discover that he doesn't know how to swim. It is Krystyna who placates Andrzej, and jumps into the water to retrieve the oar, demonstrating that perhaps it is she who is most virile of the bunch. In order to prove himself once again, Andrzej offers his hand to the young man who is holding the knife and claims to have a light touch, and would therefore never damage the deck or accidentally hurt anyone.

What follows is a very tense scene, in which we see the young man's face behind Andrzej's back. Even after all this time on the boat, we have not yet decided who the young man is, nor do we know for sure whether he should be trusted. This elevates the stakes of the game, for perhaps the young man is beyond frustrated, his hunched physicality hiding a monstrous rage. We wonder many things, as the tapping of the knife becomes faster and faster. Even when Krystyna calls out to her husband while swimming with a crocodile float, it is the sound of the knife that overwhelms. At one point, the young man looks up at Andrzej, the knife hitting the deck with an anxious rhythm. We hold our breath, wanting to prove his lightness of touch. When Andrzej cannot take it anymore, he grabs the man's hand, forcing him to stop. The young man's palms are covered in blisters. Andrzej tells him to dress his wounds, and the young man slinks inside the cabin to do as he is told, leaving the knife out on the deck of the boat.

There is a beautiful shot of the knife, so strong, so certain, lying on the boat, with Krystyna swimming in the background. It is the coveted symbol, the definition of strength. Fascinated, Andrzej bends down toward it in an almost reverent gesture. He picks it up, examines it, and tests its sharp strength out on the surface of the boat. He plays the game of chicken with himself until the young man emerges from the cabin eating a piece of chocolate—soothing himself with sweets as would a wounded child. The young man turns his back to Andrzej and shoves a large piece of chocolate into his mouth.

The wind picks up as Andrzej and Krystyna swim and play in the water, laughing and shouting. The music begins again, as the young man struggles to take control of the boat on his own. He clings to the ropes, falling this way and that as the boat moves in circles. When at last Krystyna and Andrzej are able to reboard the boat, the mood is lighter and everyone is beginning to enjoy each other's company. The clouds are stormy as Andrzej dares the young man to hang from the sail onto the side of the boat. The young man obliges. Ecstatic, he shouts, "We're sailing!"

"Sure, for sailing's sake," Krystyna replies, taking a cue from a comment the young man made earlier on. "Or walking's sake!" He smiles, pretending to walk over the flowing water, moving his legs in mid-air. He is literally walking on water and walking on air. Ecstatic, he smiles. This is the beauty of innocence that he brings to the boat, and for this moment he is allowed his pleasures. Andrzej and Krystyna even smile along with him. It is a beautiful image in which the young wanderer finds freedom and home. In fact, so liberating is this moment that the camera backs away from the boat, showing us the image of the young man suspended by a rope, and for a moment he is in command.

Watching the boat as it glides through the water effortlessly, one experiences a collective release. Krystyna and Andrzej watch the young man as he experiments with the ropes, trying out different positions like a child moves through his first steps. They play the roll of curious parents. The image is smooth, yet the fluttering saxophone riffs an uncertain warning. It begins to moan, as if blowing out sound from deep beneath the water.

All at once, the expansive scene is cut short as the boat gets stuck in shallow water. The sail is tangled, and the young man lands in the lake, the boat tipping on its side. Standing up to his waist in water the young man looks down at himself, dripping wet, acknowledging his own transformation—a baptism of sorts. While he is being reborn, Andrzej calls out for the knife to cut loose the sail. Here the knife is a source for action. It begins to rain heavily, and once they've all gotten into the water and pushed off (a moment extended by a beautiful long shot of the boat in the distance, through the fog of heavy rain, evoking longing with a soft song of piano and saxophone), they anchor in the reeds and take shelter in the cabin of the boat.

If the atmosphere was claustrophobic above, then it is even more so down below. It is a space in which tensions cannot be denied, and where hurts, when surfaced, have nowhere to go. There is no need for deep-focus photography here, for the actors fill the frame. They cannot hide behind their nudity—their bikini-clad openness, nor their tan torsos. This place is about simply being themselves, and all are revealed for who they are and what they dream of being.

When Andrzej helps untie his wife's hat, he fumbles with the knot beneath her chin. Her expression is tense, almost pained. It is unclear whether she enjoys her husband's touch. When she goes into a back cubicle to change her clothes, she tells the young man not to look, but he ends up peeking anyway when a fly travels her way. Andrzej turns on the radio and pulls out a bottle of spirits. They drink to seamen everywhere, and sit down to blow up their mattresses. Krystyna and Andrzej wear robes; the young man wears his clothes. He suggests that they compete to see who blows up their mattress first, Andrzej using a hand pump, and the hitchhiker his mouth. Andrzej happily agrees. The two rush excitedly as an announcer describes a boxing match on the radio. The young man finishes first, and Andrzej becomes angry with the announcer.

The three sit at the table, with Krystyna in the middle, the arch of the doorway perfectly framing the crowns of their heads. Andrzej initiates a game of pick-up sticks. As usual, the young man is a novice. He says that he doesn't know how to play, but Andrzej says that it is easy and he will show him how, finding assurance in his teacher's role. There is an atmosphere of cozy camaraderie as they listen to the middleweight championship while playing the game in which each must remove a piece of clothing and pay a penalty in order to get it back. The camera is slightly above them, creating an even tighter space. The soundtrack is an energizing mix of crackly radio combined with endless rain. Pieces of clothing are removed, and at one point the young man removes the knife as if it were a part of him, and throws it across the room into a board on the wall. This becomes the new activity—a game within a game, and Andrzej takes his turn, perfectly making his mark. Krystyna's back is to them, ignoring this new pleasure, continuing with the pick-up sticks.

In order for Krystyna to reclaim her slipper, the young man asks her to continue the song that she was singing before. She begins, and Andrzej shakes his head and tells her to stop. The young man asks her to continue and she complies. Andrzej shows his annoyance by plugging in a headphone so that he can listen to the game, isolating himself from the trio. The song is soft and romantic, speaking of a love that is on its way out. "We're out of words, and moons and stars," she sings. The young man listens while holding her slipper in his hands. This action recalls a young Brando in *On the Waterfront* (1954) using his possession of Eva Marie Saint's glove as a way of holding onto her presence. "Though life is empty, you don't need me," she sings, her eyes downcast while Andrzej lights his pipe. He behaves in a manner that is so self-involved that he might as well be in a room all his own. "Stupid song," he remarks, looking down at the radio.

When it is the young man's turn to pay a forfeit, Krystyna asks him to recite a poem. He willingly begins, looking up into space. "That handful of stars above. Mother, are they you?" he asks. One cannot hear this poem, knowing that it is in fact Roman's voice, without thinking of his mother. He continues, "Are you the white sail on the lake, or the waves that lap the shore?" Andrzej is sidetracked by the recitation of the poem, but quickly succeeds in ignoring the other two once again. The poet continues with, "Have you strewn my pages with stardust?" It is a tender expression rare in a film so heartily based around actions rather than words. It is a moment that shows the closeness in the age of the woman and hitchhiker, for they are connected so easily by the simplicity of art. Perhaps Andrzej is past poetry and song, or perhaps he is simply jealous, wishing to remain above it. As the young man recites the poem, we see more than a young aimless hitchhiker. We see a sensitive poet, and we feel that we know him much better than before. We see a glimpse into the source of his longing. It is through art that this longing articulates itself. In fact, it is through reciting this poem that he has lulled himself to sleep. It is a signal for everyone to take a rest.

In the early morning light, the boat seems small and harmless in the wholesome atmosphere of the misty marshes. The sounds of crickets and ducks are soothing in contrast to all of the noise of the past few scenes. Krystyna walks on the deck of the boat, taking in the atmosphere, suggesting that her inner clock is aligned with nature. She leans against the mast wearing only a sweater. Her hair is loose and she smokes a cigarette, looking off into the distance. This is a sultry image, one in which a woman is at peace yet perhaps is thinking of other things. The young man walks past, yet all that we see are his feet. He says that he heard her upstairs, claiming to be "a light sleeper." One questions their claims of disturbed sleep and close air, for they could easily be interpreted as complaints of unrest and desire. The young man sits down on the edge of the boat and blows into a reed, waking Andrzej. Andrzej packs his pipe and puts the knife in his pocket. When he comes on deck, he finds the young man at the top of the mast fixing the sail, and he is uncomfortable with this assertion of power.

Andrzej smokes his pipe while ordering everyone around as they push off. They comply, but when he tells the young man to clean and shows him how he's filled the bucket the wrong way, things begin to get tense. The camera is low on the young man as he wipes the deck with a rag. At ground level, the camera gives the characters a very large presence, creating the impression that things are about to explode. There is no longer any need for the background to be in focus, for now it is only these three, the boat, and the uncertainty of the water.

When Krystyna asks Andrzej to offer a kind word to the young man, his only response is to bark another order. When the young man sees that Andrzej has taken his knife, he claims that he doesn't require a knife in order to fend for himself, brushing off a pant leg as if preparing for a fight. Andrzej toys with him before throwing the knife. The young man ducks so as not to be hit, and the knife tumbles into the water. He lurches at Andrzej, who pushes him against the ropes. He looks down, noticing that he has lost a button from his shirt. Andrzej picks up the button and laughs, pushing the young man onto a sail. He lies on his back, looking up at Andrzej, at a loss as to where to go. Andrzej laughs as the young man scoots toward the end of the sail. Krystyna reels the sail in, and the young man jumps back onto the boat. Andrzej punches him, and he falls into the water, the boat quickly leaving him in its wake.

The music begins again, the sky dark, the young stranger farther and farther away. Krystyna worries that the young man will drown, but Andrzej is convinced that he was lying about not knowing how to swim. Either way, we cannot see him. It appears that he is underwater. Krystyna dives off the boat toward the buoy where the young man fell. Andrzej shows signs of nervousness, directing Krystyna, shouting and pointing her in the right direction. Anchoring the boat (pausing the game, suspending the conflict), Andrzej dives in after her. Andrzej and Krystyna examine the four-sided buoy, and find nothing. As they swim away, the young man resurfaces, grasping onto the black and white striped float. He gasps for air, as if he had in fact been drowning, when in reality he was simply hiding from the others.

Andrzej and Krystyna become hysterical as they climb back onto the boat. She accuses him of drowning the young man, and Andrzej calls out to him, panicking, recognizing that he doesn't even know his name. This is a moment of realization for Andrzej, who all this time felt that he was winning the game. Now he begins to see that he was not a big man, but a thought-less boar, so self-involved that he never even took a moment to ask the young man's name. This internal admission only makes him angry, and so he begins to lash out. He picks up the young man's rucksack, reaching to throw it overboard, and wipe out any trace of his existence, along with any memory of his own weakness. Krystyna stops him, accusing him of killing the young man, kneeling before him as he holds her by the wrists, ready to explode. She calls him a "Tough guy! Phony! Clown!" Each word pierces him, and he pushes her down, until she is on her back, attacking him with insults. The image is primitive, of man and wife in a struggle, half-naked and wet from the water. Andrzej tells Krystyna that "without me you'd be a whore!" This is the final straw. Krystyna pulls away, telling him that she despises him. She begins to cry, and he dives off the boat, away from her, toward his unknown fate. She shouts after him, the sail waving behind her like a flag of victory.

We watch the young man as he swims back to the boat and climbs onto the stern. Krystyna is so angry at having been deceived that she slaps him several times when she sees him. She turns around to call Andrzej back, her hair and face still dripping with water and salty tears. The young man drips from head to toe in the background. He helps her to call out Andrzej's name, but it is pointless. Her voice is hollow, an echo that falls silent in the mist. The water is silent in response, waves lapping, reminding us that nature shows no mercy.

Wet and cold, the young man shakes. Standing in the lower portion of the boat, he apologizes while Krystyna paces above him, saying that he's just like Andrzej, "only half his age and twice as dumb." He insults her bourgeois lifestyle in retort. "Bet you've got a four-room apartment," he says. "I suppose you live four students to a room," is her comeback. He says that he lives with six. She did the same once, she points out, as did Andrzej. "You're no better than him, understand?" She says. "He was just like you. And you want to be like him. And you will be, if you've got the guts." She proceeds to reminisce about the difficulties of student life. She asks him if his parents are still alive. He says that they are. She asks him if they support him. He replies that his father does on occasion. It is the first moment, other than the poem, where we learn anything practical about the young man. And though he may remain nameless, at last he is real. He is no longer a stranger, nor a possible danger, yet somehow this truthfulness also makes him less enigmatic. Krystyna throws him Andrzej's terrycloth robe and turns away while he changes out of his drenched clothes. As he undresses, he is reborn. At last he is becoming a man who needn't hide behind illusiveness anymore.

The young man is now dressed in Andrzej's clothes. He sits down, and Krystyna sits behind and above him, picking up a towel to dry his hair. He shakes off her motherly touch and turns around to face her. Coming up to her level, he is close to her, making this playing field equal, refusing to be a little boy. They kiss passionately, and then the alarm clock rings (though they've been up for hours), and they pull apart, her face on his shoulder. He looks off in the opposite direction, his profile against the backdrop of the ropes, now so delicate and humbled by his transformation, the lake in the distance. He may not have mastered himself, the boat, the water, or even Andrzej, but now he is whole, his head sheltered by the crook of her neck. Krystyna kneels down to turn off the clock.

Krystyna is in the foreground, the sail looming over the young man's head. He holds his pants in his hands and apologizes to her, addressing her formally, calling her Pany (or Mrs.). He has faltered, the little boy crawling back. Yet when he kneels beside her to pack his bag, we can tell by Krystyna's expression that she desires him. Together they hold one of his radishes that had fallen from his bag. Together they drop it and hold hands. There is great tenderness between them, and anticipation of fulfilled desire, the sail sheltering them, letting through a small pocket of light as he touches her hair. The only sound is of the water hitting the sides of the boat, and of the wind beating the sail. They begin to kiss, and the sounds become louder as he holds her by the neck, laying her down. As the sounds increase, their embrace becomes complete. And even though they make love, we never learn his name.

The following image is from the boat's point of view. The sun is rising in the distance. The water is placid, no longer something that needs to be tamed. The world is gliding by. "It's Monday," the young man says, as the shot transitions to his profile, clear as the background of sky, countryside, reeds, and water. It is a solemn expression, marking the event with the simplicity of a day—just as yesterday was Sunday, a day that changed his life. "Monday's the best day," he says, referring to how easy it is to hitchhike and find a ride. Once again Krystyna is at the helm, and while the young man looks down in contemplation, she looks out at the water and at the world. She asks him if he's ready to get off. He repeats the question with surprise. He replies that he is but is clearly sad and hurt. The saxophone begins again as he reaches for his rucksack.

Krystyna pulls over and the young man jumps down onto a loose log, which is the first of many in a row. He looks at her intensely but says nothing as he walks away. She, too, is quiet. He turns his back on her and on us, now walking from log to log, a thin figure, an anonymous form. Watching him walk on the logs, we see that he is once again on shaky ground, still haunted by a self-conscious longing. He missteps and falls into the water. He is the knife in the water. At this exact moment, the camera cuts to a new shot in which Krystyna continues to look out at the logs and the land, her expression pensive, enlivened by the wind. The stranger is gone as abruptly as he came.

When Krystyna returns to shore, Andrzej is waiting on the dock, nervous in his bathing suit. Though we only see him from behind, his anxiety is palpable. In silence they meet and bring down the sail. Andrzej lights a cigarette, inhaling shakily, looking like a man who has committed a crime. He gets dressed. Krystyna pins her hair and puts on her glasses, looking exactly how she did at the beginning of the film. Not a word is said until they drive away from the dock, which appears harmless and small when in the distance. Just as Krystyna looks the same as she did at the start of the film, so does the dock look unaffected. It is Andrzej who looks transformed, with his scruffy beard and uncertain movements. He is just as hotheaded as he was at the start, but he is no longer as confident. He senses his weakness and feels ashamed. Just as the young man became real through revealing himself, so has Andrzej, by finding humility.

She asks Andrzej if he's afraid to go to the police. He responds no, but the tears in his eyes and the lump in his throat betray his fears. She asks him again, and he admits that he is. She tells him not to go, that his fear is punishment enough. He tells her that she doesn't understand because it wasn't her fault. He doesn't believe her when she says that the young man returned to the boat and that he was fine. He asks her not to protect him. She tells him that she went so far as to be unfaithful to him with the young man, and again he doesn't believe her. He doesn't trust anyone, and now, not even himself. He has committed a crime, one of arrogance but not of murder. They arrive at a fork in the road where a sign points toward the local police station, 10 kilometers away. The howling whistle of a train is heard in the distance. Light drops of rain dot the windshield and remain, as the wipers were stolen while they were away.

The camera switches to their view of the road, and there is unity achieved between the audience and these two characters. There are no more shadows passing over them. If there were, they would pass over us as well.

The camera returns to the car, with Andrzej in the foreground and Krystyna in the back. She looks down at her hands and up at the sign, trying to decide. In the distance is the road, an endless perspective in which the narrowing horizon is also an opening to a new world. The window that reveals this road is open a crack, allowing air and clarity in, where the rest of the window is obscured by patterns of rain, bleeding reality into the soft palette of a watery world. The trees rustle in the wind. The train whistle grows stronger.

Krystyna asks Andrzej to finish the story of the seaman who stepped onto broken glass. Andrzej answers: "He got overconfident. Did the trick once too often. He was a stoker. Hard soles from walking on coke. Been ashore a year. His feet had gone soft." Here Andrzej is speaking of himself. It is the closest that he can come to admitting his mistakes. He had become too sure of himself in his manhood and his material possessions. Meeting the young, nameless hitchhiker, believing he'd let him drown, reminds him that he, too, had once been young, ambitious, and unsure. She asks him if the seaman ever attempted the trick again. Andrzej replies that he doesn't know what happened to him. A cock crows. Andrzej starts the car, and the music begins again. A lonely saxophone sounds a tribute to longing—a tribute to life.

The camera is down the road, far behind the car, watching and waiting to see what they'll do next. We are left wondering which way they'll turn, as we ponder the quivering reflections of the slippery road. Fade to black. We'll never know.

As exhilarating as it was for Polanski to make his first feature, *Knife in the Water* was a difficult shoot. Though his relationship with Basia was crumbling and he knew she was having an affair, he felt unable to discuss the matter even with his closest friends. To make matters worse, Andrzej Munk, Polanski's dear teacher and friend, died tragically in a car accident just days before the end of the shoot. Everyone was heartbroken, so much so that Kuba Goldberg and Polanski argued with a police officer on the very same day and had to spend the night in jail. On the drive home from Mazury, Polanski himself was in an accident with Goldberg and Jerzy Lipman, who was driving the prop Peugeot (used to replace the original Mercedes, as a way of getting critics off their back). Polanski suffered a skull fracture and had to remain in the hospital for two weeks while his step-mother Wanda (with whom he'd now made peace), stayed nearby so that she could bring him soup. It was a trying time for Polanski. In his autobiography he speaks of one moment during the shoot in which he sat alone, asking for the fortitude to complete the film without projecting his disappointment in Basia to the crew. Just like the young man in *Knife*, in many ways he was still a boy working to become a man, battling the ego and excess that comes with youth.

The original sound of the picture was unusable, and the film wound up being dubbed, one of the reasons the hitchhiker and Krystyna's voices do not belong to the original actors. The film did not strike a chord with Polish critics (most of whom belonged to political factions) of that time. Bossak stood up for the film against criticism from people like Party Secretary Wladyslaw Gomulka, saying he was only interested in what fellow artists—and not politicians—had to say. Yet it was a time in Poland when to reach some, one had to reach everyone. Unlike Wajda, Polanski had not captured a generation or a political mood, for what he achieved in *Knife* was far more universal. It is a film about desire—the desire to assert one's self and one's manhood, and to make something of one's life. It is a young man's story, but it is also an old man's film, a remarkably sophisticated achievement for a young filmmaker. Anyone can relate to *Knife* simply because it is about the basic struggles between men and women, and interrelationships between men. The actors in the film (except for the young hitchhiker) do not even look particularly Polish, nor does the landscape itself. In *Knife in the Water* every element takes its natural place. People are people, the land is land, and water, water. Do not ask them to be more, for they are everything they need to be.

By making *Knife*, Polanski asserted himself as an individualist who, unlike other filmmakers whom he admired, didn't need to speak to a particular audience for his message to be clear. His language belonged to the camera. It was purely cinematic, and cinema—the pure and unadulterated image—belongs to everyone.

Polanski had asserted himself as a great talent who could not be confined to the communist model. He was a filmmaker who would make his way in the West, and through this achievement, would also find himself a Polish success. He was a man in search of personal freedom, looking to exile to relieve him of constraints. Like the young hitchhiker, he was hanging from ropes off the edge of the boat, telling others that he didn't know how to swim. But he knew exactly who he was and what he was doing. It would take a little while, but he would realize every dream. Whatever he may have thought or said, in his heart he knew how to swim.

He took his car, the last vestige of his marriage, said goodbye to his family and friends, and headed west for the border.

Bridge to Freedom: England in the Sixties

Driving into Germany, Polanski began to feel a new weightlessness. It was spring of 1962; he was 28 years old and had nothing to speak of other than a car and Polish Zlotys, a meaningless currency outside of Poland. His marriage was ending, and it was clear to him that he could not make his way as a filmmaker in Poland. In spite of having experienced great tragedy as a child, in many ways he remained an innocent. He had clung to the sails of his dreams and the potential of art to give life to his imaginings. He was like a child waiting to pounce on the possibility of good fortune. Choosing the unknowable was the greatest decision that he could have made.

Exiting communism meant leaving behind the confines of social idealism turned into fascism. Although Polanski had left Poland before, this time it would be permanent. From now on *he* would determine his relationship to sex, art, and political beliefs. Going west meant becoming the master of his own dominion. The hollow echo of such freedom can be intimidating for some who find themselves strangers in a strange land, feeling that they will not exist if they aren't known. Yet for Polanski such empowerment was all that he needed.

His vast network of friends would prove to be the cushion that assisted his transition to the West. His first move was to visit his friends Ignac Taub and Marek Hlasko in Munich, both of whom were struggling to make their way. He then moved on to Paris, where he was reunited with his dog, Jules, and rented a small room in Andrzej Katelbach's house. He took a quick trip with Zbigniew Cybulski to Cannes and felt encouraged that there was plenty of fun and adventure to be had.

This time period in Paris was somewhat grim. Basia, in her transition to Barbara, had ended an affair with Italian director Gillo Pontecorvo[1] and moved on to German actor Karl-Heinz Boehm. Her marriage with Polanski was officially over. In his autobiography, Polanski writes of how he waited for her on the street outside a divorce lawyer's office, too poor to spring for a coffee. When she didn't come, he called her lover's apartment. He writes of the lightness he felt when she said that they shouldn't see each other anymore, as if all the pain of their relationship suddenly dissipated. All was not lost. After all, he was in Paris, and life still had much to offer.

Through Pierre Roustang, Polanski met Gérard Brach, a small man with a scar across his forehead—a memento left by his ex-wife's high-heel. Brach ran errands for Roustang and was so broke that he slept in his office. He would later become a recluse. Brach was an interesting character who Polanski immediately developed an affinity for, and the two became inseparable. Of Brach, Polanski writes, "We found we had a great community of ideas, Gérard and I: the same kind of humor; the same sense of the absurd." The two began to write together, working on individual scenes and subsequently building the story. They decided that the pieces would come together later, and it was with this technique that they first conceived of the premise for *Cul-de-Sac* (1966), originally titled *Dicky*, and later *If Katelbach Comes*.

Unable to get Roustang to agree to *Katelbach*, Polanski eventually signed a contract with Alpha Productions, a joint venture with the West German distribution company, Atlas Films. The deal ultimately didn't work out, but meanwhile Roustang gave Polanski and Brach small writing jobs to help keep them going. Also, *Knife in the Water* was invited to the Venice Film Festival, where it won the Critics' Prize. The film picked up some momentum at its premiere in France, and *Mammals* won first prize at the Tours Film Festival, which earned him a statue designed by Max Ernst.[2] Just as Polanski blossomed in the West, so did the possibilities for his work.

Although (with a few exceptions) Polanski did not hold particular respect for the New Wave movement (as it had a very different technical approach, which Polanski considered to be loose), it was still an advantage and an honor to work in their midst. Roustang brought Polanski together with Claude Chabrol and others, and they made a series of shorts, which when put together became *The Beautiful Swindlers*. Polanski and Brach's portion, *River of Diamonds*, was about a French girl who takes a Dutch man for a diamond necklace. Filmed on location in Amsterdam, *River of Diamonds* was shot by Jerzy Lipman, and Polanski's lover Nicole Hilartain played the girl. He was even able to enlist Krzysztof Komeda to compose the soundtrack. Even though the critics enjoyed *River of Diamonds*, the film as a whole was a failure.

In the spring of 1963 Polanski attended the Cannes Film Festival, where he saw Federico Fellini's[3] *8½* for the first time. He was blown away by the masterpiece as if it were the fulfillment of a fantasy. It was here that he met Hugh Hefner's partner, Victor Lownes, who was starting up Playboy's European division. Lownes told Polanski to keep in touch if he ever came to London.

In August of the same year, Polanski was invited to the Montreal World Film Festival with *Knife in the Water*, and once back in Paris, he discovered that it was to show at the New York Film Festival at Lincoln Center. It was the festival's first year, and there was a great deal of excitement surrounding its inception. Polanski was asked to present his film, with all of his expenses paid. Polanski's response to New York during his visit was varied. Surprised by the contrast of high and low coexisting in such tight quarters, he saw that the fantasy of a perfect America perceived by the East had been erroneous. Yet, at the same time, it was comforting to discover that the differences were not as great as he had imagined. Polanski was impressed by the casual openness of New Yorkers and their informal approach.

Introducing the film, Polanski, who spoke very little English, decided to use his limitation as a resourceful trick, saying that he was better at making films than he was speeches, and so he wanted to screen *Knife in the Water* immediately. There was an enthusiastic uproar in the audience. It was the moment that got New Yorkers hooked on Polanski, and Polanski hooked on New York audiences.

If this experience had not been enough, a still from *Knife* appeared on the September 1963 cover of *Time* magazine, along with the headline, "Cinema as an International Art." The following winter his film was nominated for an Academy Award for best foreign picture. Meanwhile, he signed a contract with the prestigious William Morris Agency's Paris office. To Polanski, Los Angeles was a fantasy, remarking that, "It was like entering a safe new world." In his autobiography, he recalls being "so naïve that I was amazed when the hotel switchboard operators, from the moment of my checking in, started calling me by my name." In the comfort of his Cadillac, esteemed Polish composer Bronislau Kaper gave him a tour of Los Angeles. When Kaper first came to pick him up, Polanski slipped in the driveway and tore his only suit. A destroyed suit was becoming a trend for Polanski, for while in New York his suit was nearly destroyed by an exploded bottle of shampoo.

Polanski was taken to Disneyland with Federico Fellini and his wife, the great actress Giulietta Masina.[4] Polanski remarked, "For all of us it was like discovering the America of our childhood dreams." He couldn't help but recall the time when as a boy he had rescued clips of Disney's *Snow White and the Seven Dwarfs* from the bins of a local movie theater.

Knife in the Water lost the Oscar to Fellini's *8½*, and although Polanski felt slight dismay, he wrote, "Losing to such a winner was no disgrace." Polanski stayed on in L.A. for a little while longer, but sadly, as is pointed out in his autobiography, the only interest he could generate in making a Hollywood film was the possibility of remaking *Knife in the Water* for an American audience with Twentieth Century-Fox. The proposed actors were Warren Beatty, Elizabeth Taylor, and Richard Burton. It was a laughable proposal, demonstrating limited imagination on Twentieth Century-Fox's part. When they asked if he would sell them the rights, Polanski responded that they could have them for free.

Returning to Paris, Polanski contacted producer Gene Gutowski, an elegant Polish-born émigré who was based in London. The two had met at Polish Film Week in Munich months before and had stayed in touch ever since. Gutowski wished to work with Polanski, and he hooked him up with Michael Klinger and Tony Tenser of the Compton Group, a company that had made its mark producing soft-core porn. Polanski hit it off with them and an agreement was made; however, they showed no interest in Polanski and Gérard's script, *If Katelbach Comes*. They were looking to move from soft-core porn to horror, and after fewer than three weeks of intense screenwriting sessions with Gérard, *Repulsion* was ready to be made. Coproduced by Compton and Gene Gutowski, along with Sam Waynberg, a Polish born producer based in Berlin who had an option on *If Katelbach Comes*, the script was translated into English, and the project quickly got off the ground.

The cultural revolution of London in the "swinging sixties" was a pleasure to behold. Polanski was given a beautiful apartment down the street from Gene Gutowski and his wife Judy, and he brought Gérard over to share in the fun. He had mod suits made to fit in with the times, hung out at the Ad Lib club, and was welcomed into Victor Lownes "Playboy" circle, which included many international celebrities, such as Warren Beatty, David Bailey, and set designer Dick Sylbert. Making contact with women was also a far more relaxed and free endeavor than it had been in Poland or France. He had found a home in which eccentricity and personal freedom were accepted as a part of everyday life. In London, Polanski felt that he could make a name for himself. In London, he belonged.

REPULSION (1965)

Shot in London, *Repulsion* would star French actress Catherine Deneuve[5] (who had already achieved notoriety in *The Umbrellas of Cherbourg* [1963]) as Carole. He likened the experience of collaborating with Deneuve to "dancing a tango." The character of Carole was based upon a young woman whom Polanski and Gérard had known in Paris. She had a quiet exterior, but when she moved in with a friend of theirs, she displayed other tendencies, often having enraged breakdowns.

Yvonne Furneaux (who co-starred with Errol Flynn in *The Master of Ballantrae* [1953], and also performed in Fellini's *La Dolce Vita* [1960]), was to play Carole's sultry sister, and British actor John Fraser (*Tunes of Glory* [1960]) was Carole's love interest. Desperate to hire cinematographer Gilbert Taylor, the famed director of photography of *Dr. Strangelove* (1964) and *A Hard Day's Night* (1964), Polanski worked hard to convince Klinger to spring for him. Taylor shocked Polanski with his unusual technique. Rather than using direct light, he primarily used bounced light (light reflected off of bounce boards, reflectors, etc.), and he was able to intuitively gauge the amount of light needed to shoot without consulting his light meter, a rare feat for even the best cinematographer. The way in which Polanski worked with his art director, Seamus Flannery, is a perfect illustration of his wholehearted commitment to film. Constructing a model of Carole's apartment, he explained to Flannery that in order to make Carole's disintegration tangible, the audience would need to feel spatial changes. Polanski intended to do this with two mechanical devices. The first would be to use wide-angle lenses. The second would be to literally build movable walls, so that the rooms of the apartment could expand throughout the film. There was also the matter of Carole's hallucinations, which would involve hands coming through the walls to grab at her. Forty years later, this trick could be done employing digital technology, but in the 1960s, this surreal imagery was executed through the use of latex and other tactile materials. The shoot would be slightly strained because of tensions with Klinger (sparked in part by Polanski's tendency to work overtime and above budget); however, the crew was so devoted to the project that they often worked overtime.

Repulsion is the story of a foreigner who, in her extreme displacement, spirals into a schizophrenic breakdown. As her life becomes more and more fragmented, we touch the horror of her disjointed experience, allowing our internal boundaries to dissipate. The reality of her terror is made palpable by our shared experience. The audience is given insight into her deteriorating world and cannot help but identify with her. While writing the script,

Roman Polanski and Catherine Deneuve on the set of *Repulsion*. (Courtesy of Photofest)

Polanski and Gérard knew that Klinger wanted straight horror, so as was often done in communist times, they cleverly put together a screenplay that was as direct as possible on the outside, with plenty of room on the inside to play with the execution of the film.

Watching *Repulsion* is a terrifying experience. It is a film executed with such care that everyday life and the subtlest moments of fear become twisted into the horrible, playing on the commonality of irrational fear. It is a masterful film, with a starkness so extreme that it is alarming in its effect. Silence becomes internal noise brought about by fear, and spaces become unreliable as they widen into chasms of mistaken thought. It is a film in which Polanski developed many visual themes that would become staples of his cinematic language, and it is also a breakthrough in the psychological/horror genre. It is an exquisite piece, subverting the form for those who are accustomed to today's variety of horror. And for those who are generally not interested in this genre, *Repulsion* is so nuanced that it makes horror seem appealing.

The opening titles for the film are reminiscent of *Un Chien Andalou* (1929) and Hitchcock's *Vertigo* (1958) in which one enters into the spiral of an eye and plummets into an abyss, laying the groundwork for multiple deceptions within the film. Here we are close to the eye of a woman, only even worse than falling into it, we are stuck in front of it. As it witnesses terror and widens in disbelief, we are trapped, forced to watch her, just as Carole will be helpless to her own experience. The credits scroll upward, as if into the ether of nightmare and dream, a direction antithetical to nature, to gravity. We sense that things are already quite wrong. The credits begin to move in contradicting directions, further upsetting any established flow, and the music consists of one high-pitched drone (soundtrack by Chico Hamilton) supported by a minimalist rhythmic pattern, endless in its anticipation. It is a primitive drumbeat, harboring anxiety coupled with the agitating buzzing of an inhuman sound.

The camera is close up on Carole's face, and then cuts to one hand holding another that appears limp, perhaps even dead. We see the face of a woman lying in repose, towel on her head, mask on her face. We immediately identify that this is a beauty salon, but the impression is already one of a strange disconnect and of death. The camera pans along the woman's still body lying beneath a white sheet, to reveal that it is Carole who is holding her hand. She stares off into space, and we realize that the opening credits were a representation of her inner world—the sounds inside her head, and the terror that she feels. The woman on the bed asks Carole if she has fallen asleep, and though she is quick to apologize, it is clear that even though we are only a few minutes into the film, Carole is in a dream.

The woman drawls, "You must be in love or something." It is as if Carole doesn't even hear her. Her dreaminess is being misinterpreted as that of a light-hearted girl lost in a fantasy, but as the story unfolds we see that it is of a much darker nature.

The salon is a busy one, filled with women working hard to beautify themselves, but Carole is effortlessly beautiful and seemingly unaware. She wanders the streets with the relaxed swagger of a "swinging sixties" baby doll, but she still seems lost. There is an iciness about her appearance, but her voice and her accent are warm. The camera is close behind her, a Polanski trademark in which the audience feels that they are breathing down the protagonist's neck, creating an awkwardness that is pleasantly distasteful, inspiring apprehension. A worker on the street calls out to her, and the camera turns to watch him as the audience also becomes victim to his lecherous gaze.

A young male suitor follows her into a restaurant and offers to take her to a better place. She seems to like him, as he is the first person to cheer her, but she declines his offer, saying that she has to get back to work. Her voice is childlike and meek, and she glances down at the table flirtatiously. When he reaches to touch her hair she shakes off his touch. The young man walks her back to work, the camera stalking once again, as he tries to convince her to have dinner with him that night. She says that she can't, that her sister is cooking a rabbit. He responds to this by saying, "I thought they'd all been killed off . . . poor bunny." Perhaps he is referring to Carole, who herself may be the cute and lovable victim.

In the elevator going home, the solemn music from the salon is carried over, indicating that she is in her own world, isolated from external sounds. She looks down at her hands and bites her fingernails as the elevator ascends, hinting at nervousness with response to movement and closeness—perhaps even an aversion to sexuality. This is the first sign of a feeling of repulsion, for she is repelled by intimacy, and as a result becomes repulsive. When she arrives upstairs, she rings the bell as if she is an outsider in her own home.

In her room Carole stands at the window undressing, looking off into the distance, hair blowing in the wind. There is a churchyard outside, and the sounds of children playing resound inside the apartment. It is one of the only external sounds that Carole filters in, a clear selection of childhood memory. Carole washes her feet, the camera panning up to her face. She sees a razor and is drawn to it, removing it from the glass. When she talks to her sister, Carole asks why her boyfriend has to leave his toothbrush in her glass. Her sister ignores her, instead tells her a story about the Minister of Health who discovered eels emerging from his sink. She finds this very funny—the story suggesting that nowhere is safe—but Carole doesn't, looking down as she hugs the rim of a wooden salad bowl. She then looks at the wall and says, "I must get this crack mended." Her sister nearly questions her but is distracted by the doorbell instead. We have only seen Carole's face, and do not know if the crack is real. The statement may be a reflection of her splitting internal landscape, and as the film progresses, cracks will begin to surface everywhere.

The dynamic between Carole, her sister, and the sister's boyfriend, Michael, is established when Michael comes home. He is a nuisance in

Carole's life—an intrusive figure, and for them, she is often a third wheel. When he arrives at the house he pinches Carole's cheek, speaking to her in French, but she pulls away, walking down the hall and into the shadows. He comments to her sister that Carole is "a bit strung up," saying that perhaps she should go to the doctor. Her sister responds by saying that she's just sensitive. Carole's sister acts like a neglectful mother, babying her at times, yet completely indifferent to her needs. When Carole asks her how long she and her lover will be away, her sister doesn't heed the signs that Carole is deeply afraid of being left alone.

The fear of being alone is connected to the fear of intimacy, and we are presented with clues, both subtle and extreme, to Carole's interest and wariness of sexual interaction. She sits at the table kissing her own arm, the sound of water dripping from the sink in the background. Like a child playing, trying to see how such a kiss would feel, she does so shyly, until she views her distorted reflection in a teapot. Catching herself in the act of love frightens her, and she turns away from herself, her hair aglow, and her face in shadow. She hears a sound, suddenly attuned to what is going on around her. Perhaps afraid that she was being watched, she goes to the door and looks out the peephole. It was only a neighbor with her dog. (The further one delves into Polanski's work, the more one sees how innocuous characters—such as this stranger in the hallway—can give birth to absolute terror.)

A clock ticks. There is a dog barking outside, leading Carole to the window, where she sees a nun walking in the courtyard, her habit flapping in the wind. She turns to a photo of herself as a child in a family portrait, and the camera pushes in. Is there an answer in the photo that might explain Carole's behavior? The photo is of a perfect family, and so we can only guess what if any horrors lie behind its immaculate façade. It is an intelligent trick, to bring us to the photograph yet never explain its purpose. By leaving the film open to interpretation, the audience is immediately engaged, imaginations running wild. We become open to hostility and fear, just as Carole is.

We begin to comprehend the extent of her problems when we see Carole in bed at night. A clock ticks nervously. She hears Michael and her sister make love, her eyes open wide, even kissing her own hand. She is trying on the guise of womanhood, yet cannot accept its form. She feels sickened by her desire, yet it is apparent as she tosses and turns that she is both disgusted and excited. Long shadows play along the ornate ceiling, and the curtains flap as if they too are experiencing unrest. She is plagued by curiosity, yet simultaneously she feels intruded upon. This is the source of her disturbance, and as she begins to unravel, these feelings will become hallucinations. The sounds of her sister's moans pervade the room. The camera pulls away from her, toward the foot of the bed.

The next morning Carole walks in on Michael while he is shaving, and apologizes, quickly retreating to her room. She is like a child who has a crush on a man yet has nightmares of him, unable to understand her physical response. Carole asks her sister if he will be there all the time. She brushes her hair, looking down at the folds in the sheets of the lovers' unmade bed. The two move down the dark hallway in an apartment that seems to consist primarily of shadows and curtains, glass panels and doors. The atmosphere is made tense by a neighbor playing scales on the piano, which creates a sense of constant ascension and anticipation. While the music plays, Carole stands at the breakfast table, picking up and then neglecting a piece of toast. She carelessly drops a few cubes of sugar into a cup of coffee, and stands while sipping it, the zipper of her dress undone, reminding us that, indeed, she is a neglected child. Basic things like feeding and dressing herself seem near impossibilities.

Back at work, a coworker cries over the cruelty of her latest boyfriend. Speaking of men she asks, "Oh, why are they so filthy?" Carole brushes at the seat beside her, as if trying to rid herself of a thought. At the end of the day, we watch as she walks down the street, the perfect picture of a "swinging sixties" bird, but when she comes across a crack in the sidewalk, she circles the spot, mesmerized. She sits down before it, as if at the mouth of a stream that divides into two paths, and choosing the one that leads into an abyss, she allows her mind to wander.

When her young suitor shows up on the scene he is angry at her, saying that they had a dinner date and that he has been waiting for her. It is becoming clear that she has time lapses and moves in and out of reality. Once he has calmed down he asks her if she is okay, saying that she looks strange. A trio plays music while crossing the street, as the duo drive away. Sitting in his car Carole stares straight ahead, her blond hair and white jacket making an icy impression. He leans in to kiss her, but quickly changes his mind when she pulls away. He lights a cigarette instead and moves away from her. He looks at her with concern. He smiles and again moves in to kiss her. She kisses him back, as the piano scales begin to play once again. The camera turns around to see her face, and her wide-open eyes hint a slight aversion. He pulls away and stubs out his cigarette. She opens her door, and jumping out of the car, she nearly gets hit. An alarming drum roll begins, and the camera is tight on his face as he calls out her name. He is trapped within the frame, just as Carole is trapped within the horrifying landscape of her mind.

This time when Carole goes up in the elevator to her flat the soundtrack becomes cacophonous. Rather than watching her from the side as we did before, sensing her anxiety yet taking comfort in the familiarity of her surroundings, we now watch her from behind, the black steel grating of the elevator casting crisscrossed shadows before her. She wipes at her mouth, trying to erase the dirty kiss. The cuts are quick, moving the action along, allowing the audience to feel Carole's tense disgust.

Back at home she brushes her teeth vigorously, working hard to wash herself clean, as would someone who has been violated. She picks up her water glass and dumps Michael's toothbrush and razor into the trash so that she is free of his masculine presence. Even when in the company of others, Carole remains isolated and alone. She passes by the darkened living room where the only source of light is a boxing match that her sister is watching on TV. She revels in the glory of strong men in battle. She is the overtly sensual one—a kept woman with a robust sex life, while Carole cannot accept even the gesture of a kiss. Her sister pets her head and tries to comfort Carole while she cries in bed, both of them completely in shadow.

In their home, light almost never dominates a space. It is always directional, emitting from a nearby source. Dogs bark and bells toll, creating a hollow, empty place. Now it is her sister's turn to pull the curtain aside and stand at the open window. Perhaps there is a shared memory between her and Carole, but what it is, we will never know.

Carole lies in bed at night, listening to their lovemaking once again, a spotlight on her face. She rolls over and closes her eyes, her face half in shadow. Sounds from the street permeate the room. Before Carole was isolated from external sounds, but now one feels her lack of boundaries, as the outside filters in. She looks at her doorknob in expectant anticipation, and it turns slowly. One wonders whether she wants someone to come in or not. It isn't a suitor, but her sister, asking Carole why she got rid of Michael's toothbrush and razor. As they prepare to leave the next morning, they stand in the hallway in the light. Carole sits in the dark in her room, begging her sister to stay. "Don't do anything I wouldn't do," Michael says cheekily, treating Carole like a normal young woman excited to have the place to herself for a couple of days. It is as if Michael is psychologically opening the door to her misfortunes. Carole watches her sister leave from the open window.

The camera cuts to a woman being sprayed in the face. "Oh," the woman exclaims, "You're killing me!" Carole demurely enters the room, and the woman looks up at her. "There's only one way to deal with men," she says, the camera tight on her mouth, nose and chin, as viewed from Carole's upside-down perspective. "That's treat them as if you don't give a damn about them." The image of her mouth is a grotesque one. The woman's harsh voice coupled with the discomfort of sharing Carole's point of view makes us feel that we, too, may fall into her mouth and swim with her callous words. It is an image that recalls the fantasy of a child, who, having no way to protect herself, feels as if she may be overtaken by the scary old lady. "There's only one thing they want," the woman continues. "They're all the same, just like children," she says. "They want to be spanked, then given sweets." Carole cowers in the corner. Her coworker asks if she feels all right, but she looks on blankly, in a daze. Her friend stops her work in order to see if she's all right. Even the talkative woman props herself up on her elbows in order to have a look. We wait for Carole to come back to attention. The camera moves with her coworker, prolonging the wait, transitioning from a wide shot to a tight one as her friend touches her hair. It is a high-angle shot, making Carole appear small and fragile. The smooth move from a wide-angle to a tight shot creates the feeling of a shrinking room. When Carole finally does acknowledge her, she looks up innocently, like a shy little girl. Unable to get through to her, her boss sends her home.

When Carole returns home from work, she uses her key to enter the apartment. She may have gained access into her home now that her sister is away, but the place feels quiet, even alien. She now faces the question of existing in the terrifying closeness of being left alone, even if only for a few days. She is like a child who has been abandoned and cannot find a way to function in the world. As she crosses the threshold into her apartment, the outside and inside worlds collide, for now we are entering a space that exists only in the mind.

Shutting the front door, she removes one shoe and then the other, kicking them off like a child who has come home from school and wants to shed their proper attire as soon as possible. She takes off her coat and puts her fingers in her mouth coquettishly, removing her gloves with her teeth. She walks to the open window, trying to get closer to the joyful sounds of the street as they flood the apartment.

Carole explores the newly abandoned space. Various motifs arise, creating images that will endure for the rest of the film. They mark time repulsing the audience with their disfigured beauty. One of these is the rabbit, the "poor bunny," which Carole pulls from the refrigerator and then forgets about, leaving it by the phone. As the film progresses, we will watch the rabbit carcass deteriorate along with Carole's mind, and we will recite the comment "poor bunny" in unison, as one cannot help but wish for Carole an alternative fate.

Another motif is the literal breaking down of Carole's environment, as signified by the cracks in the wall (perhaps a tribute to the disintegration of Roman's world as a child—the disintegration of life that came with the erection of the ghetto wall). When Carole goes to the sink to have a glass of water, she hears a loud sound, as if something is being struck by lightning. She turns to the wall, and there is a close-up of her eye. It is the same wide-eyed look as in the credits at the beginning of the film. We are then taken into her perspective when we see that a crack has formed along the wall. Fade into darkness.

As the musical scales are played once again, Carole stands at her sister's closet, pulling out a very womanly dress. As she closes the closet door, a mirror reflects a man standing behind her, and a chilling sound begins like an alarm going off in her head, resounding in us as well. The camera pushes in slowly on the mirror's reflection, showing that the man is now gone. It is as if she is being punished for opening the door to sexuality. It is a terrifying moment, simple in its execution yet completely effective. Carole's mind may be playing tricks on her, but for her, the presence of a male figure is very real. She looks around the room, and there is no one there.

At night, once again in her room, Carole hears footsteps in the hallway. A clock ticks incessantly. Where lover's sounds once kept her awake, now there are stalking sounds so real that it is difficult to distinguish whether or not they arise from her mind. Whatever the truth, she is paralyzed by fear.

The next morning she draws herself a bath, ignoring it until it overflows. She looks into the mirror and is able to see herself without the addition of an intruding stranger. When she walks outside, we are now in front of her and beside her rather than behind, making apparent the impossibility of escape. The walls are closing in. The music signals an alarming march. She looks about suspiciously, as if she suspects even the birds and the trees. The outside world is being phased out, as she seems to skip days of work, unable to behave responsibly. Day and night also seem to blend together, as the shadows in her home are overwhelming.

At home, she passes the rabbit carcass, which resembles a poor, skinned dog that appears to be decomposing. The rabbit represents the passing of time, and it is a clue to her further descent, for she doesn't even notice it— neither sees nor smells it. She flips on a light switch, and at this moment, the wall splits open. This time the crack is substantial, as opposed to the vein-like lines shown earlier in the film. It is a chasm, a clear sign that her foundation is crumbling.

Carole locks herself into her room and sits on her bed. She hears footsteps creep around her, listening attentively as they come closer. She sees the light in the hallway turn on, filtering through the edges of the door. It is a terrifying moment, especially because she is supposed to be alone. The door blocked by her bureau begins to push against the wardrobe, trying to open onto the room. It cracks slightly, and we hope that the horror will stop there. As the door opens completely, a faceless man enters the room. Carole gasps but cannot scream. The man rapes her from behind, and a quick succession of shots shows her horror as she clasps the sheets, writhing about in terror. The only sound is of a ticking clock, as she opens her mouth but cannot scream. It is an unbearable moment, one from which we wish to turn away. As a result of Carole's duplicitous feelings about sex, her fantasies have been realized. Now she must protect herself, for as the woman in the salon said, she believes that all men want is sex. She will now have a violent reaction, justified in her mind by the crime committed against her and by the darkness of the night.

The phone rings. Carole lies on the floor, waiting to pick it up. The caller is her suitor, Colin, and he is worried about her. She hangs up the phone without saying a word. All that we hear are the flies buzzing around the rabbit carcass. She goes into the kitchen, eats a cube of sugar while looking out the window and is charmed by the distant sound of children playing. We see that the potatoes are rotting, beginning to grow sprouts as her world crumbles. It is an image taken from Roman's childhood, and his memories of watching a bean grow through cheesecloth in his grandmother's house.

Carole returns to work. She holds a pair of cuticle scissors and is frozen, her lip sweating as if she is about to do something wrong. She uses the cuticle scissors too aggressively, and winds up cutting a client's finger. The woman screams as dramatic music rises, including a high-pitched sound that resembles a scream. Blood drips from the customer's finger.

Carole sits in the locker room with her coworker, who is trying to convince her to go home or go out and see a film. Carole smiles for what may be the second time in the film. Her friend describes to her a Chaplin movie that she thinks she should see, and the two laugh and carry on like schoolgirls. This moment of reprieve tricks us into believing in Carole's potential for normalcy, but she quickly withdraws and stiffens. Her friend pulls Carole's bag from the locker, and there is a look of horror on her face when she sees the dead rabbit inside. The carcass reminds us that Carole's exterior is deceptive, for however beautiful and normal she may appear, she is, in fact, disconnected from reality.

As Carole walks down the street, there is a dominant drumbeat. Her march continues. She is completely vacant, practically possessed, as she passes a crowd gathered around a car crash. This scenario is typical Polanski—the absurdity of one's own breakdown juxtaposed against the backdrop of an even more absurd and deteriorating world. It is the reality of these two elements coexisting while remaining completely disparate at the same time that makes his worlds so interesting.

At home, flies buzz by the phone. The walls continue to crack (a time-consuming trick that was performed manually, through a mechanism that opened the walls, which were painstakingly replastered for the next shot). The potatoes also continue to grow. Carole clings to the walls, which she discovers are soft, and her hands leave imprints on them like clay. Her environment ceases to have a reliable form. She is so unsafe that she can affect the solidity of her own atmosphere.

Her suitor, Colin, comes to the front door and even tries to break it down. He is worried about her, but she cannot feel his concern. All that she can feel is danger. A nearby piano begins to play scales. The intrusive presence of a neighbor is felt as she stands at the elevator watching them. Carol closes the door and clobbers Colin with the candlestick. She seems to feel no remorse. His hand reaches out from the cuff of his perfect suit and white shirt. Then she looks at his ear and a stream of blood flows from his head. There is a sound reminiscent of the shower scene in *Psycho* (1960), and Carole shakes with fear. She draws her hands to her face. Her terror subsides as she boards up the door, dragging his body along the carpet and then into the full bathtub. The image is vivid, as his perfect black suit and white-buttoned shirt become drenched with blood as it mixes with water. For a moment Carole has rid herself of impure thoughts and fears.

In the following scene Carole sits by the window, sewing and singing softly. Her voice trembles as if she were crying. Both the sewing and the singing are self-soothing acts, not to mention that the song that she sings is in French, her native tongue. She is trying to comfort herself, like a child who has misbehaved, sulking in her room, waiting for absolution. Here, Carole is an orphan of sorts, for she is a foreigner in a strange land who, in her displacement, has lost the thread of self. Her sister is away, and her parents are most likely dead. Flies crawl over the rabbit, which is now in an advanced state of decomposition. As layer upon layer of death build up around her, Carole remains oblivious. She retreats to bed, a place where one might normally look for peace; however, for the mentally disturbed, bed becomes the battleground for uncontrollable demons. The mystery man returns to her bed (let us not forget that Colin lies dead in a bathroom down the hall), and she is raped once again, feeding the fuel for her fire. This time the intrusion comes faster, and the scene is shot in close-ups. Darkness prevails.

The following morning, Carole lies naked on the floor of her room. The mailman has delivered a postcard from her sister reminding her to pay the rent. Michael has added his own special comment: "Don't make too much Dolce Vita while we're away." The irony of his note is absurd. The front of the card shows the Leaning Tower of Pisa, emblematic of her crumbling world.

Haunting music plays as night falls. Carole stalks the apartment in rhythm to the music, as if dancing in a daze. The living room is lit by a single lamp, which acts as a spotlight on her decaying world. The room becomes distorted. This is where Polanski begins to push out the walls of the room. To an untrained eye, the effect is purely psychological, and to a professional, the image is pure genius. The expanded room containing a spotlight gives the feeling of being on stage. The awkwardly large space filled by this unflattering light displaces Carole in her own environment. Her experience of mental breakdown is now consummated.

She walks down the hall into an enlarged bathroom where a string hanging from the ceiling sways back and forth. This room also has a stark, stage-like feel, and we begin to think that nothing is real. Water drips down the dark walls. She is suddenly afraid, backing out into the hallway where a hand reaches out from the wall and grabs her. Soon, two more hands reach out, one grabbing her breasts while the other grabs her stomach. It is this horrifying image that defines *Repulsion*, implanting the film in the viewer's mind forever. Now there is no sacred space. Nothing is safe.

Day breaks to the telephone ringing. It is Michael's wife, who assumes that Carole is, in fact, her sister. She calls her a "filthy bitch" and a "filthy little tart," and hangs up the phone. It is as if Carole cannot escape her feelings of sexual guilt and disgust. They meet her everywhere. She goes to the window where three minstrels are playing on the street. The doorbell rings. It is her landlord (played by Patrick Wymark), who, like Colin, wears a black suit and white shirt (with the addition of glasses and a black bowler hat). We see him first through the keyhole and then outside the dark door, ringing the bell and shouting, threatening to call the police. There is a slight echo to his voice. He uses his own key to gain access to the apartment, making the grave mistake of crossing into her world.

The landlord is cautious as he opens the door, confused by all of the blockades. He walks through the darkened room to find Carole barefoot, charming in her flimsy white nightgown. What is strange is that the apartment doesn't seem to smell, for even he doesn't wrinkle his nose in disgust. Perhaps he too is immune to the "repulsion." He examines the apartment like a detective. She hands him the rent. "Let's have a little light on the subject," he suggests, moving to draw the curtains. "No!" Carole shouts, plopping down on the couch just like an ornery little girl. He goes to the window to count the money and smiles when he realizes that he has what he needs.

"I thought I'd seen everything," he says, looking around. "This is a flaming nuthouse." He looks at Carole sitting there, unaware of her own appeal. She pouts in the sunlight, the skirt of her nightgown hiked up around her thighs. He asks her if she always wears such outfits, indicating that it is rather sexy. He kneels down before her and asks if she is sick. He smiles and offers to bring her some water. "White as a sheet," he says, speaking of her. He is in the shadows, and she, in the light.

The landlord, attempting to clean things up, returns the rabbit, which has found its way to the living room and back to the kitchen. He brings Carole water, covers her shoulders with a jacket, and offers to make her "a nice hot cup of tea." Sweating, he paces the floor, and wipes his brow with a cloth while talking about how poor and alone she is, "shaking like a little frightened animal." He touches her neck as she flinches away. "All alone by the telephone," he says and smiles. He walks into shadow at the back of the room, puts on his glasses, and picks up her old family photo. He brings it to the window just as he did with the money and comments that it is very nice.

"There's no need to be frightened of me," the landlord says. A bell tolls outside, punctuating the children's shouts. He tells her that if she takes care of him she can have the apartment without paying rent. He pounces on her. "Just a little kiss between friends," he says, pulling her onto her back and into the light. She struggles about, her blond hair shining in the light. She escapes from him, throwing him aside. He stands up and laughs nervously as we see the razor behind her back. He comes toward her. They face each other and he embraces her. She cuts him at the base of his neck, quickly removing the razor. He recoils, stepping back. He touches himself oddly, confused as to what has happened. He doesn't understand until he sees the blood on his hands. Carole begins to attack him with the razor, cutting him at an awkward angle (as opposed to the clear contact of a knife. Even here she cannot achieve consummation, only a repeated sideways attempt). She continues stabbing, until he begins to gurgle, ceasing to move, her dress covered with blood. She throws him over on his side, and the screen goes black as his body covers the camera lens.

Carole is desperate. The music is solemn, and the camera moves around her, trailing up and away, her head resting in her arms.

In bed that night, the camera closes in on Carole as she stares up at the ceiling, her eyes darting about anxiously. She looks to the right as a horizontal scar cuts its way across the wall beside her. The entire wall cracks open like a mouth waiting to eat her.

The next day, Carole hums while ironing a shirt, and as the camera pans down we see that the iron is unplugged. She sits at her sister's bureau applying lipstick. She seems to have lost her shyness and is able to look at herself. One wonders if her acts of violence have somehow liberated her. She lies in bed, her lips made up, smiling. As she smiles, the nun's bells toll and terror strikes, the male intruder of her dreams appearing in bed beside her.

Carole writes invisible words on the glass panels of the living room doors. The room is even bigger and emptier than before, with shafts of light running down the ceiling. She turns around in circles and moves back down the hallway. As cymbals crash, hands shoot out from the walls. There are many of them—they reach out to her, touching her, and even petting her hair.

Carole lies in bed once again. The camera is handheld, and it moves toward her, examining her eyes, now as wild as they were in the opening credits. It appears that she is afraid of the ceiling, and we see her perspective from behind her head. As the dark shadow across the ceiling goes out of focus, she moves up toward it. It is as if she is levitating toward the final crack, the ultimate scar, as the ceiling closes in on her.

At night, in heavy rain, Carole's sister returns home from her vacation. She pulls her luggage from the car. It is the first time that we are brought outside in a while, signaling the normalcy of other people's lives. Seeing that the door is unlocked, she calls out to her sister. Entering the apartment, she marvels at the state of the place. When she turns on the lights, she cries out. Michael comes over to her, slapping her to calm her down. She points to the bathroom where Colin lies dead in the tub, and as we see Michael's reaction we simultaneously hear a heavy male panting. It is a sound most likely dubbed after the shout, yet it creates an interesting affect. One begins to wonder, if not Michael then from whom does the sound come? Is it from the dead man? Perhaps it is a collective anxiety, as everyone has now been traumatized.

Carole's sister sits on her bed, realizing that Carole is actually underneath, hiding her thin, white hand outstretched on the floor. Responding to the screams, neighbors begin to trickle in through the open door. They stand in a semicircle around the bed. One tries to calm the sister down while the other one comments that she doesn't speak English, attempting to further alienate a woman who has already been estranged. At first they come under the pretense of wanting to help, but it quickly becomes clear that they simply want to watch. Hushed whispers are passed between them as they lift the mattress to uncover Carole. They exchange possible cures for her, such as an ambulance or a shot of brandy. The group forms a grotesquely intrusive crowd, the mark of many great Polanski films. They are made more intimidating by a deforming low-angle shot, creating an alienating image.

Michael swoops in and takes Carole up into his arms, carrying her out of the room. Her face is as lifeless as a doll's. The camera pulls back from them as they leave, giving the viewer a life that is now separate from Carole's. It pans right across a ticking clock, past various figurines, and then down to the Leaning Tower of Pisa postcard, which lies crumpled on the floor. The wistful music used in the opening scene of the film returns as the camera pans up to Carole's childhood photograph, which is now obstructed by a lattice or a grate, such as the one in the elevator earlier. It is a fence of sorts—closing off the past. It is the scar that defines adulthood and the distance from one's childlike self. The camera closes in on her picture, zooming through the grate onto her face until it comes right up against the young girl's eye. We fade out of the film just as we faded in.

Although Klinger was disappointed that Polanski had created such a work of art, complaining that it was "like ordering a Mini Cooper and winding up with a Rolls Royce," *Repulsion* turned out to be a masterpiece of horror, approved of by psychiatrists as an exact portrait of schizophrenia. This seal of approval from the medical profession allowed the film to slide right by the censors. The film received a Silver Bear Award at the Berlin Film festival, thus establishing Polanski as an international filmmaker with great potential. Sam Waynberg took this opportunity to seal a second deal with Klinger, and, at last, Polanski and Brach would have their chance to make *If Katelbach Comes*, now titled *Cul-de-Sac*.

CUL-DE-SAC (1966)

Polanski and Brach made *Repulsion* in order to make it possible to shoot *Cul-de-Sac*. At last they could make their movie. Filmed on a small island in Northumberland, England, the film would star Catherine Deneuve's sister, Françoise Dorléac,[6] Donald Pleasence[7] as her husband George, and American actor Lionel Stander[8] (who was now living in exile) to play the fugitive, Dicky. They also hired playwright Samuel Beckett's favorite actor, the slight and gifted Jack MacGowran[9] to play the second fugitive. For the first time in his life, Polanski was to work with a casting director for whom he drew a perfect image of each character as he imagined them. The result was his ideal cast.

After a successful collaboration with director of photography Gilbert Taylor on *Repulsion*, the partnership was to continue. Taylor knew what Polanski wanted, and he would give the film an extreme look to match its dramatic content. The imagery would be stark, the backgrounds dramatic. The story would take place in a castle on Holy Island, which boasted 300 residents, pubs open 'round the clock, and stories of ghosts and other mysterious happenings. The sardonic humor of the locals was in line with that of the film. Holy Island was accessible only at certain times of the day because when the tide came in the road would disappear underwater, a romantic notion for a film but not always conducive to filmmaking; likewise, neither was the environment of Northern England, with its blustery winds and dreary rain. Polanski, however, thrived on challenge, and as many of his actors have said, he loves to push them (yet wouldn't ask them to do anything that he wouldn't do).

A perfect marriage of high and low, *Cul-de-Sac* combines the wisecracking, straight-talking style of American cinema with the eccentric absurdity of false European decay. It is a film often compared to Samuel Beckett's *Waiting for Godot*. Both stories feature a savior or redeemer who is awaited but never shows, and each have various other comparisons to the "theater of the absurd." *Cul-de-Sac* is a story executed with visual and emotional originality, and though one may draw connections to all of Polanski's films, *Cul-de-Sac* has something unique. It is as if shooting on an island allowed Polanski to rid himself of every excess, and what we are left with is pure character, pure imagery.

Cul-de-Sac is the story of two fugitives who wind up on an island with a castle and take a young couple hostage while they wait for their boss Katelbach to rescue them. Meanwhile, Katelbach never does come, and Albert (Albie for short), the frailer of the two wounded men, dies and is buried in a ditch. The film is essentially a triangle of characters, as was *Knife in the Water*, only here alliances are always temporary. Even the bond of marriage is loose; it does not prevent Teresa, George's young and boisterous wife, from sleeping with a neighbor and later running off with a stranger.

George and Teresa are the young disillusioned couple who inhabit the castle, played respectively by Pleasence and Dorléac. The two live a strange Bohemian life, a direct reaction to George's previously bourgeois existence. Having married a younger woman and been with her for nearly 10 months, George has sold everything connecting him to commerce and rooted himself as an aspiring artist in an eleventh-century castle in which the story of Rob Roy was originally penned. It is here that he has erected a painting studio where his representations of their home hang limply. They are repetitive in their mundane accuracy. Together the couple lives a rather disconnected life. They haunt their oversized home, listening to records and surviving on a diet of fresh eggs provided by their chicken coop next door and shrimp. In the morning George stands at the stove overturning a minuscule hourglass, while Teresa mocks him, laughing hysterically in the background. He watches as the small grains of sand fall through the glass, expecting that nothing will ever change.

Teresa makes love with a handsome young neighbor on the beach under the guise of finding lunch but returns with a meager handful of shrimp. She is gregarious, upbeat, and strong, constantly dominating her meek and nervous husband, George. Like a teenager playing dress-up, she changes her clothes at random, listens to records and smokes cigarettes, as if there is nothing better to do in the world. She mocks George at first, dressing him in her nightgown and putting on makeup. He happily goes along, playing the part of a coquette to her playboy, but late one night when Dicky enters their lives, what seems a silly game between the pair quickly escalates. At first, George is cast in the light of an odd, slightly grotesque character. He confuses his visitors (such as when delirious Albie calls him by his wife's name, Doris), yet the game ultimately exposes him as an emasculated and weak madman.

Shot in black and white, angles are extreme, and the castle's interior arches and dramatic exteriors—the sea, rocks and long reeds of dry grass—all create a dramatic backdrop for the story to unfold. The imagery is dense, with day and night blurred. The film, which takes place over a 24-hour period (like *Knife in the Water*), finds itself confronting reality at every hour of the day. Drinks are poured at twilight, mental breakdowns had at dawn. Every change of the tide as it waxes and wanes according to the moon is felt by characters struggling to escape their predicament. Much of the film addresses the absurdity of fate.

When early in the film Dicky first goes to the house, he watches George talk to neighbors between the slats of wood that form the walls of the chicken coop. Holding an oversized kite high up over his head George looks the buffoon, as if at any moment he will fall back under the weight of a paper kite. Dicky sees George clearly for what he is, yet continues to hide himself within the shelter of nature's bliss. He naps beneath rays of sunlight in a pile of hay where the chickens roost, while his friend and partner Albie sits waiting for him in the car at the bottom of the hill. Dicky abandons himself to sleep and forgetfulness as the waves lap against the tires of Albie's car. Albie, injured and immobile, calls out to Dicky, whom he addresses professionally as Richard, but it is a futile attempt. The sea absorbs the sounds of his voice. This is one of the early images of the film, yet it is also one of the most indelible ones, for it emphasizes the hopeless absurdity of their situation. Even their car is on a causeway that leads nowhere, and half of the time ceases to be a road at all. It is a transforming highway, like a mythical creature that is woman by day and mermaid by night. This very fact lets the viewer know that reality may be slightly skewed when carried onto the island. There is something hypnotic about the near burying of Albie by the sea long before the actual burying of his dead body on shore. As the incoming tide pushes up against his car and his only chance for escape, it becomes clear that both physically and psychologically the two fugitives have met their fate. And just as the chickens fly about in the coop, the rooster has come to rest. As the story progresses, it becomes evident that the isolation of being a fugitive may also be comparable to that of unfulfilled relationships. On Holy Island, all of the characters confront the worst versions of themselves, reflections causing chaos when faced with the truth.

For each character the island represents something different. For Teresa, it is a place to have fun, a chance to get away. For George, it is an escape from the real world of business and superficiality, where fantasies of art, love and history can be met. For Dicky, it is a platform for a dream. He has not endured a lifetime of crime and presumed rejection to end up on an island from which he cannot be rescued. He can only think of Katelbach and of being saved. If Katelbach comes, then salvation can be had, and so it is Dicky's purity of desire that pushes the drama, casting the other characters' desires in a strange light. His singularity of vision obscures the needs of other characters, heightening their absurdity while simultaneously reminding us that what they all need is to be saved. Even though he is a criminal, in many ways Dicky is the good guy of the film.

Though there is some mention of love in *Cul-de-Sac*, in a sense it is a film without a heart. Aside from existing outside all moral codes, taking advantage of isolated surroundings and allowing the mind to run free, the characters do not place importance on human connections. George may weep speaking of his love and devotion for Teresa, yet in reality he hardly knows her and can only objectify her without loving her. She is his playmate, not his partner, and the relationship is one based on romping, not sex and love. They are a married couple in deep water, in over their heads. When George asks Dicky if he's ever been in love, he becomes flushed and hostile. It is no coincidence that at the same time a plane passes overhead, leading Dicky to believe that Katelbach has come in a helicopter to rescue him from his fate. When it becomes clear that it was just a mirage—a plane passing by—Dicky becomes angry and even goes so far as to draw his gun. He would rather instigate more violence than accept the possibility that he may never be free.

Dicky uses this opportunity to claim that women are "all whores." As susceptible to other opinions as George is, this comment merely loosens the ties that bind George to his life. As these strings unravel and because George has allowed himself to get drunk with Dicky, the truth begins to emerge about how he feels about his perfect bohemian life. In fact, George is a man who is finding flaws in his salvation. Drunk, he puts his arms around Dicky and whispers that "the castle is impossible to heat in the winter. It's not practical." This drunken confession confirms that George's overheated notions regarding Teresa and Rob Roy are merely fantasies, and where he will find his true bliss, nobody knows. Even though characters do connect on some level in the film, true attachments are impossible.

Where there is a need for love and a desire for friendship, interpersonal distrust and the instinct to save and protect one's self wins out in the end. When earlier in the film Dicky proposes a toast of homemade liquor between himself and a hesitant George (who moans about his ulcer), Dicky says that it is a drink between friends and insists that George imbibe. Here, friendship is a hostile form of ownership, a way to one-up the other person, not to meet on middle ground. Once drunk, George begs Dicky to decide whether or not they will be friends. It is evident that no matter how hard George tries to live outside the confines of "normal society," its habits are ingrained in him, prohibiting him from experiencing true freedom. This dichotomy makes him a weak character and a weak man, for however he strives to be a rebel and an individual, he thinks only of himself. Therefore, at the end of the film it is he who crumbles under the pressure of facing himself. Dicky may die and Theresa run away, but it is George who is left mad and wild, running aimlessly through the ebbing tide.

Cul-de-Sac is a story about fugitives in which each character comes from a different country. This combustion of archetypes and varying worlds creates an environment so fascinating and bizarre that one cannot take one's eyes off of the action for even a second. George is the meek and intellectual Brit; Teresa, carefree and chaotic, is from France (as Dicky says, "continental"); and Dicky is the gruff American teddy bear with a soft spot in his heart. Each is an outcast, everyone a stranger. And though they all speak the same language, there is a disconnect that stems (in part) from cultural differences. The shared language is visual, a connection found in jokes and imagery, even in a bottle of Teresa's homemade vodka (the only thing that she seems to make herself), rather than in a shared cultural understanding. This divide both highlights and conceals the awkwardness of each character, as they find themselves backed into a corner, finding the true meaning of a cul-de-sac, from which the entrance and exit are one and the same. This is what makes *Cul-de-Sac* so purely cinematic. Here, the image must cross many boundaries in order to reach the audience, traversing the psychological landscape of the viewer, who may also be a fugitive of sorts in his or her own mind. The viewer is carried into a land so absurd that it becomes true to life, an island of surreal inhabitants, each vying for survival on the most human level, a point of identification that can be understood by anyone.

A cul-de-sac is a dead end street, a place through which one cannot pass. *Cul-de-Sac* is the story of a fugitive who finds imprisonment on an island, a holy island no less, depicting the internal imprisonment of character that is universal. What is so fantastic and terrifying about Polanski's films is that however outlandish they may become one does not have to completely suspend disbelief in order to enter into their world. Life is well observed, and characters real, even familiar at times. There are always points of identification that draw the audience in, and as reality becomes heightened, viewers find connections to their own mad world.

The film steers clear of any moral observation or reproach. Entering into these strange lives leaves one rooting for the oversized, lovable, and sometimes brutal Dicky. As if to punish the viewer for choosing, he is the only character who doesn't survive. In some ways Dicky is the purest of the three, for he is always direct, always speaks his mind. He wields a gun and doesn't shy away from violence, even murder, yet all he really wishes for is to get to the other side—to reach his own island where he, too, can be safe, to be saved by his boss, the invisible Katelbach. Dicky is a man who may have been hurt too many times and found that being a tough guy and a fugitive was the best way to go. Being a criminal may be his mode of protection, for just like everyone else, he wishes only to survive.

When Dicky is bit, Dicky bites back. When Teresa sets fire to rolls of paper between his toes, he whips her with his belt in order to prove that they are not friends and perhaps to expel his sexual frustration. Though his tactics are not always sweet, his manner is direct, and one observes how he tries to achieve his own version of what is right. He complains when he finds George "acting snotty" with him, when he's "acting regular" with George. At one point, when Albie is lying on his death bed beneath the stars, Dicky comes to tell him that Katelbach "told me I was mentally retiring or something." Albie turns to face the camera, which tenderly captures his stunned, shriveled face made odd by his thick, round glasses, and murmurs, "He doesn't love us anymore." He is imploring the audience to listen to him, to take him in. If there is any heart that can be located in this masterful film, it is here, in an exchange between fugitives, seeking survival under a canopy of stars.

THE FEARLESS VAMPIRE KILLERS (1967)

If *Cul-de-Sac* was the next step in Polanski's developing career, then *The Fearless Vampire Killers* was a foray into a whole new world. Filmmaking in the 1960s was a remarkably fast-paced process, and while Polanski was doing publicity for *Cul-de-Sac,* he was already beginning preproduction for his next film. There was a renaissance in filmmaking going on. A new audience had arrived, and movies were turned out fast. Though his relationship with Compton was no longer a working one, Polanski had been introduced to Marty Ransohoff and John Calley from Filmways, an American production company that had a deal with Metro-Goldwyn-Mayer. Ransohoff quickly convinced Polanski that he was an "artistic" producer—one who would fight for the director's vision. Polanski was putty in his hands. Still reeling slightly from the cabin fever–inducing isolation of the *Cul-de-Sac* shoot, Polanski was content to land in the lap of an entirely new production company and feel the excitement generated by a new project. In fact, he was so happy with things that he made a big mistake—he gave Marty final cut.

The idea for *The Fearless Vampire Killers* came, in part, from inspiration taken from the snowy landscape during a ski trip in the Alps and out of the desire to work with Jack MacGowran again. As Polanski writes in his autobiography, "As with Mazury and *Knife in the Water,* the setting imposed itself before the story line crystallized." The slopes were one of the places where Polanski felt most comfortable, and one of his dreams was to make a film about skiing. Brach and Polanski decided that they would like to make a film that intended to be funny while remaining intelligent and beautiful to watch. What came out of this discussion was the script for *The Fearless Vampire Killers,* a movie about nutty Einsteinian Professor Abronsius and his young sidekick, Alfred, as they travel the Transylvanian countryside searching for vampires.

The film was to be shot in the Alps, where a perfect castle had been located. Because of an abrupt shift in weather, however, and a lack of snow, the shoot's interiors were shifted to the MGM studio in London. The exteriors were quickly relocated to the Italian Dolomites, where Polanski's love affair with Sharon Tate really began.

Sharon Tate was a young American actress who (as a result of her father's military service and subsequent travel) had been raised for awhile in Europe and spoke fluent Italian. She had always wanted to be an actress, and despite her parents' worries for her safety, had gone out to L.A. on her own. She had already played bit parts in a variety of movies, a small role in *The Beverly Hillbillies* (1962–1971), and had a multi-picture deal with Filmways (from whom, Polanski would later discover, she was being grossly underpaid). She was living in London when Polanski was introduced to her, and though her beauty struck him, he saw her as one in a million. He would soon discover that Sharon was completely different from any woman he had known, and the more she learned to love him, the more she assured him that freedom was his. That was the nature of her love.

Ransohoff may have agreed to let Polanski play the role of Alfred, but he also was pushing Sharon for the role of Sarah, the innkeeper's beautiful daughter and Alfred's love interest. Polanski had qualms about this choice, as Sharon had a very Midwestern look but Sarah was supposed to be an Eastern European Jew, yet once they tested her in a costume and a red wig, Polanski began to see the possibilities. She was cast in the film (along with Jack MacGowran as Professor Abronsius, and Alfie Bass as the wonderfully humorous innkeeper, Shagal).

The Fearless Vampire Killers explores the impact that coincidence has on our lives. One of Polanski's favorite quotes, referenced in television interviews, is one by Greek philosopher Democritus that says, "Everything existing in the universe is the fruit of chance and necessity." Viewing Polanski's films with this quote in mind helps one to better understand his fatalistic point of view. Knowing that life is uncontrollable allows for a certain freedom in the way one chooses to live, a point that often underlines his films, just as it has his life. In *The Fearless Vampire Killers*, it is through absurdist comedy that Polanski explores the subject of destiny.

The Fearless Vampire Killers is a comical depiction of a backward country world in which a Yiddish innkeeper and an aristocratic vampire king share mastery of the local terrain. In many ways, it is a tribute to Polanski's Polish-Jewish roots. Days and nights spent in the country inn, walls splattered with wreaths of garlic, are suffused with a brand of Polish absurdist humor particular to this part of the world. Shagal stomps out sauerkraut in a wooden barrel and silently stuffs himself with a handful of the cabbage. He cannot help but stare at the young barmaid whom he often visits at night, as she scrubs the floor on her knees before him, her breasts busting out of her dress. Shagal's wife is a homely woman who relies upon available resources, such as an oversized salami, to bash the snooping professor on the head. The couple has a beautiful daughter, Sarah, who is obsessed with bathing. So fixated is she with the bathtub that Shagal has gone so far as to board up her side of the bathroom. In order to circumvent her father's restrictions, Sarah sneaks into Alfred's room wielding a sponge, speaking to him of bathing as if it were a sexual act, rendering him speechless and eager to retrieve hot water for her bath. Alfred falls for Sarah. When she is bitten by the vampire king and taken to his castle, leaving only a mass of blood and snow in the tub, Alfred must go after her. What follows is a string of antics so absurd that one cannot help but delight in enjoying the ride.

There is a campy satisfaction to the film, which upon deeper examination is far more artful than it may appear on the surface. The action climaxes in an extravagantly baroque ball from which Alfred rescues Sarah, yet in the end even he cannot escape the vampire's bite. Shagal is the first of the three men to be transformed by the bite, and he is deeply offended when his coffin is permitted only in the stables, as the vampire king and his son keep theirs in a candlelit stone room. Polanski has a gift for making the morbid comical, such as when dinner guests emerge from their coffins to join the ball. Alfred's innocent response to the events around him somehow adds to the wit and charm. Polanski reminds us that within the inescapability of fate lies great humor, and here he allows comedy to lead the way.

The Transylvanian landscape is immense and eerie, filled with hungry roaming wolves and stalked by a hunchback from the castle (played by former middleweight boxer, Terry Downes). Each character is led by desire. For Abronsius, it is an intellectual desire, while the needs of other characters are far more base. As with the encroaching sea in *Cul-de-Sac*, the endless snowy hills call to mind that which is uncontainable and unknowable. Just as the vampire's bloodlust may intimate a certain deep and relentless sexual desire, so does the realm of sexuality, which once entered cannot be controlled. Young Alfred is a devoted companion to the professor (the "nut," as his colleagues refer to him). He strives to help him with his work, yet is also innocent enough to still question the morality of his surroundings. No matter how hard Alfred works to make things right he cannot win. At the last moment of the film, just as their sled is moving away from the castle, his beautiful and pure object of affection sinks her vampire teeth into him. As the last line of the film suggests, the professor winds up "carrying away with him the very evil he had wished to destroy." Despite Alfred's pure heart, even love cannot stop the wanderlust instinct of a vampire, nor the wild, old-world landscape. Alfred must accept that vampires (just as fugitives) live according to their own moral code.

The imagery of the film reinforces this sense of desire and inevitability. Though the eternally dark country landscape is vast and romantic, and the vampire palace grand and archaic, the camera still finds ways to zero in on intimate scenes. The frame seeks creative ways to contain the uncontainable.

When Alfred hears Shagal punishing Sarah for bathing, Alfred peeks through the keyhole to see him spanking her. At the castle, Alfred and Abronsius look through a telescope that manages to magically reach the inn where Shagal is climbing through the blonde barmaid's window. The moon and the dark sky are omnipresent in the scene, reminding the viewer of the futility of human interactions and the presence of intimate, celestial desire. The secret image becomes apparent when a mirror is seen before the ball, and only the non-vampire characters are visible. Suddenly, Alfred, Abronsius, and Sarah stand on their own, where minutes before they were at the heart of a gathering. For a moment they exist independent of being pursued, each seeing themselves for what they are, while the dreams and nightmares behind them disappear in their reflection. Imagination provides escape, or at least relief from destiny, and in *The Fearless Vampire Killers,* humor is the invisible sled riding above the action, helping us to laugh at others and at ourselves.

Unlike the heavy-handed austerity of *Cul-de-Sac, The Fearless Vampire Killers* is filled with color and a lightness of touch. Although it is a pleasure to watch, there is also nostalgia to the film, unavoidable when watching the lovely Sharon Tate, and Polanski's willingness to play innocent in her presence. As much as it is a tribute to Polanski's diverse talents, the film stands as a tale of innocence and care in a world that often plays according to its own, vampiric rules. It stands in honor of Tate, who was known for a gentle spirit and a lightness of touch.

Though the shoot of *The Fearless Vampire Killers* would always bring about fond memories for Polanski, at the time things were rather tense. As usual, shooting fell behind schedule, which he claimed made him "become more exacting," therefore taking more time. His relationship with Tate was blossoming, yet she became so concerned with pleasing him with her acting that at times she felt stuck. This only led Polanski to work harder trying to get the right performance, having her do multiple takes. The number of hours during which one was permitted to shoot per day were now greatly restricted by British film unions, and MGM sent endlessly detailed notes regarding the sexually overt nature of the film.

On its first showing, Ransohoff claimed not to like the film, saying that it was too long. He would cut it down, he said, and at this point Polanski really had no other option other than to agree. Thankfully, Polanski's friend Bronislau Kaper enjoyed the film, relishing in the Polish humor unfamiliar to others. Ransohoff and his associates would proceed to butcher the film, releasing it under the title, *The Fearless Vampire Killers, or Pardon Me, but Your Teeth Are in My Neck* (1967). It would be many years before Polanski's original version would be released. The primary light in Polanski's life at this time was Sharon Tate, and promise for a continuing career came with a call from Robert Evans.

Evans was the new vice-president of Paramount Pictures. A young, handsome playboy type, Evans had already celebrated a lucrative family clothing business, and acted in various Hollywood films, such as *Man of a Thousand Faces* (1957) and *The Sun Also Rises* (1957). He held great promise as a producer and would ultimately collaborate with Polanski to great success. In *The Kid Stays in the Picture* (2002),[10] a documentary about his life, Evans says of his first meeting with Polanski, "Within five minutes this Polack's acting out crazy stories. . . . They're somewhere between Shakespeare and the theater of the absurd. Maybe that's why we clicked so well. We both came out of the same school of drama."

Evans called Polanski about a proposal for a film about skiing titled *Downhill Racer.* Clever in his manipulation, Evans understood the allure of a skiing picture for Polanski, and once he was in his office, he handed Polanski the script for *Rosemary's Baby.* That night in his hotel room Polanski studied the script. As is pointed out in the documentary, *Rosemary's Baby: A Retrospective* (2000), at first glance he mistook the story for a "soap opera," but by the time that he was finished reading he was completely taken. The next morning he told Evans that he wanted to make the film. Now a whole new phase would begin for Polanski, for he would find himself living in America, shooting one of the most successful films of his career.

4

American Lullaby: *Rosemary's Baby* (1968)

The 1960s in America were a time of free love and rebellion. The sexual revolution and the antiwar movements were in full swing. Reacting to their parents' adherence to the strict social confines of the 1950s, young people led wild and carefree lives. They experimented with drugs, had numerous sexual partners, took birth control, burned their bras, and even went so far as to protest the government's choice to enter the war in Vietnam. This was the era of Gloria Steinem,[1] Bob Dylan, and Martin Luther King Jr. It was a time in which all of the disenfranchised groups found a voice, and at last many middle class, white, heterosexual citizens stood up to defend them. Though it was a dangerous, tumultuous time, it was equally thrilling.

Hollywood in the sixties was no exception. There were wild and debauched parties throughout the city of Los Angeles, and many homes were left unlocked. The hippie trend meant that everyone dressed alike, making it difficult to differentiate friend from foe. The film industry was moving into its own revolution, with movies that addressed the subject of freedom such as *Easy Rider* (1969) and *Bonnie and Clyde* (1967). The uptight moral code of the fifties had opened up, a change that made its way into mainstream America.

There could have been no better time for Polanski to come to America. Here was a country open to a new perspective, and Polanski was ready to comply. It was difficult for anyone from the Eastern bloc to come to Hollywood without feeling as if they'd just entered the gates of heaven, palm trees signaling the call of freedom.

ROSEMARY'S BABY (1968)

Making the deal for *Rosemary's Baby* was a remarkably quick process. The film was to be produced by Paramount Pictures and horror director and producer Bill Castle (credited as William), known for his gimmicky B-movies such as *House on Haunted Hill* (1959), and *The Tingler* (1959). Castle was a showman of sorts, always looking for a gimmick and finding creative ways to surprise, such as suspending a floating, glow-in-the-dark skeleton over his audience during a show. Castle had purchased the rights to Ira Levin's book of the same name and had hoped to direct the movie, but Bob Evans and Polanski knew that the film needed to be executed carefully in order to come off well. Bill conceded (and was given a small nonspeaking role as the man waiting outside a phone booth while Mia Farrow makes a call). Now that Polanski had a deal allotting him standard pay, he felt like a rich man. He went off to his house in London to write the script on his own, and soon he returned with the finished product.

As with *Cul-de-Sac*, Polanski did drawings for all of the characters as he imagined them. Many Hollywood veterans were hired to fill the smaller parts, which would enrich the film, infusing it with talent and character. One coup was the casting of the great actress Ruth Gordon (co-writer of films like

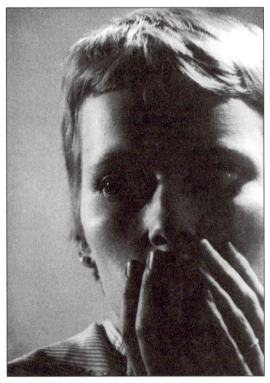

Rosemary's Baby. (Courtesy of Photofest)

Adam's Rib [1949] and *Pat and Mike* [1952]), as the nosy Mrs. Castevet, the female counterpart of the devil-raising couple. Although the book had described Minnie Castevet as a rather large woman, tiny Gordon played Minnie with such humor and eccentricity that she became a small, nosy clown with enough energy to fill a room.

For the title part of Rosemary, Polanski had imagined a corn-fed, voluptuous woman such as Tuesday Weld, or even Sharon Tate. Instead, Paramount was pushing the young and delicate Mia Farrow. Farrow was only 23 years old at the time, newly married to Frank Sinatra, and had already achieved notoriety in the primetime soap opera Peyton Place. Her mother was Irish actress Maureen O'Sullivan, and her father, Australian director, John Farrow. Although Polanski hesitated to accept her at first, once he viewed past episodes of Peyton Place he agreed that Farrow could play the part. It was a choice that he never regretted.

For the part of Rosemary's husband Guy, Polanski went through many possible actors, ranging from Robert Redford to Warren Beatty and Jack Nicholson. The part went to method actor and independent filmmaker John Cassavetes,[2] who fit the role of a handsome, all-American husband. Though Polanski admired Cassavetes's acting, even if he was not hugely enthusiastic about method actors, once shooting began rumors of tensions between the two would arise.

Rosemary's Baby was off to a hopeful start. Krzysztof Komeda would be hired to write the soundtrack, adding dimension to the film. Polanski was at last able to hire production designer and close friend Dick Sylbert (credited

Repulsion. (Courtesy of Photofest)

as Richard), who, being a native New Yorker, would easily recreate the dark, oversized New York apartment on a Paramount stage. This made it necessary only for exteriors to be shot on the East coast. Roman and Sharon rented a beautiful, 1930s-style house near the Pacific Coast Highway. At last he was living in the magical, clean, palm-tree lined Hollywood that he had first discovered five years earlier. At last he had a fulfilling love, and the opportunity to make a film in America.

Still, Polanski's past could not be erased. Referring to his first day on the set, he wrote, "I had sixty technicians at my beck and call and bore responsibility for a huge budget—at least by my previous standards—but all I could think of was the sleepless night I'd spent in Krakow, years before, on the eve of making my very first short, *The Bicycle*. Nothing would ever match the thrill of that first time; the reality would never measure up to the dream."

Rosemary's Baby tells the story of Rosemary Woodhouse, a conventionally subservient housewife whose husband Guy is an ambitious, self-involved actor. The couple moves into a landmark building (which is called The Bramford in the film, but was actually shot outside The Dakota), with a history of witches and dead babies found wrapped in newspaper. The Bramford's ominous history may be the source for many jokes early on in the film, but it also causes uneasiness in both Rosemary and the viewer. Shortly after moving in to the building, the couple's neighbor Terry, a young wayward tenant of the Castevets, is found dead on the street, having committed suicide. This is the event that brings the two couples together. The Castevets latch onto Guy and Rosemary, and soon Guy responds. Eventually we discover that the Castevets are Satanists who have enlisted Guy in an evil plot to sell his wife's unborn child (not yet conceived by the devil) in exchange for improving his career. Though the revelation of this scheme is dubious, at moments leading the audience to question Rosemary's sanity and doubt the plot's authenticity, in the end one horrible discovery proves it to be true.

Rosemary's Baby depicts a patriarchal society's oppression of one woman's basic rights (as the Catholic religion into which Rosemary was born would have done on a smaller, subtler scale), working as a misogynistic twist on a Faustian myth. Only in this case, rather than selling his own soul to the devil in exchange for love and monetary gain, Guy sells the soul of his unborn child, and in turn, that of his wife. This is in exchange for a successful career, which to an actor may signify ultimate love. Painting a microcosm from which there is no escape, Polanski removes from the story all cushions of safety and love prevalent in the book, creating a stark, private hell. This trap is portrayed literally as well as figuratively, suggesting that the mother instinct surpasses all, and that even for a Catholic schoolgirl, her devil's spawn is ultimately her baby.

The film begins with opening credits on an aerial view revealing the rooftops of ornate Manhattan apartment buildings, while a dissonant minor chord collides with a melodic lullaby, sung by Mia Farrow. Having Rosemary sing this song makes it all the more poignant—drawing us into the comfort of her sweet presence and the essence of her dreams. She is a woman who wants to have babies and to simply be good, living up to the ideal of the Catholic religion in which she was raised. We want to believe in her aspirations, be comforted by her dreams. By opening the film with a setting that is aurally and visually mismatched, a sweet lullaby is punctuated by ominous, harsh chords. Through the music Polanski suggests the disharmonious collision of good and evil that will dominate the film.

Harking back to the visually subjective approach used in *Repulsion*, Polanski takes the next step in creating a world both privately and communally experienced, the frame guiding our thoughts so that we, too, are in Rosemary's head. We identify with the character, while simultaneously being led through a story that makes us question the authenticity of her experience. Ultimately, we are questioning ourselves. This is part of what is so frightening about Polanski's films, for one need not suspend disbelief to comprehend the story.

The imagery in this film is essential to plot and atmosphere. Polanski relied upon choreographed scenes often taking place within one frame, and used short focal lenses to create a wider field of view (long focal lenses are more typically used in filmmaking because they speed up the process and because they are more flattering). Much of the film was shot in long takes and the camera handheld nearly half the time. Polanski used a harness of his own design in order to make these shots smooth. As always, he focused on the details of every shot, believing that to not do so would be sheer laziness. Precision was of the utmost importance. Cinematographer William Fraker (*The Day of the Dolphin* [1973], *Heaven Can Wait* [1978], and *Irreconcilable Differences* [1984]) used only wide-angle lenses during the shoot, alternating between 18 mm and 25 mm lenses, which created a distinct look for the film. The short or wide focal lens gives the perception of an exaggerated depth of field, and when the subject is close to the lens, distortion occurs. This means that proportions are altered, allowing the image to greatly influence the atmosphere. A grotesque quality is subsequently achieved even in the loveliest of faces. Suddenly everyone becomes suspect. Everyone is on trial.

This technique of shooting brings the viewer closer to the action. As Polanski says in his book, "Ideally the lens should be at the same distance from the subject as the eye of the notional observer." This closeness is present in many of Polanski's films—where, often from behind, we the viewers breathe down the neck of whoever is in the frame. It is generally a low-angle perspective to which we are privy, reminding us of Polanski's stature. We are made to feel his presence as well. This type of shot is eerie and unique to Polanski, generating the question of a third party. This question arouses fear, for who is watching, who is the camera, and why are we so uncomfortably close? What will happen if this middleman chooses to misbehave? The chaos will become even closer. By building this tension, the viewer is automatically involved.

As with any masterful director, Polanski is playing with us, using psychology and purely visual, visceral tools to evoke a reaction. By virtue of Polanski's courage in getting close and stepping into the film, we are left powerless to our own experience. In the epilogue of her book, *Polanski: a Biography, the Filmmaker as Voyeur*, Barbara Leaming writes, "Polanski is threatening in the way that children are: we're constantly afraid of what they're going to say or do."

Through this uncomfortable proximity to his characters, Polanski bestows upon them a suspicious quality. From the elevator operator with a knowing smile plastered across his face, to Dr. Sapirstein's secretary, to a stranger waiting to use a public payphone while Rosemary tells her doctor secrets inside the booth, one never knows what anyone might be capable of. This lends to the paranoid atmosphere, for everyone seems to know what Rosemary doesn't, and sensing this makes her afraid. Even with Rosemary's former landlord and fatherly friend Hutch, there is an eerie quality that is difficult to overcome. When he is put in a coma and murdered by the witches, our regret is not so much for the loss of his character, but more for the loss of Rosemary's ally. For our need to protect Rosemary is a driving force throughout the film.

We are brought close to Rosemary and experience her vulnerability, such as during the first time that we see her make love to Guy. She takes off her clothes, and the camera hovers just behind her shoulder. The room is dark, but her strawberry blond hair is illuminated, her face soft and expectant. She pulls herself across the floor to meet Guy, and the camera moves with her (from the same position). This camera work doesn't beautify, nor does it romanticize, but rather it makes us experience the openness of intimacy.

The casting in the film also takes on meaning, as it is one of the deviations from Levin's original text. Polanski had wanted to hire a woman marked by voluptuous fecundity. Levin had written Rosemary this way. His Rosemary was also an independent woman both in her action and thought, neither of which is implied in the film. The Rosemary of the book is closer to one of Rosemary's young friends in the film. Had Polanski been successful in hiring his choice of star to play the part, perhaps this film would have taken on entirely different meaning. What is so frightening in the book is that one does believe that Rosemary is her own woman, and she should be capable of escaping the traps set by Guy. The structure of the book is different in that Levin wants to present the story of the devil as true, whereas Polanski wants you to question its validity, even doubt it, so that Rosemary is left standing on her own.

Of course a more feminine, womanly, rather than girlish, Rosemary would not alter the fact that Polanski's script does not allow for such a dynamic character or relationship. Still, to have a sexy Rosemary would have been to invite unwanted interpretations by the audience. Because culpability is often attributed to sexy women, an overtly sexual Rosemary would have been a woman who appears more desirable, and subsequently more guilty. But to have Rosemary played by Mia Farrow, who looks more than anything like a prepubescent wife, invites an entirely new interpretation. Rosemary's goodness is a learned one; her Midwestern naïveté leaves her vulnerable in the big city, even in her own home. Therefore, it is not her sexuality that implicates her in her own spiritual rape, but rather her innocence and her religious upbringing. Rosemary is a lapsed Catholic who still swears by saints and whose devout upbringing is so engrained in her subconscious that all of her dreams invoke religious symbols. Thus, it is no coincidence that Polanski sets Rosemary's rape by the devil to coincide with the Pope's visit to New York. Rosemary's goodness makes her desirable to the spiritually bankrupt devil.

This subconscious imagery of dreams is one of the necessary elements of the film. The correlation between Rosemary's religious upbringing and the visual language of her dreams helps tread the line between good and evil. In sharing her dreams, which are often represented as half-waking hallucinations, the story splits between reality and fantasy (as is emphasized by the split-screen image in her dreams), allowing the audience to enter her subconscious; however, unlike in *Repulsion*, nightmares are represented as dreams with small touches of wakefulness. Rosemary does not hallucinate as Carole in *Repulsion* does, nor have her fears directly manifested themselves. Rosemary's fears are deeply suppressed, and so they must emerge while she is sleeping. In her dreams we witness her internal moral compass as it renders her guilty at every turn. She whispers to the nuns that she didn't mean to break a window, while at the same time we hear Minnie Castevet's voice as it comes through Rosemary's bedroom wall, emerging from the mouth of an angry nun. While the nun admonishes the viewer, Minnie yells at her husband, "Sometimes I wonder how come you're the leader of anything!" There is the sound of a book as it shuts. The effect is strong. We don't quite know what is going on, nor does Rosemary, either consciously or unconsciously, but we see the connections being drawn between a punishing, dominating nun and a witch. The presence of a guilty conscience in the dream realm (where there is subversion of one's moral code) allows for this association to be made, whereas waking life would never connect the two. Such is the rich visual dream-like element brought to the film through the character of Rosemary.

Cassavetes's Guy is a narcissist, stripped bare of a certain appeal and the affection attributed to Guy in the book. From the start of the film, Guy is hardly a likable man. Of course he has all the charm of a talented actor, but one never gets the sense that he is a man of feeling, not even toward his own wife. In spite of the fact that Guy is an artist he leads a conventional life typical of the 1950s and 1960s. His wife stays at home, and her priority is to constantly improve the family environment. Very early in the film we are aware of Guy's dominating stature, even if he is often captured in shadow. Even the name Guy implies that this man epitomizes masculinity in its most average form—hinting that perhaps he is the essence of what macho means, sacrificing everything in the name of one's manhood. Guy seems to dominate the frame, not as a result of his size, or even the framing, but more because of Rosemary's delicacy and her constant ability to adjust to his needs. Not even five minutes into the film, the couple is walking down Broadway (the framing isolating the main characters, even when outside), and Rosemary is jumping around Guy like a schoolgirl, begging for them to lease the Bramford apartment. Had Rosemary been a different type of woman, the effect could be entirely different, but this Rosemary is so willing to please, so tiny in her body and cute in her expression, that one feels she is more like a 16-year-old than an adult.

When Guy slaps Rosemary on the behind, the atmosphere is very much of a parent and child (due in part to Farrow's little girl figure). And when Rosemary is disturbed by a certain chalky under-taste in Minnie's chocolate "mouse" (which will, in fact, be the thing that drugs her so that the devil can enter), she secretly dumps the remains of the mousse into her napkin, and looking up sweetly with the cup in her hands, says, "There, Daddy, do I get a gold star?" When Guy comes home in the afternoon, a pigtailed, baby doll–dressed Rosemary runs over to him and throws her arms around his neck like a little girl. This suggests that the film is not only about Satanists and devil worshippers, but also a dramatic exploration of an unbalanced relationship. The patriarchal tone of the film is set within the marriage long before any witches come into play. This is something quite different from the more loving equal relationship detailed in the book, and it is apparent in Guy's sardonic smile and the way that he is always cocking his head and looking down into the camera, the shadows above his eyes emphasized, as if he is working to reveal his own devilish character. Rosemary remains oblivious.

This patriarchal relationship is exposed in detail throughout the film. And though there are moments in which Rosemary's submissive nature is threatened by the extremity of her situation, her passivity always wins out in the end. When Rosemary awakes after being raped by the devil and notices scratch marks on her back, Guy's only response is to smile and say that he "didn't want to miss baby night." Believing that her husband had slept with her while she was unconscious, Rosemary is momentarily outraged, but she is quickly brought back by Guy's charms and by her newly discovered pregnancy. She never speaks out against this violation. This pattern is repeated when Rosemary and Guy fight after a party they hold for a group of young friends. Rosemary wants to get a second opinion from her original obstetrician, Dr. Hill, while her own Castevet-recommended doctor, Dr. Sapirstein, has been sending her home for months despite terrible pain. When she speaks to Guy about her pain his only response is that he won't pay for another doctor, that it wouldn't be right to Dr. Sapirstein. "Not fair to . . .?" she cries. "What about what's fair to me?" Rosemary is rightfully angry, but just at the moment when she begins to express fury, the pain stops. Her relief overrides her anger, and she falls back into the role of a happy little mother-to-be, her submission keeping her home and unsafe. Perhaps the most absurd example of her meekness is in the rape/dream sequence. A very angelic Jackie Kennedy look-alike floats down the stairs and suggests that Rosemary ought to have her "legs tied down in case of convulsions." She then asks Rosemary to let her know whether she wants the music turned down. Rosemary has just had her legs tied to the table and is about to be raped, and the only thing that she can say is, "Oh no, please don't change the program on my account." She would not want to stop the rape if it would displease any-one, a heartbreaking moment in which we realize that she is incapable of breaking free of her own submissiveness.

Whereas the third presence in a film may sometimes represent an omnis-cient force, here we feel the presence of a contrary force—one that skews our perspective of the world. Polanski may not believe in evil, but he represents it well. We feel that we are looking into Rosemary's world through distorted glasses. The furniture engulfs its owners, as do the rooms and hallways, reminding us that perhaps there is an external force at work here. And if Rosemary is a doll in a dollhouse of her own construction, then perhaps those who toy with her are also being toyed with.

When Rosemary and Guy have their first visit with the Castevets, we are made blatantly aware of this portentous friendship. The dinner is an awkward portrayal of a young couple dining with their elders; however, after dinner it becomes clear what mystery is about to begin. Rosemary helps Minnie do the dishes, while Guy and Roman Castevet smoke and drink in the living room. Rosemary turns to see what they are doing, and there is a shot of the living room in which all we see is an open doorway filled with smoke drift-ing from the side. The shot is eerie, as silence permeates the atmosphere. This is Polanski's brilliance, for what he tells us in this scene without show-ing anything is that Roman and Guy's conversation is of such importance that even the audience must be excluded. One needn't see in order to know. And it is this exclusion that makes us aware that something is wrong. The smoke from their pipes evokes the fires of hell as they work their way into Rosemary's life, and again she is oblivious. Aside from growing up in a time in which one does not question one's husband or parents, what makes Rosemary so innocent to her husband's evil doings is her strong Catholic upbringing, which has instilled in her a faith that does not question. Polanski and Levin suggest that this suspension of disbelief is at the heart of Catholicism. Even for a lapsed Catholic such as Rosemary, it would be nat-ural to carry this blind faith over to her husband. Never asking, she is always expecting that her husband would have only the best of intentions, as would

God. It is not until Rosemary discovers that Guy secretly met with fellow actor Donald Baumgart, whose part he has taken over in a play following Baumgart's sudden blindness, that a floodgate opens—and suspicion becomes permissible. When she learns that during this rendezvous Guy switched ties with Baumgart, and may have helped cast a spell to cause his malady, she begins to see Guy for who he really is. This is the moment when she crosses the line from faith into doubt. It is also the moment when the devil appears, perhaps showing what destruction doubting can cause.

When Rosemary is being raped, the Pope comes to visit her in a haze, and she asks for his forgiveness. Throughout the film it is constantly pointed out that Rosemary wishes to do good, but she is haunted by her Catholic upbringing (as is shown by this request for absolution at the moment of penetration). Having come from a background in which familiarity with magic and the existence of the devil are integral to her core beliefs, it is not surprising that Rosemary is left vulnerable to the devil. In the waiting room of the doctor's office, the cover of *Time* magazine reads, "Is God Dead?" and at the end of *Rosemary's Baby* we think that perhaps He is in this film. At the end of the film, when Rosemary goes into the Castevets' apartment to rescue her baby, upon realizing that it is half devil, she is greeted with chants of "Hail Adrian, Hail Satan." Minnie tells her that out of all the women in the world Satan chose her to be the mother of his child. And so she becomes an inverted Mary (after all, her name is Rose-Mary), an unknowing mother of the enemy of God.

She has finally come face to face with the group of people who have taken over her life, and after a brief battle, the mother instinct—the good in her—begins to take over. Roman very gently coaxes Rosemary, saying, "You don't have to join if you don't want to, just be a mother to your baby." The sound of her baby crying pulls Rosemary in, and she falls in love with her baby. Even if taking care of her own baby brings great evil into the world, it is still natural to love one's own child, and after all, she may think, isn't it what God would want to her to do?

It seems that no matter what Rosemary does she is never able to break free. Even when she becomes aware that there is a plot and that everyone close to her is in on it, she is still captured and brought back. As she tries to call a friend, we see the coven as they tiptoe through the apartment toward her room, as if they were just humoring her, leading her to believe that she might have gotten away with something. Any chance for her to individuate is lost through her own submissiveness and the imprisonment of her deep religious beliefs. So that in spite of the domination of a despicable patriarchal society, in some way Rosemary is in fact complicit to her own rape.

Because of Polanski's agnostic views, the film was made under the assumption that good and evil do not actually exist. Because it was so hard for him to believe in such a story, he wanted it to appear as if the entire plot might be in Rosemary's head. It is not until the end of the film that we realize that it is, in fact, real. Polanski's dubious approach to the subject is, however, enlightening as it weaves in and out of dreams. What Polanski achieves by drawing "good" and "evil" so close together is to eliminate the validity of either as an independent force. He is subverting their importance, ultimately saying that perhaps they do not matter and that maybe the two are one in the same. As Rosemary's fragile body is hoisted toward the ceiling of the Sistine Chapel in one of her dreams, we see her as a victim of her past as well as her present. The image of Michelangelo's masterpiece associated with the profound illumination of great art is a reminder that we create our own image of God. Although the drama of the film is tense and even terrifying, Polanski is also liberating us from the inhibitions of accepted moral code. Just as Rosemary sees herself living in Los Angeles—holding a perfect baby, surrounded by friends, or naked and shivering aboard a boat—this life, too, is a dream, best enjoyed while it's still around.

By the end of the first week of production, the shoot for *Rosemary's Baby* was already far behind schedule. Part of this was due to the use of the visual techniques employed, which were painstaking and time-consuming, but Polanski knew they would prove worthwhile in the end. Paramount wanted him fired right away, but Robert Evans supported him all the way (even going so far as to put his own job on the line).

Worried about production delays while walking on the studio lot one day, Polanski ran into Hollywood veteran Otto Preminger, the Jewish-Austrian director of films such as *Laura* (1944) and *The Man With The Golden Arm* (1955). Preminger assured Polanski that even if he was behind with shooting, as long as the studio liked the dailies, there was nothing to worry about. As it turned out, he was right. Polanski was getting advice from an Eastern European who was also a Hollywood pro. He was being shepherded into his new life. Hard as it may have been to believe his good fortune, he was at the epicenter of the cinematic world.

Even though the initial setback of the shoot was soon resolved, tensions with Cassavetes made things difficult, as did interference from Farrow's personal life. When the shoot was more than halfway finished, Farrow's husband, Frank Sinatra, threw a fit. He was about to start making *The Detective* (1968) and wanted his wife to co-star. When it became clear that she wouldn't, he decided to divorce her, having the papers served to her right on set, a deliberate attempt at humiliation. Still, Farrow continued with the shoot.

Polanski was also fortunate enough to have the studio hire Komeda to compose the music for the film. This was a great opportunity for Komeda, as not only would he have his music in a Hollywood film, but he could also break away from his unhappy marriage, leaving his wife in Poland. He even found new love during his time in the United States and went on to write the music for *Riot* (1969), another of Bill Castle's pictures.

Komeda's music adds great feeling and mystery to the film. A combination of a sweet, lulling lullaby and shrill, alarming screams are punctuated by just a hint of the free-form sounds found in his other works; the soundtrack adds dimension to the film.

The film was a great success, with audiences lining up around the block. Bill Castle could hardly believe his eyes, once even offering Polanski a cut of the profits, an offer that never came to fruition. Audiences fell for all of Polanski's tricks. When Minnie Castevet hears that Rosemary is pregnant and goes into the Woodhouse's bedroom to use the phone, the camera is placed to the side, behind the doorframe. The construction of the shot was so that we hear Minnie speak but only see part of her back and feet. When her conversation began, the entire audience moved to the right, hoping to get a glimpse of Minnie's face. Such is the intricacy of Polanski's storytelling. Perhaps dating back to when he was a boy in search of escape, a true movie-goer, he understood the psychology of the viewer and knew exactly how to move them.

The audience came out of theaters convinced that they had seen the devil's baby, cloven feet and all. In truth, Polanski and editor Sam O'Steen[3] had inserted a quick shot of the catlike eyes seen in Rosemary's rape nightmare, yet it was enough to manipulate audience's imaginations into creating a complete picture. *Rosemary's Baby* is a work of cinematic brilliance, and it was recognized as such. As with many of Polanski's films, it treaded the line of commercial viability and artful splendor with perfect balance. Ruth Gordon would win an Academy Award and a Golden Globe for Best Supporting Actress, and Farrow would earn a Golden Globe nomination for Best Actress. The film received many other nominations, such as Best Screenplay for Polanski (both Academy Award and Golden Globe), and Krzysztof Komeda for a Best Original Score (Golden Globe). The movie would continue to engross audiences for years to come. It is a standout in a genre that often relies on cheap tricks and gore as a means of inciting terror. *Rosemary's Baby* was a great achievement for Polanski, and as a flood of new scripts came in, he couldn't hide his contentment. With true love on his side, he was on top of the world.

5

No Man's Land

Life after *Rosemary's Baby* was a dream. Offers for new projects came in, but most of them were too similar to the work that Polanski had done. All he wanted to do was enjoy domestic bliss. Though he still had occasional affairs with various beauties, Sharon Tate had completely stolen his heart. She showed him *her* America, and Polanski was smitten.

The two made a life together, first in the 1930s-style house that they rented from British actor Brian Aherne, and later in the Chateau Marmont. They had accumulated an interesting set of friends and would get together often, at times even going away on group trips. When on the U.S. side of the Atlantic, the group consisted of (Tate's ex-boyfriend) hairdresser Jay Sebring, actors Warren Beatty, Mia Farrow, and Peter Sellers.[1] (Sadly, Polanski's dear friend and collaborator Kzrysztof Komeda died in 1968, falling in and out of a coma after sustaining a head injury from a drunken romp with their old friend Marek Hlasko.) Polanski studied martial arts with Bruce Lee,[2] and Tate starred in a new pulp film about drug-addled beauties, *Valley of the Dolls* (1967).

Polanski knew that he belonged with Tate, but he hesitated to commit.

She wanted to start a family, as did he, though the prospect of establishing enduring connections was frightening. He couldn't help but feel the pangs of accepting love and the impermanence of life associated with it. The possibility for loss felt tremendous, especially because his childhood had left him wary of being hurt. He knew that he'd found his home, however, and could not run from it forever.

On January 20, 1968, Polanski and Tate married in a nondenominational ceremony at the Chelsea Registry office. His father and stepmother Wanda even flew in for the affair. After the wedding, there were several parties, the most publicized of which was a star-studded blowout at The Playboy Club. Roman wore a ruffled, new romantic shirt, perfectly suited to his character

Alfred from *The Fearless Vampire Killers*, and Sharon wore a white minidress with flowers in her long, blonde hair. The publicity for the party said that Sharon would keep working, and it quoted Polanski as saying that he wanted "a hippie, not a housewife."[3] Their honeymoon was spent at home.

In May 1968, the couple drove to Cannes, where Polanski was to serve as a member of the jury. Unfortunately, this was not to be the standard care-free festival experience. Not long before, French Minister of Culture André Malraux had fired the founder and director of the Cinémathèque Francaise, Henri Langlois, who was considered to be a war hero (because of his protection of film heritage under Nazi occupation). This was a low blow to film-makers and to all French citizens alike, and in accordance with the explosive atmosphere of the time, people took to the streets in protest of this affront to cinema (which would lead to an even greater explosion of riots later that year in France). Filmmakers demanded back their prints held at the Cinémathèque, and New Wave directors, particularly Jean-Luc Godard and François Truffaut, were influential in leading these demonstrations.

The Cannes Festival was their next target of rebellion with regard to the "Affaire Langlois," and they wished to disturb, and hopefully cancel, the fes-tivities. They called a meeting and invited Polanski, assuming that he would support their cause; however, having received the honor of being invited to Cannes, Polanski found himself in the unfamiliar position of being in favor of the establishment. Perhaps for someone who had lived so much of their life on the other side of the iron curtain, dreaming of making it to the West, being a juror at Cannes meant a lot more than it might to someone from around the block. It wasn't his fight. He kept thinking about Milos Forman,[4] the Czech director, and his film *The Firemen's Ball* (1967), and how much work it had taken for producers Claude Berri and Jean-Pierre Rassam just to bring it to France. Despite Polanski's decision to remain on the jury, Cannes was disbanded anyway, and Langlois was reappointed later.

It was not long before Tate became pregnant, and the couple returned to the United States to rent a house big enough for their new family. They found a place on Cielo Drive, with a beautiful garden. It had originally been rented by actress Candice Bergen and her record producer boyfriend Terry Melcher. Though Polanski's plans to shoot *Downhill Racer* had ultimately fallen through (handed over to Michael Ritchie), Polanski began to write an adaptation of Robert Merle's book, *The Day of the Dolphin*, which he proceeded to work on in his London mews home. Tate came to visit, and Polanski gave her a new Yorkshire terrier puppy that they named Prudence. (Their beloved dog, Dr. Sapirstein, had been accidentally run over by Wojtek Frykowski, who was staying at their house in L.A. with his girlfriend, Abigail Folger. Polanski only had the heart to tell Tate that their dog was missing.)

Tate was eight months pregnant at the time that she boarded the QE2 bound for the states. She looked as angelic and lovely as ever, like a Botticelli[5] painting sprung to life. In their London home, she left behind a copy of

Thomas Hardy's novel, *Tess of the d'Urbervilles*, which she had found deeply moving and thought would make a great film. Polanski planned to follow her to L.A. in a few weeks, in time for the baby's arrival and for his 36th birthday. Their goodbye on the boat was teary, and in his autobiography Polanski recalls how for a second he had the fleeting idea that this would be their last encounter. He quickly suppressed the thought and went out to meet friends.

Because of certain difficulties with adapting the script, it took Polanski longer than he or Tate would have liked to get to the United States. She was impatient waiting for him, as well as close to giving birth. Finally, Polanski decided that he would finish his work in L.A., planning to obtain a visa the following week. It was that same Saturday when he was sitting in his home with friends that he received a call notifying him of Tate's death. It was August 9, 1969. Tate had been brutally murdered in their home, along with friends Jay Sebring, Wojtek Frykowski, Abigail Folger, and an acquaintance of the groundskeeper, Steven Parent, who just happened to stop by that evening.

Polanski went into such shock that he needed sedation in order to be lovingly carted (by his friends) into the United States. The incident left Hollywood stunned. For the first time in years, everyone's door was locked. To this day many people claim that the incident was the end of the hippie era in Hollywood. People felt that they had let their guards down to a dangerous degree, and they were outraged and afraid. A paranoid atmosphere set in, particularly among stars who, in their self-obsession, took the crime as a personal threat (though, as it turned out, the Manson family[6] had planned to attack various other stars). No one knew who the killers were, and Polanski was holed up in a dressing room on the Paramount lot. Later, he moved from one friend's house to the next. He couldn't keep it together— he couldn't believe that Tate was gone. The very loss of her physical being was an unfathomable hurdle to overcome. He gave away all of his possessions. He couldn't understand the point of having things anyway.

As a way of coping with Tate's death, he became obsessed with finding her killer. In his autobiography, Polanski recalls how he allowed his mind to wander, compiling a long list of possible suspects, which included some of his friends. The first thing that he did was have the police administer a polygraph test on him, just so that they would know he was innocent and would move on with the investigation as quickly as they could. He became friendly with the policemen on the case, and at times they would work together, with Polanski meeting anyone who claimed to have information on the murders. He became an adept spy, even wearing a tape recorder and leaving bugs around friends' houses. He was fixated by the need to uncover, to understand. He was not the only one, for Tate's father, Paul, was also searching for the killers by assimilating into the hippie netherworld. The truth was ultimately discovered, not by police investigation but by a boasting prison inmate who had been a member of Charles Manson's group. Susan Atkins[7] couldn't help but brag about what she'd done, and in November 1969, the truth began to surface.

The months leading up to the Manson group's confession of the crime were unbearable. Not only did Polanski suffer tremendously from the pain of losing his wife and unborn child, but the media's handling of the event only furthered his torment. He was quoted as saying "I felt they were being assassinated for the second time."[8] The press portrayed their hippie, free-love lifestyle as an invitation to trouble. They accused them of being druggies and sex fiends, and even of practicing witchcraft. The gruesome details of Tate's death were described over and over again until the truth overtook itself and became debasing lies. These details were exaggerated, distorted to the point of sexualizing Tate's death. The press's mishandling was explosive, causing a chain reaction of unthinkable accusations. They memorialized Tate, not as the beautiful and loving woman that she was, but as a victim shamed by her killers.

Not only had Polanski lost his wife and friends, but now the lens had been turned on him and his art. The press drew connections between the subject matter of his films and the gruesome murders. Everyone and anyone wrote on the subject. From eloquent film critics to uneducated citizens, people wanted their chance to cast a stone. *Time* magazine wrote, "It was a scene as grisly as anything depicted in Polanski's film explorations of the dark and melancholy corners of the human character." As terrible as this article was, there were far worse headlines in circulation. It would take years for Polanski to excavate himself from the taint of the murders, his work now scrutinized in the context of the killings. Any touch of violence would be related back to his films, as if to remind him of his own pain, taking the knife and twisting it inside an open wound.

Being held accountable for his wife's death on the basis of his artistic work was too much to handle. The land of opportunity had turned out to be quite different than he'd imagined. He had fooled himself into believing that he could assimilate in a country that turned out to be more fickle than he could have imagined. Polanski could not help but go sour on America and its media circus. Though the country still held great significance for him, he couldn't bear to stay. Once he knew the truth about Tate's killers, he took off for Europe as soon as he could.

This was a foray into an entirely new stage of exile for Polanski, for the outside world had proved once more to be cruel and callous in its choice of beautiful and innocent prey. On the outside, his life was damaged. On the inside, he was a broken man. With the passion and spirit of 20 men, he continued to live, and eventually to love, though it is certain that the loss of Tate was the deepest wound in his heart. In his autobiography, Polanski wrote, "Sharon's death is the only watershed in my life that really matters. Before she died, I sailed a boundless, untroubled sea of expectations and optimism."

The winter of 1970 was spent in a rented chalet near Gstaad, Switzerland, where Polanski could find the solitude with which to overcome his pain. He turned to skiing—his longtime hobby since his lonely days spent in Wysoka during the war—using overexertion to quiet his mind. Eventually he was in a position to contemplate work, for his driving passion remained the same as it had as a young film student at Lodz. Film was the fuel that sparked his creative fire, and it was reason enough to continue on.

Though *The Day of the Dolphin* may have fallen through (and was later made into a film by Mike Nichols), as had a deal with Warren Beatty for *Papillon* (eventually made into a film by Franklin Schaffner in 1973, starring Steve McQueen and Dustin Hoffman), Polanski returned to London to work with National Theater literary manager, critic, and notorious character Kenneth Tynan on a screen adaptation of Shakespeare's *Macbeth* (1971).

Working again gave Polanski a new lease on life. Tynan was an expert on Shakespeare, and together they came up with ways to condense the story while remaining true to the material. The witches, who were often represented on stage as just a few, would become a large coven. Macbeth's soliloquies were often given as voiceover, a technique of pulling the audience into his mind, as they watched his face tortured by the allure of his own greed.

There is a trail of wet English mist that travels through the film—it is a sign of the witches that guide Macbeth toward misfortune, the damp earth from which no fate can escape. A streak of red permeates *Macbeth's* imagery. Upon opening, the landscape of the film at first appears as a desert of flaming red, signifying burning desire, and the flame that burns itself out. When Macbeth comes down the stairs after killing the king, he and his wife wash their bloody hands in a bucket of water. In sharing the cleansing of their sins, they invoke the darker side of their own nature. When Macbeth dumps the bloody bucket of water onto the ground, the murkiness obscures his reflection, obliterating any possibility for clarity.

Polanski decided to have the Macbeths played by a couple whose youthfulness contributes to their misguided path (as opposed to the standard middle-aged Macbeths usually presented in the theater). Jon Finch played the character of Macbeth, and Francesca Annis was Lady Macbeth. The film was shot in Wales, the perfect landscape for the piece, although weather conditions proved difficult at times. There were various setbacks during production, and the film, though it was made rather inexpensively, took longer to shoot than was expected.

Once completed, *Macbeth* received a cold response. The film opened in New York and was screened in the Playboy Theater, as Hugh Hefner and Playboy Productions funded the project. Polanski had wanted to represent violence as it truly is, acknowledging that *Macbeth* is a very bloody play, yet American critics found the violence in the film to be overwhelming.

Critics reviewed the film in the context of the Manson murders, not to mention that they found Playboy's involvement in the production to be highly distasteful. The media used these two ingredients of sex and violence to perpetuate their own picture of Sharon Tate's death, furthering their agenda, rather than judging Polanski as an individual artist. Critics simply couldn't help themselves. It was as if they had suddenly developed a puritanical streak while watching the film, when violence was certainly more extreme in other films of this time. Once again Polanski was trapped in the media's web, yet he was somewhat vindicated when the film received some rave reviews in London.

Returning to Gstaad, Polanski planned his next film, originally titled *The Magic Finger*. It was to be an erotic comedy, scripted with longtime writing partner, Gérard Brach. The matching of these two minds had always meant a spark of enthusiasm and absurdist humor, and it was certain that their new project would be a joy to make. Moving into a villa outside of Rome, they prepared for the summer shoot. The film would be produced by the great Carlo Ponti (*La Strada* [1954], *Blowup* [1966], *Dr. Zhivago* [1965)], and *The Passenger* [1975]), who was so interested in working with Polanski that he funded the movie himself.

Che?, as the film was to be called (and later, *Diary of Forbidden Dreams*), was shot in one of Ponti's villas near Naples. The film takes place on an island that can be reached only by boarding a small cable car shaped like a birdcage. It appears to be an opportunity for safety as the young American lead, played by Sydne Rome, runs away from some lascivious Italian truck drivers and into the arms of even greater sex fiends. She is not as shy as she seems, however, as she spends much of the film walking around with a napkin discreetly tied around her neck to cover her breasts and otherwise remains rather exposed. Later she replaces this bib with an oversized diary in which she writes all of the mundane details of her day.

Che? is an absurd and playful sex romp in which Marcello Mastroianni[9] is Alex, her love interest, a former pimp and presumed "fairy," who has a penchant for dressing up in animal skins. Polanski also acts in the film, playing the character of Mosquito, a wild, mustached man, who is easily offended. Though *Che?* was not a great success in the United States, where it was ultimately shown as soft-core porn, it did do well in Italy. It appears to have been fun to make. So effortless is its storytelling that at times it seems more like a documentary than a proper film. *Che?* is an absurd fairy tale in which the day begins just as it did yesterday, and nobody is ever transformed.

Though Polanski and his collaborators were smitten with Italy, it soon became clear that he needed to try something new. He wanted to remain in his heavenly villa, but the upkeep of such a lifestyle wasn't cheap. Though he and his friends were working on various projects, Polanski needed something big. It was around this time that his friend Jack Nicholson called him about a script called *Chinatown* by Robert Towne (known as script doctor of *The Godfather* and writer of *Shampoo*, and who, along with many of his contemporaries, got his start in Hollywood working for B-movie hero Roger Corman). When Bob Evans began to badger him as well, he started to take the offer seriously. As difficult as the trip back into the United States may have been, Polanski met with Evans (now the producer of *The Godfather*), who made him an offer that he couldn't refuse.

6

Redemption: *Chinatown* (1974)

Hesitant to return to Hollywood, Polanski was lured to Los Angeles by his dear friends and the possibility of venturing into an entirely new genre of film. The prospect of making a classic detective story was very appealing, as was its subject matter, which exposed the greed that helped mold the city of Los Angeles's boundaries. Though film noir may have been uncharted territory for Polanski, it was a perfect fit. Treated with the kid gloves that friend, producer, and Paramount vice-president Robert Evans provided, for once Polanski would be able to make a film just as he wished.

Los Angeles had undergone a transformation since Sharon Tate's murder, and in his autobiography, Polanski recalls these changes as a depressing turn of events. Not only did he have his personal loss to contend with (it seemed to follow the line of every road, just like the waterways in *Chinatown*), but there was also a general sense of emptiness in the city. People had turned from soft, peace-making drugs like pot and mescaline to hard ones like amphetamines and cocaine, which only heightened the edgy, paranoid environment of the 1970s. Gone was the open-door policy and the clarity of intention associated with the heart of the civil rights movement. People were now operating in a veritable haze, and the atmosphere was a disappointment for anyone who had been familiar with the Hollywood of the sixties.

At first Polanski stayed in the homes of friends Dick Sylbert and Jack Nicholson, who was also an old friend of Towne's and set to star in the film. Soon Robert Evans helped Polanski find a house of his own, with a view of all of L.A. Before preproduction was to begin, Polanski felt that work needed to be done on the script. More interested in his artistic integrity than in making it big in the industry, Towne had been working on *Chinatown* for nearly two years, and he found it difficult to accept Polanski's criticism. In the midst of a heat wave, however, the two soon began to work day after day on the script and, despite a few differences of opinion, were able to come up with a complex, magnificent screenplay full of quick, biting dialogue, a testament to Towne's wit. The underlying sentiment of the script recalled another time.

Most of the exteriors of the film would be shot on location, as Los Angeles had many architectural relics still standing from the 1930s. Robert Towne knew these places well and had integrated them into the screenplay. The remaining interiors would be built on sets, resulting in perfect period replicas created by Dick Sylbert (who had also designed *Rosemary's Baby*).

Towne had come up with the original idea for the script when a policeman told him that cops in Chinatown were told to do absolutely nothing. The police department looked upon Chinatown as a proverbial no man's land, ruled by customs and laws incomprehensible to them. Because the Chinese system couldn't be penetrated, the police felt it better to leave them alone. Therefore, in Towne's mind, Chinatown became symbolic of "the futility of good intentions."[1] With the exception of an ending that was not in the original script, *Chinatown* doesn't actually take place within Chinatown. The neighborhood becomes a metaphor essential to the story. It is a space that exists internally, a realm of exile and regret. As *Chinatown* so eloquently pushes on, the viewer falls deeper into the trap of longing, and just like detective J. J. Gittes, we lose out, only to be reminded of our own internal exile.

The opening music of *Chinatown*, written by Jerry Goldsmith (*Lilies of the Field* [1963], *Stagecoach* [1966], *Papillon* [1973]) hits like a wave of longing—a song of haunting desire. This is Los Angeles in the 1930s, a place where there are no regrets, no wasted time. At least this is what is portrayed on the surface, until love calls and the memory of an old flame ignites a new perception of time. One can sense all of this, intimating things to come, as the credits roll upward, back into their archaic home. The edges of the picture are softened, fuzzy, just as the iris of an early model movie camera might have blurred the periphery of the frame. We are being introduced to the conventions of the past—to stylistic devices derived from film noir.

Film noir is a genre that began in the 1940s in America. Defined loosely as a shadowy cop drama, the film noir story initially found benevolence in the conventions of society. This would change in later noirs, in which corruption reigned supreme, and the good guy, often a cop or detective, slowly moves outside of the accepted social norm. Defined by the moody rhythm of writers such as Raymond Chandler,[2] who could wax poetic about the Santa Ana winds just as easily as he could a lust for violence, noir was an evocative language bringing life and inspiration to bleak surroundings. Dialogue consisted of witty back talk and memorable one-liners. These were the kind of conversations where one rarely came up for air; hence the rich language of *Chinatown* forced Jack Nicholson to speak faster than his customary drawl.

According to Richard Peña, associate professor of film at Columbia University and program director of the Film Society of Lincoln Center, film noir was formed primarily by "the influx of German, Austrian and Central European directors and cinematographers who brought with them the legacies of expressionism and psychoanalysis, which found fertile ground to develop in an America undergoing vast sociological change in the postwar period." Rich was the imagery imported by directors such as Billy Wilder and Fritz Lang, who now incorporated into American cinema what was perceived by Westerners as a Kafkaesque paranoia, contributing to the underworld style of film noir. This new cinema, at times loosely defined yet easily recognizable, became a point of understanding for a culture undergoing change and for foreigners attempting assimilation. In a sense, film noir became the language of exiles. Not only were some of noir's greatest contributors exiles themselves, but also their intrinsically flawed characters relied upon the conditions of their alienation (at times hurled upon them by society, and sometimes self-imposed) for survival. Therefore, it is no surprise that Roman Polanski would find a home in this form. He would also effect change by being one of the first to move film noir from the black and white of its past to the color of the present. In his able hands, noir could withstand this transformation, emerging from its hideout, its customary shadows.

Detective J. J. "Jake" Gittes is the perfect film noir male. In an attempt to hide a painful past and shed his former life as a Los Angeles cop working in Chinatown, he has started his own business as a private eye. "I do matrimonial work," he says to his love interest, Evelyn Mulwray (played by Faye Dunaway). "It's my métier." Gittes is at home in a world in which he can live in society yet operate according to his own rules. Stepping out of the role of policeman has earned him a certain freedom. After all, he works for himself. He is content smoking cigarettes and exchanging cheap jokes with the boys. He stays out of trouble while investigating other people's problems, remaining unaffected and aloof. This is true until he becomes involved in a mystery involving the Los Angeles Power and Water Department, a love affair, one beautiful woman, and the ongoing battle between her husband (who is murdered partway through the film) and his partner, her father, who represents all of the greed and corruption consuming the city of Los Angeles.

What unfolds is a mystery with numerous twists and turns, and the discovery that the Los Angeles Power and Water Department is dumping water in the outskirts of L.A. while setting up dams that create droughts in other parts of the city. This is being done so that the city can expand into the valley and more property can be sold, all under the names of unsuspecting residents of an old age home. The illustrator of this scandal is Noah Cross (played by film giant John Huston, director of *African Queen* [1951] and *The Misfits* [1961]), estranged father of the striking Mrs. Evelyn Mulwray, who was married off to Hollis Mulwray (a sensitive, slight man with good intentions) as a teenager. In the midst of all of this controversy is Hollis's very young girlfriend, the reason that Gittes's investigation started (when a woman posing as Mrs. Mulwray hired him to investigate her husband), for

whom Mrs. Mulwray seems willing to do anything to protect. It is a meandering plotline that, just like the waterways of Los Angeles, carries the viewer
through to a dark side of the truth culminating in an ending so heartbreaking that one is left questioning the relationship of love to destruction.
Chinatown is a film that begins with a glance into the past. And from the first
notes of the soundtrack, we know that we will always wish to return to that
nostalgic moment of entry.

This doorway into a long-forgotten world is established by the impeccable imagery of the film. With sets designed by Dick Sylbert, and costumes by
his sister-in-law, Anthea Sylbert,[3] the stylish atmosphere of the 1930s is perfectly replicated. This era carried memories of Polanski's boyhood, and
Evelyn's look was modeled after a clear image of his mother. In interviews
he has often recalled the pencil-thin line of his mother's eyebrows, and the
way that she redefined her cupid's bow with the line of her lipstick. One cannot look at Mrs. Mulwray without acknowledging this connection. Thematic
nuances are captured subtly, not only with the placement of shots but with
color choices as well. *Chinatown* has a rather strict palette of earthy, bleak,
dry colors mixed with shocks of the occasional primary color. When Jake
stands by the ocean, the quiet blue sky offsets the browns and grays that
we have grown accustomed to. Brown and gray are the suits, the walls, even
the Venetian blinds. The contrast provided by bright color gives the viewer
the sensation of a cool drink of water after a walk through the desert, and it
emphasizes the distinction between the interior and exterior worlds. The
outside world provides a chance for color, life, and love, while the inside
world has a bleak palette that exists somewhere between black and white,
between truth and fiction. As the film progresses, this line becomes less recognizable, allowing both internal and external alienation to come together
as one, heightening the dreamlike quality of *Chinatown*'s experience.

Just like the drought-ridden city of Los Angeles, Jake's world is comfortable yet parched, which is one reason why Evelyn Mulwray's entrance into
his life sparks a fire. As with the striking color of the orange groves that Jake
drives through, nearly getting himself killed, the red of Evelyn's lipstick is a
signal of danger, yet simultaneously it excites. It is only in Evelyn's world
that we are permitted the glory of color. When Jake meets her in a restaurant the seats are red leather. Red carnations litter the table. Red is the color
of her lips and nails, a lush green the color of her lawn. Though she may
reside in Los Angeles, just like Curly (the overweight client who tears up the
Venetian blinds over images of his wife sleeping with another man), Evelyn's
L.A. is totally her own. Though she may be a product of greed, basking in
the glory of its bounty, she does not subscribe to its code.

The conflict of Jake's internal exile as it connects with the outside world
can be found in the turn of a Venetian blind, or in the freeing of a dam as it
rushes toward the camera, sweeping Jake up in its strength. As with many of
Polanski's films, the viewer stands with the protagonist, and where he falls,

we do, too. Dualistic imagery is important to the look and feel of the film. Shot on Panavision using anamorphic format, *Chinatown* would boast a wider image.

This visual duality is supported by shots designed to emphasize this notion. Clarity and obscurity become threads weaving in and out of the film, reiterating the separation between internal and external worlds. When J. J. Gittes follows Hollis Mulwray one evening, the perfectly circular side mirror of his car reflects an image disjointed from the background. The background becomes the foreground, as it is at the center of the frame, a reflection of Hollis standing at the gates leading to the ocean. The foreground, which in this shot becomes background, is of trees in the late afternoon sun. Here two images become one, the internal defying the external. This visual thread is carried through with the use of binoculars in an earlier scene in which Hollis stands in the desert sand, two adjoining circles coming together to create one perfect image. And when Hollis stands in a courtyard with his young "girlfriend," Jake leans over a tiled roof, holding a camera, trying to get a shot. As he raises his camera, we see the lovers' embrace as it is captured in the reflection of the lens. Again, we are privy to the beauty of a picture within a picture, and a shot that is also a work of cinematic genius. This early sequence in which scenes are captured within a lens, magnified, reflected and limited to a circle signals an entrance into investigation, as well as Gittes's initial penetration of a darker world.

Visual exposition is one aspect of a mystery founded on the duplicitous, dualistic nature of *Chinatown's* world. The power and water department is meant to support the city of Los Angeles, when really it is diverting water, squeezing the city dry. The city is supposed to be in a drought, yet people are coming into the morgue with water in their lungs. Every character has a psychological complex motivating their behavior and influencing their demise. Noah Cross and Hollis and Evelyn Mulwray each have a secret, as does Gittes, which pushes them forward into the story. For Gittes, it is a past life as a cop and a love that was destroyed by his meddling in Chinatown. For Hollis, it is his participation in a crooked scam that betrays his gentle soul and good intentions. He wishes to emerge from beneath this scandal, making the water system public, rather than scamming the community. He is also hiding a love affair with a young woman, who is tied by blood to his wife and his father-in-law. For Evelyn, it is the deep shame of having been raped by her father and having given birth to a sister/daughter at the age of 15. It is this young woman—Katherine—this protected product of Evelyn's misfortune, who has come to be known as Hollis's lover. Despite the pain of her circumstance and her implied inability to love as a result, Evelyn will do whatever it takes to protect this child, a reminder of her shame. Her dualistic existence is further complicated by the presence of an older woman (played by Diane Ladd), who hires Gittes at the start of the film, claiming to be Evelyn.

For Noah Cross, Evelyn's father, it is his lack of moral discernment that has freed him completely from the conventions of society. He is a symbol of total corruption and the greed that makes *Chinatown*'s world go round. Because he lives according to his own rules, he is never held accountable. He always makes it out on top and doesn't pay, for he feels no guilt. Though everyone around him may be on edge, he is cool as a cucumber, sitting at the table in his suspenders and cowboy hat and listening to a private mariachi band. He claims that his daughter is disturbed and can't be trusted. Playing the role of a protective father, he works to earn Jake's confidence, even going so far as to ask whether he is sleeping with Evelyn. He is so effective at convincing himself of his innocence that we almost believe him. His persistence reveals a steely quality, also present in his daughter, which is indicative of his corrupted depths. When he looks at Jake, all of his venom becomes evident. He smiles lasciviously, and says, "You may think you know what you're dealing with, but believe me you don't." Jake is standing at this point, wanting to get away. He smiles, saying, "That's what the district attorney used to tell me in Chinatown." In fact, Cross becomes synonymous with Chinatown, an impenetrable place that operates according to its own rules. One of the tricks of the film remains that the impenetrable holds a certain mystique, just as women do. This is a world where allure is a sign of danger and where the hollow echo of desire lingers in the streets.

As he delves into the mystery of the L.A. Power and Water Department, Jake comes face to face with a tidal wave of greed, each blow more earth-shattering than the one before. As with many other Polanski films, water is a strong presence, signifying the fluidity of nature that cannot be dominated by man. The closer Jake gets to the mystery of water in L.A., the more elusive greed becomes. In the penultimate sequence of the film, Jake meets with Noah Cross in Evelyn's garden and discovers that it is Cross who has murdered Mulwray. Jake questions Cross. "How much better can you eat? What can you buy that you can't already afford?" Cross looms over Jake and hisses, "The future, Mr. Gittes." For Jake, this is a comment that warrants no response. Having spent his life trying to ward off the past, he has met someone who believes himself capable of buying time itself.

When Cross whines about having lost Evelyn a long time ago, Jake asks him whose fault it is. Cross says that he doesn't feel responsible for having raped her, allowing fate to carry his guilt. "Most people never have to face the fact that at the right time and in the right place they are capable of *anything*." With a villain who feels no sense of culpability, anything becomes possible, and it is no surprise that he will prevail. One begins to see that, in *Chinatown*, the better your intentions and the purer your character, the more likely you are to get physically hurt. For Jake this means a slit nose, and for Hollis, and ultimately for Evelyn, this will mean death.

From the start of the film it is clear that Jake operates according to his own rules. He has a nice setup, including an office, assistant detectives, and even a pretty secretary who will run to the ladies room just so that he can tell a dirty joke. He no longer has to deal with the bureaucracy of the police department, nor the pain of haunting Chinatown, face to face with the memory of a lost love. And though he may devote his hours to peeping on other men's wives, as he defensively says to the mortgage broker in the barbershop who dares insult him, he makes "an honest living." His belief in what he does allows him to take things a little further when he gets involved with Evelyn Mulwray. Yet as he delves deeper into the mystery of Evelyn and her family, he comes close to being swallowed up by their corrupt world.

The signs of transition are slow at first, beginning with spying on Hollis as he goes through his day. It takes Jake a little while to know that he is in danger. When he is swept up in the breaking tide and thrown into a fence, he begins to suspect that something fishy is going on. Minutes later, when he walks toward the fence in his dripping wet suit, two men approach him. One is a fellow ex-cop, Claude Mulvihill, who we already know Jake dislikes. The other is a small man in a white suit, hat, and bow tie who wields a knife. He is played by Polanski. A distinct character, he is charming yet horrible because he appears so clean, so odd, so threatening in his unassuming impishness.

"Hold it there, kitty cat," Polanski says, approaching Jake with the knife. Burly Claude holds Jake back while Polanski attacks him. "You know what happens to nosy fellows?" he asks. "They lose their noses." He says this while slitting Jake's nose, sending a spray of blood up the side of his face. Doubled over in pain, Jake begins to experience the consequences of penetrating this broadly corrupt world. He is doing exactly what he was told not to do while a policeman in Chinatown. He is trying to understand, working to effect change.

As a result of this injury, Jake wears a bandage over his nose throughout the remainder of the film. (To have the star of the film encumbered by a bandage that covers half of his face was the sort of freedom awarded a director at this time in film history, whereas, as Polanski points out in the DVD extra documentary, *Chinatown: Filming* [2007] with the creative board now required by most studios, this purposeful blemish would never be allowed.) The effect of this bandage is that Jake looks wolfish, like a boxer who has taken too many hits. When Mr. Yelburton, who works for the Power and Water Department, suggests that his injury must be painful, Jake's cheeky response is, "Only when I breathe." This injury has affected his sense of smell, as well as his intuition, making him more attuned to insight and vulnerable to human emotions. As the past is slowly uprooted, his internal wound finds this physical manifestation. Toward the end of the film when he makes love with Evelyn Mulwray, the bandage comes off and his scar is exposed.

At the start of the film we see that Jake copes with his life by remaining aloof, allowing him to do his job without ever getting involved. It is as if he has taken the old credo from Chinatown of doing as little as possible, and made it his modus operandi, a result of his damaging past. He has separated himself from his own history and from the chance of getting hurt again. Emptiness resounds in his sarcasm, his sleek approach to life. It is as if nothing can touch him, which makes him appealing but distant as well. It is almost as if he lives in a dream, his feet planted on the earth, his heart and soul floating above. Yet as the film progresses, he cannot help but get involved.

This dreamlike quality is subtle, and it can often be found in even the most grounded film noir. It stems, in part, from a singular perspective, often experienced through the main character's voiceover, which carries us through the film. From *Double Indemnity* (1944) to *In a Lonely Place* (1950), it is a trend that rings through this genre, allowing for a certain working-class poeticism rarely encountered in film. Even the neo-noir *Blade Runner* (1982) by Ridley Scott originally began with Deckard's voiceover, designed to set the scene. This narrow position of one voice sparks a sense of uncertainty in the audience, as we are kept locked in the mind of the protagonist, and the possibility that we are experiencing a distorted reality arises. Through Polanski's decision to keep the camera as an extension of Jake's perspective, this "voice" (captured in image rather than sound, Polanski's way of revolutionizing the form), is perfectly achieved through the visual language of *Chinatown*.

Just as the lens captures Jake's experience, we, the audience, feel closely connected to what he sees. Unlike other films in which an omnipresent eye often overlooks the story, allowing the viewer to soar above the action, here we are tied to Jake's perceptions and to the boundaries set by a deliberate frame. One might even say that as we experience life with him we are also privy to his subconscious mind. Though *Chinatown* never indulges in fantastical imagery the way that *Repulsion* or *Rosemary's Baby* does, there is still the lingering sense that with all of its straight talk and violence there is still something that is not completely real. This sensation comes from a deep sense of longing and regret, which allows every moment of life to express hollowness, an echo that reverberates with each step. It leads the audience members to question where they are, knowing that this story takes place in a metaphoric world, perhaps too true to be real.

"In this incoherent brutality, there is the feeling of a dream." These are words expressed by early noir theoreticians Raymond Borde and Etienne Chaumeton in their book *Panorama du Film Noir Américain* (1955). Applied to *Chinatown*, this thought resonates well, for here is a world in which nothing can be explained.

When Jake meets Evelyn for the first time, he is rendered speechless. She asks him if he knows her, and he, the fast-talking, witty private eye, struggles to find the words with which to say that he does not. She is beautiful, elegant, and self-possessed, and perhaps she also sparks for him the memory of another time. In this arid desert, she is his tall drink of water. She holds the possibility for fulfillment of another dream, one in which love makes a person feel real again. This is the promise that they hold for one another—the chance to become whole. *Chinatown* is not only a mystery but also an expedition into the heart of a potential love.

Though their liaison ends up as a question mark—wondering what if, what might have been—Jake and Evelyn's points of connection are invaluable to the pulse of *Chinatown*. At first glance, Evelyn is pure perfection. Every hair is in place, her outfits fit perfectly, and her makeup is immaculate. Her posture and decisive movements betray her need for achieving perfection, an indication not only of her financial status but also that she is hiding something deeply imperfect. As we discover, Evelyn is damaged. Raped by her father as a teenager, she gave birth to his daughter. A great portion of her life has been devoted to hiding this truth. She lives with great shame and anxiety, and as the prospect of the truth being revealed inches closer, her panic is heightened. As she says to Mr. Gittes (which she calls him, while he respectively calls her Mrs. Mulwray) the first time that they meet in private, "I don't see anyone for very long, Mr. Gittes. It's difficult for me." She also tells him that she was grateful for her husband's affair. She is not your average woman, her wounds establishing a more personal moral code. Carrying through with this train of anxiety, we see her react anytime her father is discussed. She shakes at the mention of his name, stumbles over the word "father," and unknowingly lights a fresh cigarette when talk of him begins, even though she already has one lit. While sitting naked before Jake after they have made love, when she discovers that he has been to see her father, she rushes to cover her breasts with her hands and jumps back on the bed. All of the signs of her secret are there; Jake just has to dig a little deeper to discover the truth.

Although Jake and Evelyn's chemistry is palpable from the start, the turn of events comes when Jake finds himself (after a crazy night of narrow escapes) alone with Evelyn in her house. As she pours him a drink, he clears his throat nervously, even goes so far as to adjust his tie and fiddle with the bandage on his nose. For a cool cat like Jake, these subtle gestures demonstrate anticipation and excitement. They go into Evelyn's bathroom so that she can clean his wound, and as she takes the bandage off of his nose, she flinches at the sight of his cut. By cleaning his exposed scar she is brought closer to him, and here the camera is handheld and slightly shaky, tentative as are they. He looks at her closely and carefully, saying, "There's something black in the green part of your eye." Evelyn smiles. "It's a flaw in the iris," she says. At last she has exposed her own imperfection to Jake, and it is this weakness that brings him close to her, and into a kiss. Having found her vulnerability, Jake finds the courage to embrace her, and perhaps he even wants to protect her, for as the audience can see, she is already so exposed—right down to a flaw in her iris, her most basic way of seeing.

Roman Polanski in *Chinatown*. (Courtesy of Photofest)

In the sequence prior to this seduction scene, it is Evelyn that rescues Jake, and she does so more than once. The first time is when he has been beaten unconscious by farmers in the orange groves, and the second time is when they escape from a corrupt old age home, whose prissy proprietor has called in Claude and the nose-slitting man dressed in white. She drives up in her car, and he jumps in. They have joined in the investigation together, and for a moment one is reminded of the role for which Faye Dunaway is most famous, that of Bonnie in *Bonnie and Clyde* (1967).[4] As she drives them along in her convertible through the California night air, it is she who is protecting him. The camera rests in front of the car, and there is a two shot of Evelyn and Jake, her hair flapping in the wind. What is so interesting about this image is that each of their sides seems completely different. On Jake's side of the car, one can distinguish the glass of the windshield, for it shines in its reflections of streetlights, as they whizz past his head like a revolving halo. Evelyn is in the driver's seat, and she appears to be completely exposed. It is as if the glass on her side of the windshield is missing, and it is she who is taking risks, she who needs protection and assurance. Ultimately, this will be true, as she will be shot while driving away in this very car. The image is a portent for what is to come.

This moment in the car externalizes each character's vulnerability, for as Jake looks over at Evelyn and the trumpet soars, one feels his longing and the sense of abandonment associated with falling in love. Jake's encounter

Evelyn Mulwray—the idealized woman of the 1930s. (Courtesy of Photofest)

with Evelyn is just the excitement that he needs to be awakened from his dream and brought back to life. For her, it is a chance to be a complete woman and to feel for a moment that she can trust and is safe. When they stand together in her garden in a moment of flirtation, Jake tells Evelyn that this is the first time in years that he has gotten into such trouble. Here trouble hints at excitement. Their dialogue about Chinatown begins.

When they lie in bed together in postcoital bliss, Jake is on his back smoking a cigarette, while Evelyn leans on her side facing him. She looks at him adoringly. "You must have looked cute in blue," she says smiling, as her fingers graze his lips. Her makeup has come off, as has her stoicism that previously made her look older than her years. She is glowing, glistening in fact, as if she has been reborn. They speak of his time in Chinatown and how he doesn't like to talk about the past. He says that he couldn't always tell what was happening in Chinatown. "Like with you," he says, and rolls on his side to face her. Now it is her turn to roll onto her back and drag off a cigarette. This is their dance. One evades examination, yet enjoys the attention, while the other basks in his or her appeal.

"Why was . . . why was it bad luck?" she asks, returning to the subject of Chinatown. He answers, "I was trying to keep someone from being hurt. I ended up making sure that she was hurt." Finally we clearly understand where Jake is coming from, as well as perhaps where we are headed. "Cherchez la femme? Was there a woman involved?" She asks. "Dead?"

"Cinema of exile." (Courtesy of Photofest)

The phone rings right on cue. The past will be repeated by nightfall the following day.

Jake intends to protect Evelyn, but because of his own painful past, he jumps the gun and distrusts her too quickly. When Evelyn leaves the house, he follows her, and misinterpreting her interaction with Hollis's girlfriend, he begins to turn on her. When she weeps to him that the girl is merely her sister, he doesn't console her, rather he leaves her alone when she asks him to come home with her. He turns on her just when she begins to feel safe.

The night proceeds down this spiraled path. Jake goes home and tries to sleep, but is called over to the fake Mrs. Mulwray's house, who turns out to be dead. It is there that he meets the police, and more twists of fate follow. He winds up at the little house where Evelyn has been hiding Katherine, and she blushes when he enters, so happy is she to see him. He goes straight to the phone and calls the police. He has made a morbid mistake, though he doesn't know it yet.

When Jake wants to get the truth out of Evelyn, he slaps her repetitively until she crashes into a vase, having emptied herself of her darkest truth. And even though Jake feels regret and decides to do everything he can to help her, just as had happened before, he winds up making sure that she is hurt. By helping her to arrange a meeting in Chinatown, a place that he knows can't be trusted and which operates under foreign rule, he makes a fatal mistake. This is where the corrupt come to meet. Not even the police can save her, in fact, they wind

"Forget it, Jake. It's Chinatown." (Courtesy of Photofest)

up killing her, allowing Noah Cross to take young Katherine away. We watch in disgust as he shelters his daughter's eyes, chilled by the thought of him being her guardian. We are outraged by this injustice, as is Jake, who is once again rendered speechless, just as he was when he and Evelyn first met.

The flaw in Evelyn's iris reflects the lack of clarity in an imperfect world. As Evelyn is shot from a block behind, we fear that she is dead as the car stops mid-escape. As her car horn resounds incessantly, her daughter screams. It is a chilling sound—the numbness of the horn met by the shrill horror of the scream. Together they touch every part of the viewer, reaching both the gut and the head. The screams draw the crowd forward, toward the car. Everyone is there—Jake, in handcuffs, the police commissioner, Noah Cross, and Evelyn, who, as they open the car door, slide back to reveal a hideous bullet hole running straight through her left eye. It was the eye with the flaw, the same one that drew Jake close to her hours before. It is a devastating moment, made blood curdling by Noah Cross's perfectly heartless exclamations of "Lord! Oh Lord!" He is the villain of the film, yet he is walking away free, and with the girl.

"Forget it, Jake. It's Chinatown," his friend Walsh says, and puts his arm around him. As Jake walks away, the crowd pushes in, lured by the grotesque, trying to get a closer look. For the first time in the film, the camera is separated from Jake, pulling back and over the Chinatown street and crowd. They are the impenetrable foreigners, to whom Jake also belongs. He is alone now, left to wander in his dreamlike state, and we are no longer privy to joining him. In this separation we feel abandoned as well, and as the camera rises and the music swells, there is a hint of returning to the beginning. "In this incoherent brutality, there is the feeling of a dream." Perhaps Jake is doomed, for every time that he loves, his emotions invite tragedy. Caught in the undertow of nostalgia, we are drowning in the emptiness of life's regret.

Robert Towne has often referred to Polanski's choice of ending as "a tunnel at the end of the light."[5] The ending had been much debated over and was decided upon at the last minute, with Dick Sylbert dressing a set to look like Chinatown and Jack Nicholson helping to arrange the scene. Having such a simple ending to a complex film made a tremendous impact. Polanski knew that audiences would walk away distressed by the injustice of the story and would therefore continue to think long after the movie was over.

Chinatown turned out to be perfect in many ways. With one of the tightest scripts in Hollywood history; a sleek yet arid aesthetic; impeccable camera work by John Alonzo (*Scarface* [1983]), who replaced Stanley Cortez (*The Magnificent Ambersons* [1942]); an excellent cast; and constructed by editor Sam O'Steen, the film exceeded Towne's aspirations for the story. Though Faye Dunaway had caused problems on set, everyone, including Polanski, agreed that she gave a wonderful performance, completely embodying the character of Evelyn Mulwray. Jack Nicholson, who was now moving into a successful acting career (he had finally broken through with *Easy Rider* in 1969, after years of struggling in Hollywood), injected humor and sarcasm into the character of J. J. Gittes, and his subtle performance makes us believe his every move. The musical score was the only piece of the puzzle that needed work. Feeling lost because of Komeda's absence, Polanski had agreed to a composer whom he soon realized was not going to work out. At the film's first preview, he discussed with Robert Evans—who was also a perfectionist—the possibility of hiring a new composer. The result was a score written by Jerry Goldsmith in nine days, which contributes greatly to the atmosphere of the film.

Audiences emerged from the theater completely silent. The film was a hit. Everyone kept waiting for a bad review to come in, but it never happened. *Chinatown* was a highly intelligent film, yet it had been worked through to such a point of clarity that everyone could relate to it. It was an appealing film, a nihilistic take on noir, now socially acceptable to a skeptical public willing to examine surrounding corruption, something that would have been impossible at the genre's inception.

Chinatown won four Golden Globes and was nominated for seven. It was also nominated for 11 Academy Awards yet only won one. Robert Towne won for Best Screenplay, and no one could deny that he deserved it. To this day, the screenplay for *Chinatown* is revered by many aspiring filmmakers, as is the film itself, which is still screened in film schools across the United States as a work worth admiring. After all these years, it is a film that appears as fresh today as it was in 1974.

7

The Stranger Upstairs:
The Tenant (1976)

It seemed like a moment, but two years had passed since Polanski made his last film. Soon after completing *Chinatown* he had returned to Italy to direct Alban Berg's *Lulu* in a Roman amphitheater in Spoleto, and subsequently he began writing *Pirates* with Gérard Brach. It was to star Jack Nicholson, but the deal fell through, and Polanski was in a hurry to make a film. He was still working with Paramount, who held the rights to Roland Topor's novel *Le Locataire Chimérique* (translated as "The Tenant"), which he decided upon for his next film. He would approach the project with such passion that less than a year would pass from the time that he began writing the script to the first showing of the film. Strange yet fascinating, *The Tenant* (1976) would prove to be one of his most penetrating films to date.

The film was to be shot in Paris, the city in which he was born and where more than once in his life he would find home. It was once the source of fantasy for a boy who, during the war, dreamt of a place where his family had once been happy and free. It was a place of memory (fabricated, perhaps), and where he'd first lived outside of communism more than a decade before. Polanski applied for French citizenship and rented an apartment in town.

Preparing for the shoot was a quick affair. It was agreed upon that the deteriorating French apartment building in which much of the action takes place was to be built as a set by the talented designer Pierre Guffroy, who had worked on the films of some of cinema's greatest directors—Bresson, Godard, Bunuel, Truffaut, and Cocteau. Polanski would also have the great fortune of working with Sven Nykvist, the celebrated cinematographer best known for his close collaboration with Ingmar Bergman[1] and considered by some to be one of the greatest masters of light in the world. Of Nykvist's work, Polanski once said, "You can see the air in his movies."[2] Polanski would play the role of Trelkowski, the sweet-natured Polish bank clerk who suffers a mental breakdown, becomes a transvestite, and kills himself. For the part of Trelkowski's love interest, Polanski cast ethereal French actress Isabelle Adjani,[3] who needed to be deglamorized for the part. He also brought over veteran American actors Melvyn Douglas[4] and Shelley Winters[5] to play supporting roles. Although *The Tenant* would be shot in Paris, the film was to be in English, as were all of Polanski's films following *Knife in the Water*, a key to staying in the running as an international director.

Bearing some resemblance to the premise of *Repulsion*, *The Tenant* is the story of an immigrant who succumbs to paranoid schizophrenia. Unlike *Repulsion*, however, here the violence is not directed outward, as it was with Carole, but rather Trelkowski turns against himself. A Polish Jew, Topor had hid as a child in the region of Savoy during the war (one imagines Polanski and Topor like two ships in the night, both seeking a new, strange life in another land). Topor was a writer, filmmaker, and painter, with a unique and interesting career. His illustrations were recognized for their surreal content, which was at times grotesque, even violent. He worked alongside filmmaker René Laloux, and together they made the animated film *Le Planète Sauvage* (1973) and various other shorts. He worked on a project with Chilean psychomagician and filmmaker Alejandro Jodorowsky (*The Holy Mountain* [1973]), and performed in Werner Herzog's film *Nosferatu: Phantom der Nacht* (1979). His colleagues were all like-minded rebels, creating art with personal meaning and not with the intention of pleasing the masses. *The Tenant* addresses questions of identity and alienation, and was perfectly suited to Polanski's particular way of seeing the world.

The basic plotline of *The Tenant* is that of a youthful Polish immigrant, Trelkowski, who is also a French citizen. He rents a flat in an old Parisian apartment building, taking it over from a woman, Simone Choule, who has just attempted suicide and is in the hospital on her deathbed. Inhabiting the apartment he discovers that his neighbors are overbearing and insulting, blaming him for everything, and he begins to develop a paranoid streak. The harder he works to gain approval, the worse things become. Paranoia develops into schizophrenia, as he takes on Simone's mannerisms, even going so far as to dress in her makeup and clothes. Completely alienated from himself, he feels compelled to follow her lead in leaping from the window, and when the first jump is unsuccessful, he drags himself upstairs and does it again.

Trelkowski is timid. He dresses carefully. He is an immigrant who carries with him the respect for material goods learned in another world. His shirt is pressed, his tie and suit in perfect order. He smiles politely. As was pointed out by New York Times critic Vincent Canby in 1976, "He inhabits his own body, but it's as if he had no lease on it, as if at any moment he could be dispossessed for having listened to the radio in his head after 10 p.m. People are always knocking on his walls." He doesn't mean to offend. He may even buy the wrong brand of cigarettes just to please someone else or order a hot chocolate when he wants a coffee. He is battling an unstable sense of self, and the more he tries to fit in, the more difficult things become for him.

An example of the foreigner who strives toward assimilation while fighting against his second-class position created by society, Trelkowski experiences dissimilation through his efforts to belong. They bounce back against him, just like the ball outside his window, which reveals itself as a bouncing version of his own head. The image of his head as it is dropped from sky to pavement, and vice versa, reminds him that he will never be one with those around him, and though it is the source of his own internal decrepitude, it is also a reflection of a greater social problem.

The place of a foreigner in a modern Western world is addressed repeatedly in literature and film of the twentieth and twenty-first centuries. He has become essential to society yet is permitted integration under the assumption that he will remain second class. He is denied papers permitting him basic rights, while he works twice as hard to have half of what a native of his new homeland may possess. He is the worker who supports a society, who plugs up all of the holes that no native wants to fill yet he is almost always treated as an outcast, particularly in any environment that upholds strict nationalistic traditions, such as France. Even when he has his papers, his accent betrays him, and so, as is pointed out by linguistics professor Julia Kristeva[6] in her book *Strangers to Ourselves*, as he works to learn his adopted country's tongue and customs, he slowly lets go of his mother country, his home. He becomes a man who belongs to no one. His new friends feel comfortable with this disconnect, for it allows them to feel superior, and he often plays this role in hopes that eventually he will feel a sameness and cease to be a stranger.

This is only one concept of the foreigner among many others, yet it is one essential to the examination of *The Tenant*. Kristeva believes that, "A secret wound, often unknown to himself, drives the foreigner to wandering . . . No obstacle stops him, and all suffering, all insults, all rejections are indifferent to him as he seeks that invisible and promised territory . . . The foreigner, thus, has lost his mother." She continues by asking, "should one recognize that one becomes a foreigner in another country because one is already a foreigner from within?"

The Tenant addresses these thoughts and questions, exhuming them from the mental disintegration of one man who, in his shy bewilderment, wishes to find home, and in some ways, to win. He accepts abuse in exchange for acceptance, but there is a limit to what even he can take. The body can manage, but it is the psyche that folds when faced with the question of personal identity. He fights this pressure until it is easier to lose himself than to continue to try to be what others want him to be. He is the ultimate stranger, his estrangement made palpable by his identification with ancient hieroglyphic text. He plows through a torrent of noise, until all he seeks is relief, and, as Kristeva says, "between two languages, your realm is silence."

The Tenant takes many of Polanski's visual and thematic elements from past films and brings them to the next step of integration. Here the breaking down of one's environment, both internally and externally, is addressed with complete abandon and clear social (as well as personal) implication. The concept of duality is carried over, only in its most extreme form, as man becomes woman, sublimating his identity to hers. As always, the image is the vehicle, but here it exposes rather than conceals. This is apparent from the opening shot in which Trelkowski stands at the apartment window looking out into the courtyard. A long, continuous shot plays behind the opening credits (we wish to push them aside, so beautiful is the fluid take). The camera travels like a bird of prey, stopping at points, grazing the rooftops and gazing into windows. Unlike the opening of *Rosemary's Baby*, the scene immediately reveals to us that this is not a lighthearted film as Trelkowski's gaze switches to that of a beautiful, mysterious woman who we imagine to be Simone Choule. The image is eerie, even frightening, a sign of things to come.

The film presents Trelkowski as a shy and cautious foreigner reaching to belong. This is essential to understanding his mental breakdown. Trelkowski has an accent, a soft Polish intonation, while most of the cast, who are supposed to be French, have strong American accents, heightening the atmosphere of estrangement. The only exception to this rule is his neighbor, Madame Gaderian (the mother of an imaginary and beautiful crippled daughter), played by Russian actress Lila Kedrova, who implores Trelkowski to take her side against the rest of their neighbors who are out to evict her. She praises him for being a good man—a comment that has significance for him, as everyone else treats him as if he is a nuisance. When he first arrives at the building, the gruff concierge, played by Shelley Winters, hesitates to even let him in. She talks to him without looking in his direction, and when he goes to pet her dog, even the little Dachshund tries to bite him on the hand. When he knocks on the landlord's door, the landlord's wife, Madame Zy, tries to shut him out, saying, "We don't give to charity."

There is nothing about Trelkowski's appearance that would make one assume that he is asking for donations, but his overreaching politeness implies a sense of inferiority. When he goes to have a drink with his love interest, Stella, he changes his drink order three times. First he asks for a beer, then a coffee, and when Stella orders a glass of wine, he quickly switches to a martini, like an adolescent unsure of who he wants to be. Choosing a drink that sounds sophisticated seems the best way to go. Nervous, he tells Stella that he must excuse himself to make a phone call, but instead he goes to the toilet to relieve himself, too shy to tell her the truth. He would never dream of imposing his own bodily functions on a woman so fine as she. And, when moments later they walk on the street, he steps in dog shit, and wipes his shoe discreetly, raising his sole against every passing pole, while still smiling at her, showing only his interest in her company.

Trelkowski carries all of the marks of an immigrant who is afraid. He hesitates to make waves and always makes an effort to do the right thing. When he moves into the apartment, he beams with the smile of relief that comes with finding home and unpacks his carefully organized suitcase bearing few possessions. He fits them into the corners left unoccupied by Mademoiselle Choule's things, her framed images of Egyptian mummies (she was an Egyptologist, after all), dried flowers on a shelf. His shoes are tucked into neat plastic bags. He happily places his cookware on the kitchen shelves, and finding a flower print dress in the mirrored wardrobe (recalling *Two Men and a Wardrobe* and *Repulsion*, as well as the wardrobe moved at the start of *Rosemary's Baby*), he leaves it where it belongs so as not to disturb the peace. This careful behavior highlights the absurdity of his neighbors who constantly accuse him of making noise.

Though Trelkowski maintains a respectable job as a bank clerk, his role is that of the immigrant who fills society's needs. This is especially true with people whom he encounters, who need him to be less than they are, need him to be a pain, if only to pump themselves up. Different expectations are placed on him simply because he is not one of them. He befriends a man who doesn't even pay for rent—his brother is in Peru, and he stays in his beautiful duplex where nobody bothers him, while Trelkowski pays a high sum to live in a crumbling, stained flat with no toilet (indicating the inability to achieve privacy). When Trelkowski first speaks with his landlord, Monsieur Zy says, "I like you. You seem to be a serious young man." This is why he is accepted into his new home. In fact, he is required to be what he seems, to avoid making noise of any kind. It seems as if the surrounding environment has created a niche for him so constricting that if he missteps at all, he will fail.

This idea of the holes left open by society is essential to the imagery of the film. From the spaces left open in Simone's bandages, to the gash left in the awning by her fall, everything points to an emptiness in the environment and within people. When the concierge first shows Trelkowski the apartment, she pushes him toward the banister outside the window to show him the splintered gap in the glass awning below. "She's not dead yet," she grumbles. She laughs over the previous tenant's misfortune, which only makes Trelkowski feel more ill at ease. It is a cold world that he is entering, and we the audience wish to toughen him up, or at least protect him. He is nervous about Choule's condition.

"What if she gets better?" he asks. The concierge tells him not to worry, that she won't. But he does worry. He worries about Choule, while simultaneously coveting her home. He worries about the lack of a toilet in the apartment—"Suppose I got sick . . . and I had to relieve myself in the middle of the night?" he asks, exposing his self-consciousness. Excited by the prospect of getting the apartment, he remains uncomfortable about taking it over while Choule is still alive. He goes to the hospital to visit her. Standing over her bed, he cowers over her stiff, bandaged body, completely covered except for her left eye and mouth, which remain exposed. She is missing one of her front teeth. He holds a small brown paper bag filled with mandarins—a tribute to his old world mentality—and wears a tie decorated with a single white circle that reminds us of the eternal void.

A friend of Choule's, Stella, played by Isabelle Adjani, stands behind Trelkowski and startles him into dropping his bag of mandarins. It is a beautiful shot that watches him as he crouches down to collect the small oranges. He smiles nervously and is shy about his clumsiness, his lack of containment. The audience feels deeply for Trelkowski in this moment. We recognize the polite awkwardness of his behavior, his perfectly combed hair and the sweet little mandarins—an offer of consolation made absurd by the condition of the patient. It reminds us that he comes from a place in which such gestures are de rigueur. It defines him as separate and alone.

When Stella asks Choule if she recognizes her, Choule inhales, making a croaked, guttural sound, and exhales a horrid scream. It speaks of torture, of horrors, and is a scream so base that it belongs to a category not normally shown in film. It does not fit with the picture-perfect idea of pain normally portrayed on screen, and it indicates to us that as absurd as events to come may be, this is for real and we should be afraid. Stella later says that Choule was screaming at the sight of Trelkowski. This seems a strange comment at first, though as the film progresses we perceive this to be true. Choule's scream is a call for help—emerging from a place so horrible that we are not privy to enter it. Trelkowski looks at Choule's face, and the camera pushes in on her open, gaping mouth. This gives the impression that we have fallen into her as well. "You mustn't give in to your grief," Trelkowski says to Stella as they walk to a café.

Once Trelkowski moves into the new apartment, he holds a small party at his house. Friends and coworkers come over, and together they play music, drink, and have a good time. One colleague discovers a dirty sock from beneath the bed, and teasingly throws it in Trelkowski's face. He also takes a leak in the kitchen sink rather than go across the hall to the bathroom. There is the feeling that his friends take advantage of him, but he is happy to be surrounded by their warmth. A neighbor knocks on his door to complain about the noise. His friends laugh and heckle the neighbor, but Trelkowski is clearly unsettled. He pulls the neighbor back into the hall, and closing the front door so that his friends won't see his timidity, he apologizes for the disturbance. He kicks his friends out of the apartment, allowing his insecurity to get the best of him. As they noisily descend the oriental carpeted spiral staircase, he watches as any chance for normalcy is lost down a hole.

As the film progresses, this intrusion of sound, this accusation that he is making too much noise, begins to close in on Trelkowski until he is so afraid of his home that he rents a hotel room resembling a padded cell. His neighbors do not permit him the basic right of freedom in his own home, and any sound that he makes becomes a personal affront to those around him. It appears that even the walls are insignificant, and that however he tries to shelter himself, security and a sense of belonging are impossible. It is as if these insignificant walls are pointing to the breakdown of self and of environment. When Trelkowski returns home after a night with Choule's friend to discover that his apartment is trashed and has been burglarized, he throws a shoe against the wall in frustration. A neighbor responds by banging on the wall, and Trelkowski shouts out that he knows he is making noise. It is unbearable to have his every move examined, and also to know that while his apartment was being robbed, no one was bothered by that sound. As things progress, we come to understand that the close watch on Trelkowski's behavior has moved into his mind. He is criticized externally for making a racket, but the buzz has found its way to his internal landscape as well. The noise in his head becomes so intolerable that only silence will equal peace. He apologizes repeatedly for his imposition, for his sounds, for his very being.

The morning after his party, as Trelkowski walks downstairs, his arms loaded with two bags of garbage (one of which looks like an oversized copy of the brown paper bag full of mandarins that he brought to Mademoiselle Choule), he meets Monsieur Zy, who has just returned home from a walk. He apologizes to Monsieur Zy, saying that it will never happen again. As he speaks with Zy, standing above him, we see that bits of garbage appear through a hole at the base of the bag. He is embarrassed by this exposure, and by his inability to contain his waste. As he walks downstairs, garbage begins to fall out the bottom. The first piece to drop is a mandarin peel.

Trelkowski's world takes a strange turn as the breakdown of boundaries becomes realized. This motif of environmental disintegration arises again and again in Polanski's work. Sometimes it is woven into the fabric of the story, while at others it is concretized. In *Repulsion*, the cracked walls in Carole's apartment are symbolic of her mental state. In *Che?* Sydney Rome stuffs her oversized pencil into a hole in the wall above her bed. As she closes her eyes, at peace with the thought that she is safe, we watch as her pencil is pulled through to the other side. There is always someone watching, always a chance for instability, and a sense of displacement perhaps originated in Polanski's experiences as a child in the ghetto, where being walled in was just one expression of the loss of basic rights.

Toward the beginning of the film, Trelkowski goes to church to attend Simone Choule's funeral. At first he is quiet and calm, but soon he is overwhelmed, sweaty, and confined. The priest's sermon turns to the smell of rotting flesh, and a graphic description of a worm penetrating the corpse's face. The camera reveals this change in Trelkowski's perceptions, moving closer to the subject and enlarging the background. The image is flattened and dominating. When Trelkowski goes to the doors to get out, he finds that they are locked.

The priest's singling out of the ears and mouth precludes a fixation with cavities of all kinds. These orifices allow the body to absorb and expel sound.

They facilitate communication, and the possibility of their violation is unbearable to their possessor. Trelkowski begins to experience his break-down with the priest's words ringing in his ears. His material disintegration is brought to another level when he moves Choule's dresser in the night and discovers a tooth stuffed into a hole in the wall. Frightened, he puts it back, but even if he smoothes over the piece of cotton that holds it inside, there is no way to contain the thoughts that arise.

Trelkowski lies in Stella's bed before they make love, and he tells her of his discovery of the tooth. She ignores him slightly, undressing him while he speaks. He tells her the story of a man who lost his arm and wanted to have it buried. "Tell me," he says, "at what precise moment does an individual stop being who he thinks he is?" Descent into oblivion is imminent, as these thoughts press against Trelkowski's mind, pushing him away from himself (his second self, for, after all, all immigrants already have two—one for their mother country and the other for their adopted one), and into a reality of unknown variables. He is the tenant, implying that he is only permitted to stay on a temporary basis.

Trelkowski's identity is being pulled from him, as the world around him seems to conspire for him to take on Choule's persona. The owner of the café around the corner always serves him hot chocolate and a roll, Simone's breakfast of choice. He pushes her American brand of cigarettes on him, when he would rather smoke Gauloises. It seems that he is no longer even permitted to smoke French cigarettes. When he finally gives in to smoking Simone's Marlboro Reds, he lights the cigarette and holds it away from his body, looking at it in question. The hand becomes alien to him, and soon effeminate; we find him posing with the cigarette as a woman would.

As Choule's identity is pushed onto Trelkowski—the concierge hands him her mail (a postcard of an Egyptian tomb, bearing a message of love)—he begins to transition into a female, transvestite character. It happens only at night, when madness takes over. At first his transformation is unknown to him, for he wakes up with makeup on, not recalling how it was applied. Soon we are invited into his feminine activities: buying a wig, trying on a dress and stockings, and primping in the mirror with genuine coquettish admiration. "I think I'm pregnant," he says to himself, the reflection highlighting his split personality. We are an invisible viewer, and trapped in the mirror, we experience the deepening of Trelkowski's mental chasm. Though at times we share his perspective, we are not always one with him as we are in other Polanski movies. It is all the more terrifying to watch Trelkowski unfold, knowing that he is delusional, aware that he is mistaken in his perceptions of truth.

Heightening this loss of self, the camera begins to switch perspectives, moving from subjective to objective as a means of demonstrating his miscon-strued reality. At night Trelkowski returns home to find a frightened tramp in the entrance to his building. We see that she is as shaken by his presence as he is by hers, but what Trelkowski sees is his dominating neighbor, Madame Dioz, who begins to strangle him. Returning to an objective perspective, we understand that in fact Trelkowski is strangling himself, and he does so with such force that he winds up falling to the ground. This swapping of perspectives continues to happen as Trelkowski descends further into madness, drawing closer to suicide. In the final sequence of the film, when he has jumped for the first time, he drags himself in fear back to his apartment. The audience sees that his neighbors are concerned for his safety, but to Trelkowski, they are giddy over his fall and preparing to finish him off. As always, the Polanskian crowd hovers, leaning into him, smothering him, and this time it is taken further, with a blanket held above, as if he is a wild animal that needs to be caught, and with Madame Dioz's forked tongue emerging, slithering, trying to get at him. He can see only the bliss of empowering himself by ending his life.

As Trelkowki becomes a woman he becomes more afraid. Having emigrated from Eastern Europe, where masculine behavior in men is emphasized, it has become necessary for him to take on a feminine persona in order to allow for a new kind of expression. He is a sensitive man, but he feels that he needs to control this element of his personality, though the more he suppresses, the more things will rise to the surface. As he plummets into a schizophrenic breakdown, he draws on Choule's identity as a channel for his own abandonment of self. He shuts out the male part of himself that has always strived to maintain order in his environment as well as within his psyche. As he lets Trelkowski go, he invites in chaos and disorder.

As with *Repulsion*, the wardrobe is used to block intruders. Where Carole blocked a second entrance to her room, Trelkowski places it in front of the window. Even so, a hand creeps around the side to come through. Nothing is so frightening as this hand with no master—appearing to belong to no one, yet still wishing to invade Trelkowski's world. It is a sign of a disjointed mind and an indication that the violence Trelkowski feels is now turning inward. He rids himself of this hand by using a large kitchen knife to stab at it until the window breaks and the vision is shattered. The sound brings him to his senses as he looks in horror at his own bloody hands.

Trelkowski is being watched. Every night he is drawn to the window and stares across the courtyard into the communal bathroom. A woman in black looks at him. A man in a hat and overcoat stares blankly. A woman, Simone, wrapped in bandages, dressed as a mummy, caresses and unwraps herself. She laughs at him, exposing her missing tooth.

There is often a faded, golden tone to these images of the strange and lonely individuals who haunt the bathroom. The sepia tone that surrounds them leads us to believe that they inhabit the past. They call out to him, like long-lost family members left behind in Poland. They are victims of defeat. They are his guilty conscience, the reason for his estrangement from himself—Simone included, to whom he feels guilt for taking over her life and needing her death in order to find home. They call out to him without ever saying a word.

Trelkowski tells his friends about these people who stand in the toilet "absolutely dead still." They laugh with him about it; however, such moments of reprieve are becoming less and less frequent.

One night Trelkowski goes to the toilet, sweaty and confused. He looks around as graffiti on the walls slowly turns to hieroglyphics. He reads these ancient, universal symbols as if to find himself. Perhaps the distant call of an ancient language feels closer than the current, rejecting environment. Trelkowski turns to the window to look at his apartment. There, in his home, someone is watching him. Upon closer look, we see that it is Trelkowski watching Trelkowski. He has answered the question of at what point an individual ceases to be an individual. In fact, he has now completely lost himself. As the boundaries of his mind have disintegrated, he has turned to an ancient language as a means of communication with himself. It is a terrifying moment in which no sense of safety is possible because reality has broken.

This self-conscious guilt is evident in much of Trelkowski's breakdown. At night he sees his neighbors in the courtyard; they are torturing the crippled girl and her immigrant mother. He worries for them, perhaps feels somewhat responsible and that he ought to help, but when they put a mask and jester hat on the girl, we see that it is a mask of Trelkowski's face. The child points up at him—it is he who is responsible for their suffering. Such is the guilt of

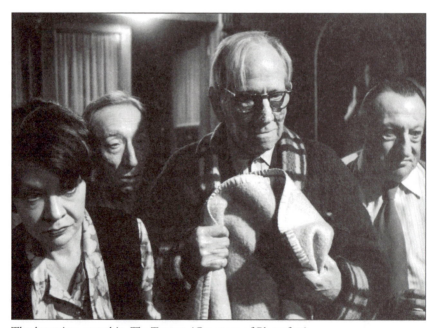

The hovering crowd in *The Tenant*. (Courtesy of Photofest)

the immigrant who has left home and never turned back, struggling to make his way in a new world.

Trelkowski is buckling beneath the instability of his reality. He is just about to completely crumble when he runs onto the street and is hit by a car. A crowd assembles around him, including the kind, elderly couple who were in the car that hit him. They apologize profusely, but Trelkowski is terrified, as he believes them to be his neighbors. He shouts at them, calling them murderers. They are disturbed by his accusations, as they feel terribly guilty for what they have done. Even in his madness, Trelkowski experiences the inability to communicate. Now his language barrier is caused by schizophrenia, a barrier of separate reality much greater than that of a foreign tongue. The couple brings him to a store where a doctor tends to him, and as he becomes more hysterical, the doctor decides to give him a shot to calm him down. Trelkowski feels that he is being attacked and sedated, while the crowd around him is only trying to help. As the couple drives him home, there is a beautiful moment of reprieve. He leans back against the seat of the car, calm and quiet as a result of the sedation. We see what he sees—a series of shining lights suspended beneath archways along the street. There is the dark and then the light, a constant, an insistent dance, and we watch as Trelkowski's face reflects these changes of light. For a moment he has found peace, and perhaps this reminds him that his answer is in silence. He knows what he has to do.

Rosemary surrounded by the grotesque crowd in *Rosemary's Baby*. (Courtesy of Photofest)

Trelkowski is on the spot—placed in the limelight by repeated accusations. He decides to provide his "hunters" with a show that they will enjoy. He thinks that he is showing them, when really he is ending his own life. Dressed in drag, his Choule-like missing tooth apparent, he steps into his window frame. He looks out over the crowd, consisting of Stella and his neighbors. Everyone has gathered to watch this great event. People have brought picnics. They sit on rooftops and watch from their windows, clapping. The camera pans across the inner courtyard, as elaborate chandeliers, velvet curtains, and orchestra boxes appear around neighboring apartments. It is a black tie affair (except for casually dressed Stella, who is most eager of all). There is a drum roll as Trelkowski stands in the window, long curls flapping in the wind. It is a strange image, Trelkowski resembling a faux Hitchcock blond contemplating her own demise. Trelkowski jumps, and as he falls to the ground, he renews the gash in the wooden awning that has just been repaired. There is no way to stop this cycle, to prevent the chasm from opening again.

When the first fall is unsuccessful, Trelkowski drags his contorted, bloody body back to the top of the stairs, and with all of his strength, manages to jump again. In order to kill both the Pole and the Frenchman, both the man and the woman, he must kill himself twice. And still he is alive.

In the final scene of the movie, he lies, like Choule, in a bandage that spans from head to toe, with only his eye and mouth exposed. He sees himself as he was before, circular tie, sweet face, with Stella crying beside him. And like Choule, he gives out a howl so profound and destitute, that one would turn down the volume if one could. Trelkowski has found himself at the beginning, caught in a horrific cycle. It is becoming evident that there is no way to go back, and there is no way to end. The camera pushes in on his mouth, and we cower at his scream, wishing that there were a way to turn away from his truth.

The Tenant received mixed reviews and was not a commercial success. It would come to be respected and enjoyed by some arbiters of film, but at the time, it seemed to be a failure. Armed with his newly acquired French citizenship, Polanski was less than eager to make a new film, so he took some time to direct opera, which allowed him to keep his creative juices flowing. He became involved with the beautiful, estranged daughter of Klaus Kinski,[7] Nastassia, who had already appeared in Wim Wenders's *The Wrong Move* (1975) and clearly had the potential to be a film star. Though still very young, Kinski was a strong and independent individual, and even if their love affair was short-lived, it evolved into a deep friendship that would last a lifetime.

Polanski threw himself into Nastassia's education. He treated her as an intellectual equal and encouraged her to grow. He helped her to enroll in acting school, take English lessons, and gave her books to read. They were developing together, and when he was offered the chance to guest edit

French *Vogue* (a privilege previously bestowed upon the likes of Fellini, Hitchcock, and Salvador Dali), he wanted to shoot Nastassia for the spread.

The Christmas issue guest-edited by Polanski was a great success, so much so that *Vogue Hommes* invited him to do a shoot for them. It was to be of young girls from around the world. This assignment was to be the cause of Polanski's demise. He had always liked young, beautiful women, but in what he considered to be European tradition, never feeling there to be any moral question with regard to such affairs. Consensual sex was just that. He didn't ascribe to American laws that prohibit one from sleeping with a minor, and when in the spring of 1977, he did have sex with his American model (a 13-year-old girl, as it turned out), he did not expect to suffer any consequences.

There are many discrepancies with regard to the Polanski rape case. In fact, there are so many suppositions with regard to this event that one could easily get lost in hearsay. In the documentary film *Wanted and Desired* (2008) by Marina Zenovich—an exploration of the L.A. justice system through the lens of Polanski's trial—many of these questions are addressed. What can be said for certain is that Polanski was held accountable for breaking American laws, and now and forever, he would have his name attached to two media circus events in American history. He would never, in the eyes of the average American, be able to live these connections down.

With shock and anxiety Polanski felt as if his new project had sprung to life and he was the lead suspect (for at this time he was working on preproduction for a picture with Columbia called *The First Deadly Sin*, based on the book of the same name, by Lawrence Sanders). Research for the film had required him to spend time with two veteran NYPD officers weeks before his arrest. When the police booked Polanski, he felt as if he were being filmed. No longer the examiner, he had become the subject, a cruel joke to the maker of films that addressed individuality and identity. He was the target, and the thought of being looked at as a criminal was unimaginable to him.

Polanski was able to post bail and stayed with friends, some of who would always remain true. He had to hide out from reporters and onlookers everywhere he went. Though his deal with Columbia had fallen through, he was able to strike a new one with Dino De Laurentiis, producer of *La Strada* and builder of the Italian film studio Dinocitta, for a remake of John Ford's *The Hurricane* (1937). Securing work gave him the chance to focus on something other than the trial, and it provided the funds needed to pay his lawyers. He was also allowed to leave the country on several occasions to do location scouting or scriptwriting for the film, spending time in London, Bora Bora, and Germany. De Laurentiis was committed to Polanski as *Hurricane's* director, and even when Judge Laurence J. Rittenband decided that Polanski ought to undergo a second diagnostic study while in a state prison, De Laurentiis insisted on working the picture around Polanski's imprisonment; however, once Polanski was in prison, he decided to replace him with Swedish director Jan Troell.

The trial was endless, and Judge Rittenband was hungry for media attention, basking in the limelight generated by the case. He would shift his stance on Polanski's sentencing more than once, such as when a photograph was taken of Polanski in a German beer garden with the girlfriends and wives of some of his friends. Details were unimportant when the media was involved. On December 19, 1977, Polanski was taken to the California Institute for Men at Chino to undergo his 90-day diagnostic study.

Though apprehensive at first, prison proved to be an interesting experience for Polanski. Under the advice of the prison board that worried for his safety, he agreed to live in a separate area for inmates under protective custody. He exercised, read, swept the floors, and got to know his fellow inmates. He began to comprehend why convicts become addicted to prison life.

On January 29, 1978, six weeks after he'd been admitted, Polanski was released from prison. This turned out to be a tease of sorts. Judge Rittenband wanted him to return to prison for the remaining 48 days of the sentence, on condition that Polanski request subsequent deportation. There was also the possibility that Rittenband would put him in prison for longer. The options were grim, and Polanski felt the walls closing in on him.

He drove directly from his lawyer's office to that of Dino De Laurentiis, whom he informed that he was not coming back to work on *Hurricane* because he was leaving the country right away. The two embraced, and off Polanski went, driving to the Los Angeles airport, where he was just in time to board a flight to London that night. He had become a fugitive from justice, like his childhood hero James Mason in the movie *Odd Man Out*. He left America, entering into another life in exile.

8

"A Pure Woman Faithfully Presented": *Tess* (1979)

Feeling uneasy, even in his own home in London, Polanski boarded a flight to Paris the day after he left the United States. He was fortunate to have recently received French citizenship, for this meant that he was safe. He would still have a chance to remain within the international pool of filmmakers to which he belonged. Once again he was at the center of extraordinary circumstances, and he had to adjust to the fact that he would never be able to live or work in the United States again. Gone were the advantages (and the hassles) of working within the studio system. The implications of his exile were many. Were he to return to America, he would be arrested immediately. There was no turning back, only moving forward.

Broke and disheartened yet eager to work, Polanski wanted to make a film that would inspire the viewer (maybe even himself). Perhaps searching for a softness not present in his life for awhile, the story of "Tess"—with its Old World complexities and its representation of nature and simplicity—was just what he needed. For a few years, Polanski and his longtime friend producer Claude Berri (who was distributing films such as *Apocalypse Now* [1979][1] in France) had wanted to make *Tess*. He went to bat for Polanski, gathering the support necessary to adapt Thomas Hardy's novel, a memento that Sharon Tate left behind years before. It was to be one of the most satisfying filmmaking experiences of his career.

Ever since meeting Nastassia Kinski, Polanski had felt that if she could improve her English, she could surely play Tess. Others were doubtful that she would be able to lose her German accent and adopt that of a peasant from Dorset, but Nastassia worked fearlessly, living in that region of England and surrounding herself with its sounds, hoping that if she succeeded in retaining its dialect that she would get the part. She did.

The story of Thomas Hardy's novel *Tess of the d'Urbervilles* takes place in England, but the film was to be shot in France so that Polanski could avoid extradition. Numerous locations throughout France were chosen to mimic the English countryside and the changes in season essential to the tone and rhythm of the story. The crew was to become a gypsy family, always traveling, sometimes losing a day of shooting in relocating, or even, as would happen on the first day, repainting a garden hothouse white and placing pink silk roses throughout a canopy of trees. All of the crew pitched a hand for this event as they always would, for those who work for Polanski know that he does not ask for anything that he himself is not willing to do.

The crew became very close during the long, protracted shoot (extended from its original seven month shooting schedule to nine because of several Société Française de Production strikes). There was something about working in the French countryside, of moving with the landscape and the changes of season that made the experience of *Tess* so extraordinary for everyone involved. Polanski had brought with him from his *Tenant* crew, production designer Pierre Guffroy, who faced one of the most demanding roles, as there were numerous locations to dress in order to recreate the nineteenth century. Polanski had insight into establishing this world, for his time in rural Poland during the war had taught him many things about peasant life. "It was in the forties, but it was nineteenth-century Poland," he remarks in the DVD extra, *Filming Tess* (2004). For Guffroy, swampy puddles had to be created and trees added to the landscape, old cottages built and even a replica of Stonehenge constructed for the final scene of the film. Power lines were brought down and erected, and roads temporarily repaved.

Polanski also rekindled his working relationship with the charming hairdresser Ludovic Paris and makeup artist Didier Lavergne, who always managed to steal the show. Included in the team was the magnificent British costume designer Anthony Powell (*Papillon* [1973] and *Indiana Jones and the Temple of Doom* [1984]). Powell and Polanski had an excellent working relationship because of their shared attention to detail and authenticity. Powell would incorporate Victorian pieces with newly made costumes, and even when they were fraying at the edges and falling apart at the seams, there was always a way to make them work. Performing in costumes of great detail, such as an exquisite tiepin worn by Alec or the burgundy dress donned by Tess after she has committed murder (a spot of blood emerging on her petticoat as she rides the train—an aspect immediately captured by Polanski's camera), helped the actors to totally embody their characters.

Cinematographer Geoffrey Unsworth was also a tremendous influence on the overall atmosphere of the shoot. Admired by all, Unsworth was famous for his work on *2001: A Space Odyssey* (1968), *Cabaret* (1972), *Murder on the Orient Express* (1974), and countless other films. He had a gentle, loving nature and was a consummate professional. Not long into production while shooting in Brittany, Unsworth suffered a heart attack and died in his hotel room surrounded by Polanski, Kinski, and other colleagues who were desperately trying to save him. A team of medics was unable to bring him back to life. It was a tragedy for everyone. It took awhile to adjust to his absence, with the camera operator, Jean Harnois, hesitantly lighting the following day. Eventually Unsworth was replaced by Ghislain Cloquet, a veteran in the business having shot *Night and Fog* (1955), *Au Hasard Balthazar* (1966), and *The Young Girls of Rochefort* (1967), who would come to be respected, and even more remarkably, give a seamless fluidity to the look of the film.

"Tess of the d'Urbervilles: A Pure Woman Faithfully Presented" (as it was originally titled when printed as a newspaper serial), is the story of a young Dorset peasant who, upon her father's discovery that the family is in fact of an aristocratic name, (d'Urberville, rather than the working-class Durbeyfield), is sent to request help from a distant cousin, changing her life forever. Alec d'Urberville (Leigh Lawson) is a man whose family's real name is Stoke, having bought the title of d'Urberville. He hires Tess to work in his poultry farm so that her family can buy a new horse, and after a long-endured seduction, he rapes her. Tess leaves Alec's estate when she discovers that she is pregnant, returning home to give birth to the baby. She cares for him, breastfeeding him during her lunch break while working in fields of wheat. The baby dies without having been christened so she christens him herself. When the vicar refuses to grant him a Christian burial, she mounts a rough yet tenderly constructed handmade cross on his grave, placing beside it a marmalade jar of wild flowers that will surely blow away. Her life seems over before it has started.

She moves to another village where she can maintain her autonomy and works on a dairy farm. She makes friends, laughs again, and falls in love with the son of a preacher, Angel Clare (Peter Firth). All of the girls are in love with Angel, but he thinks only of Tess, and it is not until after their wedding that she tells him her story. He abandons her on the spot.

Devastated, Tess returns to work with her friends from the dairy farm, now enduring harsher conditions in fields of snow. Her father dies, and when her family is left destitute—parked on a four-poster bed in the churchyard beside a crypt that holds the family name, she succumbs to Alec's offer to care for her family in exchange for being his mistress once again. When a repentant Angel returns weak and ill from an unsuccessful mission in Brazil, he comes to the seaside to find Tess. She kills Alec as a means of escape, so that she can be with Angel. Together at last, the couple walks for days, sharing one blissful night in an abandoned estate. They eventually wind up at Stonehenge, where she sleeps on an ancient slab of stone. At dawn the police corner them, and it is implied that she is taken to the gallows, as a pensive sun rises through the gaps in this ancient site.

Tess is a story about the nuances of fate and the misfortune that often accompanies sudden monetary and social gain. It is implicit in the story that to remain close to nature is to remain good and true. The imagery of the film depicts the cyclical quality of the ever-changing seasons, the milking of the cows, the harvesting of the wheat. Animals stay close to Tess, just as she does to nature. A stag comes to visit her while she sleeps in the forest at one of her darkest hours, and peacocks call alarmingly when she goes to visit Alec for the first time. These elements remind the viewer that sometimes no life is sweeter than that of the peasant who lives simply, and in earnest. The more societal truths that Tess encounters, the more wounded she becomes. She is a victim in many ways, but she is also a heroine, for, like Polanski, she continues on.

Tess is a three-hour, plot-driven film, in which the mise-en-scène is created not to dominantly lead the viewer, but simply to tell a story. This is not subjective filming, but objective, allowing the audience and the local surroundings to draw in the viewer. One subsequently observes the story rather than entering into it, as is Polanski's customary fashion. The countryside as it moves from dusk till dawn, summer's green as it becomes the color of scorched wheat, and a misty water's gray all coexist with the fluidity of Tess's character, for being a child of nature, she endures the complexities of life with a steely acceptance. She lives with the knowledge that being close to the earth gives. Life and death are her masters, and despite her suffering, she moves through both of them with an open heart.

Tess is strong and proud, but she also remains a casualty of her family's poverty and weakness as a result of its patriarch's alcoholism, and of the conditions and morality of her time. She is a victim, yet she accepts her place in life. She does what she can with what she has, and though she may be resigned to her fate, we almost never see her smile. It is only when the possibility for love and renewal come (the remembrance of spring), that she feels alive once again and begins to smile. She becomes young and almost carefree, independent of the weight of her past. It is only the loss of Angel and his rejection of her shameful truths that makes her question her ability to continue.

Though Tess's fortune is determined by a callous fate and the narrow-mindedness of highly moralistic times, she does not carry the mark of a scarred woman. Restricted in her options, she does her best to forge her own path. Devastated, she moves from town to town, becoming one with the earth, at times fighting the urge to die and literally merge with the soil. She spends much of her time milking cows and catching chickens, but she is as much at home in a fancy dress as in the dairy. At one of the lowest points in her life, she stands at the gates of the d'Urbervilles crypt and asks herself, "Why am I on the wrong side of this door?"

When we are introduced to Tess she is with a group of young women like herself, dressed in white with flowers in their hair. They giggle with excitement as dusk settles into the half-light of crickets and fireflies. They are waiting for the men of the village to come and join them so that they can begin the May dance. It is here that Tess, the most strikingly beautiful of the group, first lays eyes on Angel, who is not from the town and just happens to pass by. He is a mark of her fleeting innocence, which is to leave her in no time when her father discovers that they are d'Urbervilles. Angel will be the source of great joy and pain. He is (even more than weak and egotistical Alec) her exterminating angel, for he is the cause of her demise. Were Angel not to destroy Tess's heart, she would not be dead inside, and she would never have returned to Alec. Angel is the only one who can understand and help harvest Tess's dreams. We first begin to see a connection between them when Tess tells her coworkers that her soul leaves her body at night when she looks up at the stars. To her audience it is foolishness, but for Angel, who sits on the sidelines with his face buried in a book, her voice alone is reason to look up. It is Tess who can understand why Angel is so absorbed by the sunset and all of the other murmurings of life that have remained private until now. Together they enjoy life, but it is not meant to be. On their last night together, Angel watches over Tess as she lies on a great ancient stone, sleeping with the peace that comes from his protection. He regrets the pain that he has inflicted by his own callousness. His revelation has come too late. And as Tess is taken to jail, the sun rises over Stonehenge, reminding us that in this sacred neolithic monument, "older than the ages, older than the d'Urbervilles," life will continue. Thus, we come to the end of the life cycle of Tess, who was born a child of nature and will now return to the earth from which she sprang.

The aesthetic of *Tess* demonstrates Polanski's agility as a filmmaker, though it is a departure from his other work and in no way captures the strange intensity of his past films. Each shot is carefully constructed; the costumes, performances and sets all exquisitely executed. Though certain exterior shots do break this thread, they contribute an altogether different sensation of a misty, false beauty in the tradition of 1950s American melodrama. Polanski's talent for cinematically expounding upon the tensions experienced in life can also be found in its purest form in *Tess*. This is best expressed in the scene in which Tess reveals her story to Angel, a monologue shot in one long take, the camera zooming in and out. The only sounds are of the crackling fire and a ticking clock (that minutes before intended to signify the ever-approaching moment of marital consummation). The sounds are a reminder that time is running out. We come closer to Tess as she speaks, then zoom out, with Angel out of focus, sitting quietly in the background. When Tess finishes her story, the camera racks focus, revealing Angel's blank expression. He rises to feed the fire and then leaves the room. This is one of the cruelest, tensest scenes that Polanski has ever put on film, for in an instant an entire relationship has changed, and rather than forcing the camera to convey it subjectively, he has used the movement of the lens to quietly guide the audience's response. This smooth influence is one of the strengths of *Tess*.

Though at times we are drawn in emotionally (particularly in the midportion of the film), there is a lacquer to the piece that prevents total involvement of the viewer. Though Kinski gives a wonderful performance, her natural exoticism and elegance make it difficult to believe that she could ever be an English rose. In other Polanski films, such exacting criticism might be unnecessary, but here, with the intention of total authenticity, her separateness is palpable. Tess is different from her ruddy English family, so much so that she appears to be a foreigner in their presence. It is as if she doesn't belong to them at all. This incongruence does work for the story, in that it accentuates her feelings of exile in her own society, but it also adds a level of imbalance and falsity to the film, which boasts an otherwise British cast. It is said that writer Thomas Hardy held the character of Tess very close to his heart—perhaps Polanski did as well, these discrepancies obfuscating his vision for her.

After much deliberating over the length of *Tess*, it was ultimately left at its three-hour length. Francis Ford Coppola (who was working with producer Claude Berri at the time) considered distributing *Tess* in the United States through his Zoetrope company but believed the film should be drastically cut. This was a tenuous time for Polanski and Berri, for *Tess* had been a long shoot—roughly nine months—and at first, the film had a negative response. The opening in Germany received poor criticism, and as Berri had risked a good deal of money and connections in the making of *Tess*, he needed the film to be a success. Luckily, as time went on, French audiences warmed to it, and eventually a U.S. distributor was found in Columbia Pictures. *Tess* would go on to receive great success, earning numerous awards in 1981, more than a year after it premiered in Europe. Kinski's performance was critically acclaimed, earning her a Golden Globe award for New Star of the Year. *Tess* won a Golden Globe for Best Foreign Film, and Academy Awards for Best Art Direction, Cinematography, and Costume Design. It was also nominated for Best Director, Best Original Score, and Best Picture by the Academy, and won César awards for Best Director, Best Cinematography, and Best Film.

Tess was dedicated "to Sharon," as it was she who had brought the story into Polanski's life. He honored Tate in this film, demonstrating his love and eternal devotion. He was bidding adieu to a kind and gentle soul who, like Tess, had been destroyed by the callousness of fate.

Making *Tess* was the doorway to a new life, and a new direction into a more varied approach to filmmaking. There would be many ups and downs, but with these explorations would come great accomplishments, both creatively and personally. In this transition into exiled life, Polanski would alter his cinematic perspective from subjective to objective, from singular to universal. A very unique vision would be lost, but with this transformation would come the possibility for influencing audiences in an entirely different way. A new life was beginning, and in his return to Paris, Polanski would at last find the home that he had dreamed of for so many years.

9

Where Is Polanski?

Making *Tess* was a cathartic experience for Polanski, and the atmosphere of renewal was palpable; however, the debacle that followed (with regard to distribution) once the film was finished, had turned him off somewhat to making films. In fact, for a time, he even considered himself an "ex-filmmaker." Invited by Tadeusz Lomnicki (the diminutive Polish actor whom Polanski had admired since childhood), he returned to Poland to work in the theater, directing and starring in Peter Shaffer's *Amadeus*. In the play, Mozart is portrayed as crass and childish, as well as brilliant.

The production coincided with the height of the solidarity movement. Poland was undergoing a dramatic change. Though the confines of communist life were in many ways the same—evident in the numerous hours one had to wait in line merely to buy a loaf of bread—the upheaval started by Lech Walesa[1] was powerful and transformative. Anticipation (and some fear, sparked by the threat of a Russian invasion) only heightened the atmosphere in which the play opened. It was a terrific experience for Polanski, who also took the opportunity of being in Poland to revisit many of his childhood places, including Wysoka and the ghetto. Old friends flocked to his performances, and the play received international attention. A reminder of the ever-changing nature of life, Polanski reveled in the thought that Poland had found its gateway to freedom. Now it seemed that anything was possible.

As the play was moved to Paris, an announcement of martial law was declared in Poland, and the thrill of recent months diminished. Now the sense of narrowing borders were enforced again for Polanski, and the feeling that history repeats itself, a dull reminder of the past. However, it had been a shining moment to witness the bright star of the solidarity movement, and see how luminous Poland could be when freedom was close at hand. As he opened in the role of one of music's great geniuses, in Paris, his new hometown, he was moved by his own capacity, his history, and how things had appeared to come full circle.

PIRATES (1986)

For his next big project, Polanski would at last be able to make *Pirates*, a film that he had been pushing ever since finishing *Chinatown*. In a 1995 interview with Laurent Vachaud, Polanski was quoted as saying that at this point in time, he "had it up to here with arty and *auteur*-driven films. Sometimes you just want to have fun when making a film." Working from a script written with Gérard Brach and John Brownjohn, *Pirates* was shot on the Neptune, a beautiful and massive ship (that has since been transformed into a museum) and was filmed in Tunisia. Again Polanski returned to the instability of the sea, creating a raucous romp starring Walter Matthau.[2]

Pirates depicts an uprising led by Captain Red (Matthau) and his French cohort, Jean-Baptiste, also known as The Frog (played by Cris Campion), on a Spanish ship, The Neptune, in the seventeenth century. Red is a notorious pirate, an Englishman with a wooden leg and a penchant for storytelling and scheming. His drive is treasure, believing that it is "easier to live without a head than without gold." Meanwhile, his young French sidekick is a romantic who fights "for glory, not gold." We follow their adventure from sea to land, watching as the ever-revolving underdog fights to dominate, and as Red works to obtain an Aztec treasure. The Frog longs for a beautiful young Spanish woman, Maria-Delores de la Jenya de la Calde (played by Charlotte Lewis), and though their attraction is momentarily consummated, the two are ultimately separated.

There is an element of classic adventure and childhood fantasy in *Pirates*. No effort is made to soften the grime and decay of slave quarters and life on the boat. Though there is a wide divide between upper and lower classes (as supported by camera angles), the difference in cleanliness is minimal. *Pirates* is written with a comedic touch, yet sometimes it falls short of comedy and is simply laughable, or worse, boring. Still, there is an amusement that periodically shines through, as can be observed in the great irony of the film. The two men end up on a lifeboat identical to the one at the beginning of the film. Were it not for the massive golden throne upon which Captain Red sits, encouraging Frog to fatten up, you would think that no time had passed at all. It is only humor that rescues *Pirates* from being a completely unrecognizable Polanski film.

The fact that *Pirates* was made on a very big budget did not prevent it from being a tremendous critical and commercial disaster, but it was nominated for an Academy Award for its beautiful costumes designed by Anthony Powell. Once again, Polanski was left to contemplate his next move.

FRANTIC (1988)

Frantic opens on a Paris highway at dawn, the half-light causing car lights to sparkle where normally they would blend in to the light of day. We move forward, and the credits do as well, appearing in the foreground and then diminishing as they move down to the background of the frame, so small that they disappear. There is a sensation of movement and also of narrowing, with everything pointing to one word: frantic. The cab suffers a flat tire while the woman in the back of the cab sleeps, passed out on her husband's shoulder (indicating her lack of presence for most of the film). The middle-aged American couple from the cab check into a hotel—Le Grand Hotel, which looks more like a Holiday Inn (here we move from the apartment drama to that of a hotel). Things begin innocuously enough, but before we know it, everything will change. The man is Richard Walker (played by Harrison Ford, best known for his work with Steven Spielberg and George Lucas), and his wife, Sondra (Betty Buckley), who will be kidnapped while he enjoys his shower. For the rest of the film he will sink deeper and deeper into the underworld of Paris life. He may have come here in 1968 for his honeymoon and enjoyed all of the lights and privileges of a tourist on vacation, but now he will come to know the real Paris, as well as its seedier side, anything to find his wife and return home once again.

Upon arrival at the hotel, Walker and his wife are very playful with one another. Like two kids on vacation, they dance around, letting us know that they are a couple that, after all these years, are still in love. Sondra showers and sings, "I love Paris in the springtime . . . why oh why do I love Paris?" She orders breakfast while Walker showers, and it is here that the tension begins. While his eyes are closed, and his face drenched, we watch from behind him as Sondra receives a phone call. We already know that she requested that the concierge hold all of the doctor's calls, so it is strange that the phone is ringing. We cannot hear what she says. We see her speak to Walker, but he is blissfully oblivious. She holds up a red dress and shouts something else, then, we watch as her suitcase is dragged out of frame. The camera pushes in slowly, until it reaches the shower wall, drops of water covering the glass. These are the parameters of suspense permitted in this scene (suspense created by limitation, a very Hitchcockian ploy), the slow movement of the lens heightening the viewer's anxiety, for we are not permitted to see what we know is most important. Rather than being a subjective camera, here the lens becomes a third eye, drawing the viewer into secrets as yet unknown. Walker comes out of the shower to find his wife gone, and, while he waits for her return, succumbs to a jetlag-induced stupor. When he realizes that she has not come back, the thriller begins.

We discover that Sondra has left the hotel with a tall, dark, mustached man with "an accent." Here the plight of an American who thinks no ill can befall him is taken to the extreme. Walker is victim to his own vulnerability. He does what he can to communicate with locals, and his sense of isolation in dealing with the police and American embassy mounts as cultural differences arise. The Americans behave as if they, too, are merely vacationing in France and have no power over local authorities, while the French policemen sneer and snicker over a saga that they believe to have an obvious explanation. The consensus is that Sondra was having an affair and simply wanted to get away from Richard. Walker's estrangement builds as he struggles to understand what has happened to his wife, and as he discovers that her suitcase was swapped with another woman's (holding a switch for a nuclear reactor inside of a small ceramic statue of liberty), all of the reasons for her kidnapping begin to unfold. It is through the phone number on a matchbook that Walker discovers Michelle, a feisty young girl who smuggles for a living. She seems hard at first, but soon the two become partners in crime, and as they watch out for each other, all of her sweetness emerges, turning her into someone who would do anything for Richard Walker.

As is customary in many Polanski films, Walker's world is gray and bleak until the arrival of the femme fatale (Michelle, played by Polanski's new love interest, Emmanuelle Seigner) It is Michelle's absurd underworld, filled with clubs such as The Blue Parrott (she has dangling earrings with birds to match), and her bathroom mirror that has the word "cocaine" written in Coca Cola–style lettering, which all add flavor to Walker's tense, staid world. Michelle is ballsy, perhaps too much so, for it is she who in the end must pay the price. She carries with her life an edge that has the freedom of youth but also the irresponsibility. For her, it is no big deal to scale the roof in order to enter her apartment through the window, but when Walker joins her (as they try to retrieve the suitcase that has fallen to the ledge), she nearly falls. The inclusion of Walker's awareness is dangerous for Michelle, for as she softens toward him, she becomes more vulnerable.

In any other film, Walker and Michelle's relationship would turn romantic, but in *Frantic* it remains a partnership in which sexual gain is not at stake. Even when the two dance at a club—Michelle writhing in a tight red dress—Walker embraces her for a moment, his emotional strain heightened, his expression impassioned, yet theirs is more of an estranged embrace (it is no coincidence that the song which plays in the background repeats the word, "strange"). As we move into the final segment of the film, Michelle makes way for Sondra's return. The shocking red of Michelle's dress is a portent of things to come. We know that Sondra is also wearing a red dress, only hers is less sexy and dull in color.

When Walker and Michelle at last meet up with the gangsters on the Champs-Élysées, the two women pass each other, their red dresses doubling up to momentarily become one. They are two sides of one coin, but it is the woman who has a family and a life to return to who will live on, while the young girl who hustles for a living and has no one to account for will die before this dramatic scene is over. Walker does try to save her from being held by one of the gangsters, even leaving his wife's embrace to beat up the guy, but few men are fast enough to overcome the speed of a bullet. Michelle runs awkwardly, her breath slowed as we begin to understand that she has been hit, collapsing in Sondra's arms, the Statue de la Liberté standing proud in the background. She asks Walker to hold her, and he does, carrying her away toward the Eiffel tower, his understanding wife by his side. The film ends with Walker leaning on his wife's shoulder in the taxi going back to the airport. Their places have changed, and for a moment one questions whether it was a dream. Walker cries to his wife, and tells her that he loves her.

Frantic explores a Paris that is not normally seen on film, such as the houseboat where Michelle's friends live and play music, parked in front of the Statue de la Liberté. This emblem of freedom is referred to again and again throughout the film, a mocking jab at the innocence of America, and the idea of freedom that Polanski had left behind. During their final night together prior to the showdown at dawn, Michelle and Walker wait on her friend's boat. She sleeps, awkwardly passed out in a chair, her thumb in her mouth, her childish action betraying her womanly body. Walker looks out the small window onto the misty river at a tour boat gliding by. Silhouetted tourists rise to greet the Statue de la Liberté shining in the night. The passing boat's many lights blur and travel upward like long tubes of white and blue. Shining past the statue, they continue on. It is a quiet moment, oddly beautiful and emotional, a silence rarely permitted in an otherwise busy film.

Frantic does have potential as a thriller, though its modern atmosphere is a bit of a shock to Polanski fans who feel as if they have suddenly been catapulted into the future. *Pirates* and *Tess* belong to centuries past, *Chinatown*, the 1930s, and even though *The Tenant* was shot in the 1970s, it has an individual, isolated aesthetic (the only retro aspect is found in Isabelle Adjani's costumes and her red lava lamp, which seem more costume than current). If anything, Trelkowski seems to belong to another time—his words, his gestures, his clothes convey a politesse and a willingness-to-oblige that betray his roots. Therefore, viewing *Frantic* we feel as if we have jumped forward at least 20 years, and the look of the film is rather flat and appalling. The transformation from the rich tones of the past to the texture and quality of a contemporary lighting scheme doesn't serve Polanski as a filmmaker, as did the gaudiness of earlier, more primitive film stock. It is as if all of the nuances have been dispensed of, the intensity of color and depth eliminated as we enter into a generally flat landscape. In essence, the film looks just like many other films of its time. This lack of connection to the image is only suspended on occasion throughout the film.

Despite these disconnects there is still suspense, and Polanski captures the awkwardness of a foreigner who desperately needs to communicate with the locals. Walker fumbles through the tension of being on his own and in a for-eign land. At times this is tragic, confining him to the isolation of a frantic man with an unexplained mystery on his hands. At others, it is funny, even absurd, such as when he asks the flower shop attendants if they have seen his wife and they begin to gather roses for a bouquet, or when he meets a man at the Blue Parrot and winds up sniffing cocaine from his finger, a misunderstanding over the man's mention of the "white lady," who Walker assumes to be his wife.

Even the soundtrack by Ennio Morricone (of Sergio Leone's spaghetti westerns), vacillates between tensely effective and over-the-top melodrama. Though *Frantic* is in no way representative of Polanski's capability as a film-maker, it is again a foray into a new genre, and at times it still manages to entertain. This is in part because of the inclusion of Polanski's new love, Emmanuelle Seigner, who plays the part of Michelle and remains charming at every turn. A dancer and a natural beauty, Seigner has high cheekbones and exotic eyes that could lead one to believe that her origins are Polish rather than French. Born to an artistic family, Seigner is the daughter of a journalist mother, photographer father, and the granddaughter of actor Louis Seigner. At last Polanski had found someone with whom he could build an enduring life in Emmanuelle. They were to marry one year later.

BITTER MOON (1992)

"How far are you going?" Fiona asks the young woman with makeup smeared all over her face. "Further," she says, a far-off look in her eyes.

There is no extreme too great for *Bitter Moon*. As a cruise ship headed toward Istanbul faces increasingly tumultuous seas, the emotional tension also reaches its climax. First, there is the repressed English couple, Hugh Grant's Nigel and Kristin Scott Thomas's Fiona (who have been married for seven years, and are trying to rekindle their passion on a voyage to India). Second, there is the raunchy match of Oscar (Peter Coyote) and Mimi (Emmanuelle Seigner). Oscar, a lascivious paraplegic lures the blushing Nigel into his cramped room to tell him the intimate details of his love story with Mimi. Nigel is uncomfortable with Oscar's forwardness, his lewd com-ments, and description of Mimi's anatomy, so detailed that he often longs for escape, but he is nevertheless enthralled. Mimi is beautiful. Mimi is seduc-tive—vulnerable and tough, erotic and afraid, she is everything that elegant and refined Fiona is not.

The film plays in flashbacks dotted with excerpts of the present. Fiona plays bridge with a playboy shipmate, is seasick, and observes her childish husband as his tail wags for Mimi. Oscar plays tricks on Nigel, going so far to lie in Mimi's bed and allow Nigel to kiss his hand thinking it is Mimi's, only to discover (to his horror) that it is not. Mimi dances, finally going to bed with Fiona, not Nigel, in a sequence that takes place on New Year's Eve and culminates in a fight on the dance floor, a storm that rocks the boat, and

Oscar ending the game by shooting Mimi (who sleeps naked, beside an equally nude Fiona), and then himself.

The incessant rocking of the boat coupled with the (at times) unrestrained movement of Oscar's wheelchair allows for a present that has no moorings, and a camera that moves constantly. Were it not for the steadiness of memory (both visually and metaphorically), the audience would likely become seasick as well. As difficult as it is to hear Oscar's story emerge from his foul and embittered mouth, it is even more uncomfortable to witness his tale as it is revealed in flashbacks, for we soon discover that Oscar and Mimi have destroyed each other more than once.

When Oscar first met Mimi, he was an able-bodied, middle-aged, unpublished writer living on a comfortable trust in Paris. She was a beautiful young dancer and waitress, still childlike in her red polka-dotted dress and white sneakers. They meet on a bus. She has no ticket, and so Oscar discreetly forfeits his own, going so far as to be thrown off the bus in order to help her. The memory of her image burns in his mind, even appearing on his primitive computer screen as he wrote the story of their encounter. Yes, Oscar writes the story, so not only is it recounted to Nigel, but it is memorialized on paper at the same time. Needless to say, the two meet again and fall madly in love. They can't get enough of each other, ravaging one another until the relationship becomes dull and they search for something to bring it back to life. They turn to sadomasochistic games, and Oscar sleeps with other women. Mimi weeps often at Oscar's feet, begging him to love her as he did before, but each time he despises her more. He mocks her, and slowly her beautiful glow turned pasty. She cuts off her hair, so that it is short and matted. She dresses awkwardly and is ashamed. He comments that she is "losing her looks, her figure," and she cries that she can no longer dance. She tells him that "Dancing comes from the heart . . . my heart is broken."

Mimi becomes pregnant, and Oscar arranges for an abortion. He comes to visit her in the hospital and shows her two tickets that he has bought them for a vacation. Through her exhaustion, she smiles. Having boarded the plane together, Oscar tells Mimi that he wants to check his bag, and exits the plane just as it is to take off. He gazes up at the moon knowing that she is doing the same. For her the moon is a sad and bitter image, even "poison," but for him it is "sweet relief."

Time goes on, and Oscar enjoys his bachelor life wholeheartedly, enjoying a different woman every night. It is at dawn one day, when he is leaving a club with two women, that a car hits him. Mimi comes to see him in the hospital. She is strong and beautiful again, only different now, harder, and looking for revenge. She offers Oscar her hand, and pulls him off of the hospital bed, leaving him to writhe in pain. When he awakes, he discovers that he is paralyzed from the waist down—punishment for abusing his sexual freedom—and now it is Mimi's turn to "care for" Oscar, as she takes on the role of torturer.

So it is here, on a cruise to the mystical East, that these two couples collide. Oscar and Mimi know all along that this boat trip will signal the end of their lives, as they have corrupted each other too much to survive. They prey on Nigel and Fiona, looking for one last game, one last story to tell. After all, if Nigel's books were never published, then who else will hear his tale other than us, the passive viewers?

Bitter Moon explores a corrupted and defiled love, leaving very little purity intact, and a sour feeling does come at the end of the film. This is Vladimir Nobokov's[3] novel *Lolita* turned on its head and defiled until nothing remains. Here, Daisy is a woman of feeling and Humbert Humbert an arrogant, cruel, and repellent man (though we see him as having once been almost charming). The obsession is not of the other, but rather of the self. The need to be reflected in another's perfection is a trap for each character, even Fiona, although her desire is less visible, even displaced. As her wish for a family has been diverted, she turns to other, more ephemeral pleasures. Each character reveals his or her ugliness fearlessly. It is deeply uncomfortable—disturbing even—to watch as Oscar debases Mimi again and again, and how she in turn treats him as the helpless child he has become, torturing him sexually and every other way that she can. *Bitter Moon* holds nothing back, and in its exposure it is almost brave. There is no transcendence, however, achieved in a story as debased and cruel as this, and ultimately there is no reward, no deeper understanding, only a strange relief at the sight of Oscar and Mimi's sheet-covered bodies being hauled off the boat on New Year's Day.

Based on the book *Lunes de Fiel* by Pascal Bruckner, *Bitter Moon* was written by Polanski, Gérard Brach,[4] and John Brownjohn. It starred writer, activist, and narrator Peter Coyote in the role of impotently oversexed and crassly self-centered Oscar. Polanski's wife, Emmanuelle Seigner, played Mimi, showing great emotion and vulnerability, at times shamelessly so. Playing Mimi requires courage, and though she is not always consistent, Seigner comes through. Kristen Scott Thomas is the perfectly distinguished Fiona, and a young, as yet unknown Hugh Grant plays Nigel. Grant is so perfectly suited to the role that one imagines him actually blushing in the wake of Oscar's tirades.

As was becoming customary, the film received mixed reviews, attacked for its melodrama and for being overly contrived. In the *Chicago Sun-Times*, Roger Ebert wrote that Polanski's "portrait of a doomed marriage may be high porn but it is low art." *Bitter Moon* still managed to garner plenty of attention, perhaps in part because of its explicit content. Some applauded Polanski's audacity, perceiving the film's outlandish sexuality and overt callousness to be a deep foray into dark and disturbing material, while others shuddered at its laughable and unconscionable storytelling. Despite the varying response to *Bitter Moon*, it was clear that Polanski's next movie would require great thought and effort, for it was time to make a film that would return him to his own standards.

Return to Suspense

When Polanski first began working in the film industry in the late fifties, the New Wave was blasting through France and a revolution was going on. Getting a project approved was like playing a game. If one avenue didn't work out, another would pop up. Films were made quickly and for less money. Where it once took about one year to make a film, the process was now much more involved. There was also the advantage at that time of youth, enthusiasm, and the momentum associated with success. Nevertheless, things had changed, and however young Polanski remained, defying his age at every turn, there is the sense that he had grown tired of fighting (perhaps the stability of his home life had also grounded him). Now, as the control of producers and creative boards (often run by business men more familiar with selling commercial product than with the various aspects of film) had taken precedence, things had really changed. Although filmmaking remained his calling in life, the question arose as to whether Polanski was running out of steam. This makes witnessing the return of his eagle eye all the more thrilling.

DEATH AND THE MAIDEN (1994)

Death and the Maiden takes place in an unnamed South American country following the fall of a dictatorship. Nearly all of the action occurs in a small, remote house by the sea, with the exception of two scenes on the edge of a nearby cliff and a concert hall where a quartet plays Franz Schubert's[1] "Death and the Maiden." It is a film that focuses on dramatic tension and underlying theme, and it could take place anywhere. It seems to have been a perfect choice for Polanski at this time in his career, for it could be shot in the controlled environment of a studio, and it provided him with the strong material needed to make a condensed and powerful film.

Tired of doing big budget movies such as *Tess* and *Pirates*, Polanski was enthusiastic about constructing a film intimate enough to allow emphasis to be placed on camera movement, character, and story, and not on extravagant cast, costume, or location. A story in which every character must fight and defend their honor, *Death and the Maiden* makes many statements about the nature of torture and life in a post-dictatorship democracy. Here is a society in which one may come face to face with his previous torturer—in this sociopolitical climate, equality takes on a new and varied meaning.

When Polanski came into the picture, the project of *Death and the Maiden* was already in the works. Warner Brothers had bought the rights to Ariel Dorfman's play of the same name, and novelist Rafael Yglesias who, at the age of 18 had published his first novel, *Hide Fox and All After*, was hired to adapt Dorfman's play. Dorfman is an award-winning writer of human rights plays such as *Speak Truth to Power: Voices from beyond the Dark* and has been prolific in poetry, novels, essays, and works of nonfiction. Born in Argentina, he grew up in America and Chile, and he was temporarily exiled from Chile in 1973. He wrote of his exiled experience in the critically acclaimed book, *Heading South, Looking North: A Bilingual Journey.*

In preparing the adaptation, a few changes would be made, the most important of which was the addition of Dr. Miranda's admission of guilt at the end of the film. The film encourages its audience to question Miranda's innocence until the end when he finally confesses to his crimes, whereas the play left its audience without any definite answers. Here Polanski would work his magic once again, making it clear that whether he liked it or not, "arty and *auteur*-driven" films were in fact his milieu.

The film was to star Sigourney Weaver (*Gorillas in the Mist* [1988], *Working Girl* [1988], *The Year of Living Dangerously* [1982]), who actively sought the part of Paulina Escobar. She had experience volunteering with victims of abuse and believed that this was her opportunity to be the voice of a collective group of women. Weaver's inclusion into the film also guaranteed a green light for the project. British actors Ben Kingsley (*Gandhi* [1982], *Schindler's List* [1993]) as Dr. Roberto Miranda, and Stuart Wilson (*Lethal Weapon 3* [1992], *The Age of Innocence* [1993]) as Paulina's husband, Gerardo Escobar, were added to the cast. The film would be shot at Studios de Boulogne in France, and the seaside exteriors, in Spain. Tonino Delli Colli (*Once Upon a Time in America* [1984], *The Canterbury Tales* [1972], Pier Paolo Pasolini's *Accattone* [1961]), who had collaborated with Polanski on *Bitter Moon*, was to be the cinematographer, and Polish composer Wojciech Kilar was to write the score. The classical Schubert piece would play a large role in creating the dramatic, incessant atmosphere of the film. Although the story takes place in a South American country, it was to be shot in English, creating a strange disconnect that casts everyone in the light of an exile.

Death and the Maiden is an examination of torture and its repercussions. Having been kidnapped and tortured as a young woman, raped while forced to listen to Franz Schubert's piece "Death and the Maiden" by a seemingly kind doctor who slowly changed as he joined the torture game, Paulina has never recovered from her ordeal. She was a student at the time of the regime, and though she was abused repeatedly, she never revealed her boyfriend's name. Had she done so, he most likely would have been killed. The two are together still, and they have been ever since her release. No longer an activist, Gerardo is now an esteemed lawyer, who, at the start of the film, is appointed to head a commission investigating torture for a new, democratic government.

Into their life walks Dr. Roberto Miranda, who gives Gerardo a lift home when he is stuck on the road with a flat tire. Paulina has been home cooking dinner, waiting for her husband, angry over his acceptance of the new position, as it only investigates crimes against the dead. She is alive. She wants to be acknowledged. Paulina and Gerardo fight when he returns home, but they soon make up, their love for one another evident. When a knock comes on the door an hour later, it is Miranda, who has come to bring Gerardo's spare tire. Miranda shyly confesses that his wife is away, and he is lost without her. He has tremendous respect for Gerardo and is hopeful about the commission. Perhaps it will bring justice, he says, and "those fucks will have to face their own flesh and blood." We wonder later whether he is referring to himself. The two sit and drink, while in the adjacent room, Paulina experiences a meltdown. She chokes on her own laughter (or are they sobs?), and writhes on the floor. She panics, takes money, rope, a bag of things, and sneaks out onto the porch, into the night, and, driving Miranda's car away, leaves the two men stranded. He runs after her, though he is no match for Paulina's fury. He remains behind with Gerardo, drinking and debating the absurdity of women and quoting Nietzsche.[2] "It's probably Freud," Gerardo quips. "He said everything. If it's quotable, it's probably Freud." The two men laugh, enjoying their newfound friendship. Gerardo admits that his wife is crazy, but also that she has her reasons.

Having pushed Miranda's car through the rail and over a nearby cliff, Paulina returns home. When it is apparent that the two men have gone to sleep, she enters the house, holding her trusty gun that will, with the exception of momentary scuffles, remain in her hand from now until the end of the film. With the gun as an extension of her body, an externalized symbol of the blatant violence and terror that she has endured and wishes to inflict, she finds a way to take her power back. She knocks the doctor out, stuffs her dirty underwear in his mouth, and ties his hands and feet. Gerardo is appalled when he awakens to discover what his wife has done to his new friend and when she threatens to shoot him if he messes with her plans.

The remainder of the film is a struggle directed at finding what is true. Paulina will do anything she can to get Miranda to confess what she believes to be the truth—that he was her torturer. Gerardo struggles with his sense of justice, wanting to give Miranda a "fair trial." Gerardo doesn't believe

Paulina, though he wants to help her, as he feels he owes her his life. This feeling interferes with the one that tells him he owes the justice system his life. The confession is taped. The confession is filmed, but the only true confession comes at the edge of the cliff, when everyone is exhausted, and truth resounds in the overpowering echo of the sea.

Unlike the opening of *Frantic* in which the credits flee down the road ahead, here they rise to greet the camera, alerting us to an overwhelming experience to come. For throughout *Death and the Maiden*, there is no relief, no break from the action. There is a connection with other Polanski films here, for again we arrive in a tense situation in which a triangle of characters fight for their lives. Unlike *Knife in the Water*, there is no blossoming love affair, and the need to assert one's masculinity arises more in Paulina than it does in her male counterparts. Gerardo resists any level of violence or physical action, and Miranda uses force only to protect himself. Here the men show their weakness, as a counterpart to Paulina, who highlights her strength using brute force.

Though this trio is crowded into a small, isolated space by the sea, as are Dicky and his companions in *Cul-de-Sac*, their predicament is hardly ironic. The violence and revenge carry over, though here it is deliberate, premeditated, and at the forefront, whereas in *Cul-de-Sac*, violence is sporadic, untamed, and messy. Nevertheless, connections can be made between all three films, each addressing the tension between three characters fighting to stand their own ground.

Paulina was a victim of torture, yet she also tortures herself. She cries out, "I don't exist," and whispers to herself, "Be a good girl." Perhaps she feels that she was too good a girl and paid tenfold in her life as a result. Tough as she is now, as she shows in her every movement—the clenching of her jaw and rolling of her eyes—she confesses to Gerardo that she remained silent on the day that she was taken away. She complied with the men who arrested her for being a member of the student movement. She cannot forget this, nor can she forgive herself. Paulina is angry with Gerardo for agreeing to participate in a commission that will only investigate stories of torture involving the dead. This means that he will not investigate her troubles—that she doesn't exist. Yet she punishes him by punishing herself. Though her movements are abrupt and large, as is her presence, she nevertheless inflicts pain upon herself, insisting that she was and will always be a victim. When she eats dinner while waiting for Gerardo, she sits on the closet floor with a candle and a bottle of wine. She stands in the pouring rain allowing her clothes to get soaked through while waiting for him. She has changed her looks, saying, "What time didn't change, I have," out of fear that Miranda would recognize her. "I didn't want to recognize me," she says. She hurts herself to get back at her torturer, but this night presents the chance for her to be set free. Though she seeks a confession, she, too, confesses, breaking 15 years of silence. Having Miranda before her, at last an image of a man attached to a voice and a smell that she had come to know intimately (she was blindfolded during torture), inspires her to tell Gerardo the truth about having been raped. Though she speaks often in monologues, there is no sense of urgency regarding the resolution of the outcome of the story; the telling of the story is enthralling.

Polanski once remarked that he likes working with female actors because they are particularly committed. Watching Weaver embody Paulina may be one of his strongest examples yet. Though Weaver may not be as natural an actress as Farrow or Deneuve, she puts herself into the role of Paulina with abandon and determination, giving everything that she has. Regardless of her surroundings—whether in the cramped living room where Miranda is being held, sitting on the porch like a cowboy, smoking in the night air, or perched on the side of a cliff, Paulina dominates the spaces that she inhabits. She is tall and strong, this fact emphasized by her muscular arms and cropped hair. She is a column, a pillar of deep despair and rage. She dominates in every way. Standing over Miranda, holding the gun to his throat, the camera behind her in a high-angle shot she yells, "Out there, maybe you bastards are still running things behind the scenes, but in here . . . I'm in charge." She fears that once the gun leaves her hand she will lose this battle, but she does not know her own strength. One might even say that Paulina is the protector of all of Polanski's heroines. Not only does she come to avenge her own torturer, but also that of Rosemary, of Carole in *Repulsion*, of Tess, and even Trelkowski in *The Tenant*. She may be slightly off center in her need for violence and revenge, but she also knows where she stands and of what she speaks. Finally she receives the confession that she needs, is liberated, and no longer yearns for Miranda's death.

Paulina's husband is the mediator for this drama. His commitment to the law is challenged by his allegiance to Paulina. "She's crazy, but so is the whole country," he says to Miranda early on in the evening. Whether she is crazy or not, Paulina risked her life for his, and as a result, Gerardo will do anything—almost anything—to help her. This situation puts Gerardo in the middle of a brawl and at the center of his own conscience. He is rendered frozen in moments when he could act, caught between one side devoted to fairness, and the other, which must embrace action to save his wife. If Paulina and Miranda are representative of the old regime, then Gerardo is an emblem of democracy. At times, this is his greatest limitation. Miranda is astonished that Gerardo hasn't jumped in to save him when he could have. He shouts that he has just stood there. "Of course he just stood there, he's the law," Paulina admonishes. When Gerardo and Miranda are enjoying a drink at the start of the night, Gerardo smiles and says that Miranda has taught him a lesson. "In a democracy, the midnight knock on the door can be friendly," he says. On the other hand, it can also be not so friendly. Polanski has chosen another film in which a mere coincidence is the spark that lights the whole story aflame. If Gerardo's car had not broken down and Miranda had not picked him up, then Paulina would never have come to know her torturer.

Gerardo loves Paulina. This love has been "the logic of my life, but I have the feeling that it's going to destroy me," he says, while discussing what to do with Miranda. Miranda is seen through a glass door beyond Paulina, hands tied behind his back and nervously pacing the floor, while they discuss their plan. Paulina and Gerardo share two of these private discussions. This is where Paulina confesses, describing her torture by the doctor, and her inner torment over her passivity while arrested. Gerardo also reveals that if the tables had been turned, and if it had been he who was being tortured to give up Paulina's name, that he would have done so. It is here that a frailty in Gerardo, a dynamic of their relationship, and Paulina's deep conviction and strength are all exposed. We are given insight as to why, in the end, his need to support his wife must override his pragmatic mind.

At first Gerardo doesn't believe that Miranda is guilty, and he behaves as if he is going along with Paulina's game. This changes when Paulina tells him that she was raped. The truth, plus a corroborated fact that appeals to Gerardo's lawyer mentality, challenges his manhood and his honor. Suddenly, Gerardo displays a strength and assertiveness that we have not previously seen. As if a dark cloud has passed over him, he becomes more suspicious, more passive with Miranda. Even so, when Miranda conceives of his confession, it is still Gerardo who helps him to write it down, giving him tidbits of information when he can. While Miranda is in the bathroom urinating, the president calls Gerardo to tell him that his life has been threatened and that policemen will be arriving at his house at daybreak. The dramatic tension is heightened, as is the image of Gerardo's passivity at finding himself in such an absurd bind. The irony of this moment is not lost on the audience, for even in a democracy, Gerardo's life is still in danger.

Gerardo is put to the test when Miranda, kneeling beside a cliff, finally admits to his wrongdoings. He describes his pleasure in raping Paulina, and as she walks away empty, Gerardo lunges at Miranda, ready to put him away. He grabs him, groans, and then lets him go. "I can't do it," he says, resigned. He is active in his mind but not his body. He must leave that role of strongman to his wife.

Miranda is a duplicitous character. With his gentle manner, elegant suit, and shifty eyes, it is hard to determine whether or not he is guilty. He has arrived in their world as a result of doing a good deed, and he pays deeply for his overture. While shooting the film, Polanski told Ben Kingsley to play the character of Miranda as if he were innocent and so even though we doubt him, we feel for Miranda, right up until the end. His past actions seem to exist independently from the man that we meet. Gerardo is equally fooled, for the two drink together, laugh, and discuss women and Nietzsche. Even Paulina describes her torturer as being kind at first. He gave her a shot to stop her pain, cleaned her, played her Schubert, but he succumbed to his desire soon enough. He was sorry when it was over, he says at the end of the night.

Miranda is an example of what can happen under an extreme regime. Faced with a new sense of power, he has buckled, leaving in the dust the honorable man he could have been. Miranda is so convincing in his innocence that one begins to feel that there are several different Mirandas. There is the man who first arrives at the house and is lost when his wife is away, who lovingly musses his son's hair at the opera house. There is also Miranda the doctor, Miranda the torturer—a persona left behind in a room where he raped many women, where not having to charm or seduce, he enjoyed having the upper hand. Just as Paulina says that here she is in control, so, too, was Miranda once. How does Miranda reconcile these disparities within himself? His darker side shines through in the shifty nervousness of his eyes, rings in the quivering uncertainty of his voice. The eyes reveal what a face that wishes to deceive cannot, and Miranda's eyes run, like a rat in a cage, nervously to and fro. He pleads innocence and fights to support this truth, until there is nothing left to win. One wonders why he has decided to come to the house of a man who will be persecuting torturers just like him. Perhaps he is looking to reveal his secret, or else, with the security of knowing that he has an alibi, to secure his position as an innocent man. Just as he returns to women because, as he says, he gets his "balls cut off" and wants them back, he has arrived at a place in his own life where only confession can return his manhood.

Miranda bares a resemblance to George from *Cul-de-Sac*. With a shaved head and thin moustache, at times he approaches the absurd world inhabited by George. When Miranda is drunk and enjoying his time with Gerardo, one can almost see a hysterical George giggling and fumbling along with him. George found his violent impulses, however, in sexual frustration and madness, and Miranda is far more calculating and insidious. George lets loose, spiraling further and further away from himself, running wild into the ocean, away from stable ground. Miranda retreats into himself, denying the truth about his past until the very end. His admission is his salvation, for it is at this moment that he finally stops shifting and becomes real.

With the constant playing of Schubert's "Death and the Maiden" and the tight space (reminiscent of the boat in *Knife in the Water*) in which the action takes place, there is no room for even one extra breath in this film. The confines of the house restrict the victim in search of the truth. The weight of each confession pushes the parameters of the space until finally an answer comes. The frame is precise in its encapsulation of the three characters so that the dramatic tension is heightened with a third expression, a third point of view.

As often as possible, all characters are seen together on screen. No one is left out, and so not for one moment is the audience allowed to forget the tension in the room. The dramatic music is pushing us over the edge, just as

Miranda may go over the cliff in the end. Just as the camera will move over the edge, to face the sea and then fade out, we feel ourselves losing ground.

Because Polanski establishes the frame as he shoots, waiting for the actors to walk through the action, there is a unique vision that comes across (and had been missing for some time). Being on set and conceiving of the image when already inside the action helps Polanski to make unusual choices. Whether the camera is focused on a pair of feet or Gerardo as he retrieves his dinner from the garbage pail, we still know precisely what is going on outside the frame. Polanski chooses visual clues that hone in on subtext as well as the action, and as a result, the audience is engaged on multiple levels. So exacting are his choices, whether the frame is close or wide, we know exactly where we are and what is going on. Here, almost the entire story takes place during a power outage, under the low-key lighting scheme established by candles and small oil lamps. These light sources separate every subject from its background, giving each character a duplicitous existence. Shadows loom (although they don't really dance, as they ought to in candlelight), each person inhabiting their own shadow world.

Death and the Maiden tries to understand where ideals fit in a democratic society. In the old regime it was easier to know where one stood, but in this new state one may sit in a concert hall just feet away from his or her former torturer, contemplating freedom. This is the price of equality, and in some ways it proves to be much more difficult than the old ways of right and wrong. Miranda is an example of this dichotomy, for when he sits listening to music with his wife and kids, he completely inhabits the role of a respectable, honorable family man. We know his secrets, his wrongdoings, and his lack of remorse. Noticing him looking down at Paulina and Gerardo on the orchestra level, his son turns to him and there is an anxiety and a momentary uncertainty in his face. To reassure him, Miranda smiles and plays with his hair. Do not worry, it is I, your father, he seems to say. In the eyes of his children he sees only the good parts of himself, yet he continues to live with what he has done.

Miranda's confession emerges at the end of a long night. There is a progression in which he is first taped and then videotaped. Finally, he is taken outside, presumably to his death. While being filmed, Miranda sits at a table, an oil lamp beside him, as well as a piece of paper from which he reads his script. He still cannot admit guilt, and the large bandage taped to his bald head is more foolish than serious. The entire setting appears staged, and he delivers his speech without conviction. Only his tremendously boxy shadow reveals what he cannot. It is not until Miranda is taken out to the cliff, the camera and all artifice removed, that the truth comes to light. In this half-light of ocean mist and roar, he kneels before them in submission. Paulina removes his blindfold and holds his face in her hands, and she asks him if, in the light of day, he is able to really see her and admit to what he has done. This is not a sentimental plea, but a simple telling of horror, waves crashing against the cliffs beyond his head. It took him the longest, he says. He tried to resist. When Gerardo is unable to push Miranda off the cliff, Paulina unties his hands, and she and Gerardo leave in silence. In the relief that they find in truth, each one of them is set free.

Death and the Maiden was a critical success, even though it would only appeal to a selective audience. Polanski had found the right material with which to return to his element.

THE NINTH GATE (1999)

Based on the book, "El Club Dumas" (1993) by Arturo Pérez-Reverte, *The Ninth Gate* was Polanski's next project. The story follows the premise that clues in an ancient text (which proves to be a MacGuffin-like device),[3] "The Nine Gates of the Kingdom of Shadow," cowritten by Aristide Torchia and Lucifer himself, carry the key to raising the devil. Corso is a seller of used books hired by Boris Balkan, an expert on dark magic and an avid collector of antique books. Balkan enlists him to track down the remaining two copies (Balkan already has one), so that he may check their authenticity and subsequently become one with the devil. Balkan cuts Corso a large check (powerful enough to illuminate his glasses in reflection) and assures him that he will do anything to get his hands on those books. This proves to be true, for as Corso travels through Western Europe, any obstacle is suddenly lifted, his path often cleared by another's death. These coincidences are furthered by the presence of an enigmatic blonde beauty, who appears anywhere and everywhere that Corso happens to be. She is his shadow. Her angelic looks are belied by her devilish abilities, and ultimately it is she who leads Corso into the kingdom of shadow. Though Corso is not initially interested in attaining this power, as the film progresses he is compelled by a desire that appeals to his apathetic personality.

Set to be a Spanish-French coproduction and financed by the American company Artisan Entertainment, *The Ninth Gate* was to be shot in numerous beautiful locations in Toledo, Spain; Portugal; and France. Costume designer Anthony Powell (who worked on *Tess, Pirates,* and *Frantic*), rejoined Polanski's crew, as did Polish composer Wojciech Kilar (*Death and the Maiden*), whose score perfectly enhances the suspenseful atmosphere of the film. Also to join the crew as cinematographer was Iranian-born Darius Khondji (*Se7en* [1995], *The City of Lost Children* [1995]) who would lend an accuracy of vision, and consistently light each scene with a beautiful, soft, golden glow. Production design is by Dean Tavoularis (*Apocalypse Now* [1979], *The Godfather Trilogy*), and art direction by Gérard Viard (assistant on *Frantic, Dangerous Liaisons* [1988], and who designed *Bitter Moon* along with Willy Holt). The creation of sets involved building numerous private libraries, fixing and also making shabby various apartments and chateaux, as well as constructing numerous antique books, mastering watermarks, aging, and texture to perfectly resemble the originals. Johnny Depp stars as Corso, Polanski's first choice for the part, and Frank Langella, as Boris Balkan. Swedish-born actress Lena Olin (*The Unbearable Lightness of Being* [1988], *Romeo is Bleeding* [1993]), was cast as the decoy devil woman, who also happens to be Telfer's wife, and cast as the true devil woman was Polanski's wife, Emmanuelle Seigner.

As with Polanski's films of the sixties and early seventies, even secondary parts are filled perfectly by actors such as Allen Garfield and Barbara Jefford. Every character has their quirk, defect, even disability, and everyone is exactly as they are meant to be. Polanski even filled two smaller roles with nonactors, which gives one the impression that he enjoyed the making of this film, for he did not feel obliged to follow every tradition. Just as the man who owned the old age home in *Chinatown* was in fact store owner Jack Vernon, from whom Polanski had bought his Edwardian wedding jacket, here, the man who hangs himself in the opening sequence, Mr. Telfer, was in fact Willy Holt, a veteran production designer who had worked on *Bitter Moon* and who Polanski felt fit the part. Also, the Spanish brothers who own the used bookstore in Toledo from which Mrs. Telfer had bought the book were both played by José López Rodero, the Spanish production manager, using a blue screen and various costume changes to differentiate between the two.

From the opening scene of *The Ninth Gate*, it is apparent that Polanski is in his element. It is as if all of the disparaging aspects of the past years of filmmaking, the flat texture of the eighties, the garish nineties, and all of the various techniques used to convey a feeling of exile have at last come into focus, and Polanski has returned home. The rhythm is right, with a varying pace that one might compare to Alfred Hitchcock's *Vertigo* (1958), and it is evident in Polanski's willingness to take his time with telling the story. The camera is in steady, confident hands, lingering for just as long as is necessary. And even if the tension is not upheld throughout the entire film, it is nevertheless pleasing to witness this cinematic belonging. As Johnny Depp pointed out in an interview with Charlie Rose in 1998, the premise for *The Ninth Gate* is "classic Polanski."

The opening scene shows a man with white hair, dressed in a robe, seated at a desk in his library. He seals an envelope. The camera glides through the room, past a wooden footstool before arriving at Telfer's desk. It returns to the center of the room to reveal a noose hanging from the chandelier. Telfer closes the letter, rises, stands on the footstool, and, pulling the noose over his head, falls, monogrammed slippers twitching until death. The chandelier blows out and is extinguished in the process. Once his feet cease to quiver, the camera (here, as a third character) pushes past death, into the room, leaving Telfer in the background. The movement ventures into another kind of drama. Tension mounts as the camera passes over the desk, and scans shelves of antique books. There is a presence to this movement, and as we approach a missing slot in the bookshelf, we break through to the darker side. Now speed is inherent in the movement, as we pass through ornate, archaic doorway after doorway, under the assumption that we, too, are entering the kingdom of shadow. The credits expand toward us, as we pass through them, just as Corso will do with dead body after body, as he moves into the devil's realm. There are nine gates in total, the final one opening onto a bright light, a final illumination. We traverse dark cobblestone roads as the haunting score engulfs the viewer, heart beating in anticipation, dancing this devil's waltz. Polanski once made a remark that he couldn't remember experiencing such excitement over laying down the soundtrack to any other film.

Imagery is essential to the mood and atmosphere of the film. The aesthetics are exacting, with a cold, linear quality dominating the New York scenes, and a classically decaying European air hovering throughout the rest of the film. Consistent is the calculating distance, both of Corso and the camera. Certain characteristics do carry over, however, such as the apricot-colored practical light, from a large standing lamp to small wall lights, which carries from one bourgeois apartment to the next. It is symbolic of the contained fire, not fully realized, for one must remember that many of these characters aspire to make contact with the devil. Not only does this shade of light flatter its surroundings, but it also establishes a continuous thread. When in the presence of Balkan, the quality of light is white/blue, often in linear tubes, highlighted by the lights of an office building in the distance. His lecture hall is decorated throughout with lights of this kind, and his private library, with its sliding glass doors, resembles a mausoleum, only with glass windows that look out over the New York night sky.

With the exception of second-unit shots of the New York skyline, the majority of U.S. scenes were constructed on a stage, exteriors as well when necessary, using backings or real footage to make the background more realistic. In another film, one might find this incongruity unrealistic and distracting, but here, the eeriness is merely furthered by the estrangement of existing in a reconstructed New York, in which everything is in place, yet awry at the same time. There is something slightly off and hard to put your finger on about not inhabiting the real thing. As Corso pulls up in a yellow cab at his colleague Bernie's bookstore on the way to the airport, the faux New York street encourages us to focus deeper, as if asking us to discover what is off. Though Polanski is happiest working in the studio, and is, as we know, unable to work in the United States, one cannot shake the feeling that it is the devil's work that makes us shift in our chair, trying to pinpoint every uncertainty.

With his trim goatee, glasses, and slick black hair, Corso has the look of a weasel at home in the underbelly of the world. Johnny Depp is the perfect choice for Corso. Just like Cary Grant[4] in Hitchcock films such as *Suspicion* (1941), *North by Northwest* (1959) and *Notorious* (1946), Depp is adept at approaching dark material with a feather-light touch. Both of these actors have the ability to observe any difficult situation with a sardonic smile, and even though Depp plays Corso on a very flat plane, one can always sense the enjoyment that lies beneath.

Corso squirms his way into any situation from which he can benefit, never stopping to think of the consequences for others. He does this with a charm and a panache that make him impossible to dislike. This is apparent from the start of the film. The first scene that follows the opening credits finds Corso in the New York apartment of a book collector who has recently fallen ill and cannot speak. His offspring wait eagerly to discuss the value of his collection. Corso talks them up on the price of the collection, while simultaneously walking out of the apartment with a valuable four-volume edition of *Don Quixote,* at an extraordinarily low price. When Balkan asks him if he believes in "the supernatural," he responds by saying, "I believe in my percentage." When Corso discovers his only friend, Bernie, hanging from his foot, dead in his own bookshop, he panics. He calls Balkan to say that he is finished with the charade, and Balkan suggests adding another zero to his price. This puts an end to any hesitations.

Though Corso has a feel and respect for books, he is indifferent to their contents. He flips through Balkan's copy of *The Nine Gates*, listening to the sound of passing pages. He is so keyed in to the details indicating the authenticity of a book that he bypasses the content's importance. This may account, in part, for his getting in way over his head, for before he knows it he, too, is a pawn in the devil's game. When he first arrives home to his dull and impersonal bachelor pad with the book, he sits down with his microwaveable dinner and opens to the print of a man on horseback. As if alerting the viewer, the man holds up his finger, saying no, proceed no further. But watermarks and varying signatures are what captivates Corso's mind, not obvious deterrents. The audience knows more than the hero.

Like Polanski, Corso does not believe in evil or the concept of the devil. This gives him the confidence to travel into an unknown realm without thinking that he, too, will get caught up in the desire for it—for achieving and acquiring the inaccessible. For Polanski, the reason for making a film about the devil is simple. He is an amusing subject, to be treated ironically here; however, as in *Rosemary's Baby*, he is understood to be real. Polanski is playing with these ideas, and with Corso himself, enjoying his investigation, which leads Corso slowly into belief. This game of cat and mouse is dimensional, palpable. It involves Corso, Balkan, the devil, a woman known as "green eyes" or "the girl," and even Polanski, who gets a kick out of characters discovering faith.

Even though the camera isn't strictly subjective, as it was with *Rosemary's Baby* and *Chinatown*, it does portray Corso's experience, at times looking with him and at other times representing a mysterious, malevolent, and sadistic force that sometimes hurts Corso with the intention of helping him in the end. Just as the devil toys with him, the camera plays with these two characters, until ultimately it steps back, observing as the two become one.

This, however, does not exclude subjective imagery from the film. A magnifying lens is used to uncover the nuances that differentiate the three volumes, just as Corso's eyeglasses are a means for immersion into his experience. Whenever they are taken off, or broken, his clarity is obscured. When he is in the library delving into Balkan's book, he takes off his glasses and rubs his eyes. Looking up at a balcony he sees a fuzzy image of the girl who has already appeared both at Balkan's lecture and, minutes before, through a crack in the bookcase. When he replaces his glasses Corso sees that she is gone. When engaged in a fight on the banks of the Seine, his glasses fall off. The girl comes down the steps to help him, and for a moment it appears that she has flown. It is the first supernatural occurrence in the film, and it is also an indication that his vision is changing. Once the fight is over, he steps on his own glasses, shattering their clarity for good.

Applying various ways of seeing is just another way to play with the cinematic form and to spark the imagination of the viewer, allowing secondary images to arise in the audience's mind while watching the film. As with the camera lens in *Chinatown* that reflects a lover's embrace, when Corso calls Balkan from a phone booth, after finding Bernie, there are multiple aspects to the mise-en-scène, or frame, which subliminally ask the viewer to pay close attention. Red, blood-like graffiti covers the glass walls, and an overhead light flickers on and off. Meanwhile, Corso's attendant cab driver watches him, a beautiful, dim image of silhouettes playing basketball in the distance filling the upper left corner of the screen, reminding the audience that somewhere else normal life does exist, while simultaneously reinforcing that this is a game that we are witnessing.

Following the fight on the Seine, the telephone booth is revisited in Paris. This occurs after he and the girl sit in his hotel room, and she seductively smears blood from her nose onto his forehead, enchanting Corso, her eyes glowing with catlike fervor. He stands in a booth in the lobby of his hotel, blood on his forehead and glasses shattered, obscuring the vision of at least one eye. It is an amusing moment in which we realize just how little Corso cares about the opinions of others. This is the point at which his way of seeing has been permanently altered, for now that he has had insight into the devil's charm (through the mysterious girl), he will not rest until he succeeds. Having crossed over to the dark side, he is unaware of his appearance, and even though he will have his glasses repaired, he will never see things the same way again. When the Baroness Kessler tells him to "Get out before it is too late," he responds by saying, "I'm afraid it already is."

In *The Ninth Gate*, the devil is surely a woman. At first it appears that Liana, Telfer's feisty widow, is Lucifer incarnate. With her sexy black thigh-high stockings and her serpent's tattoo, she seduces Corso and then attacks him when he tells her that he doesn't have the book. She grabs his hair, bites him, and hits him over the head with a bottle, his vision blurring, as seen in the third person. But soon we discover that Liana is merely a decoy. She may head the club of bourgeois Satan worshippers known as the order of the silver serpent, dreaming of raising the devil for her own benefit, but she is powerless against Balkan and even more so against true power.

The girl, on the other hand, is devil and angel combined. With her long blonde hair, soft voice, and innocent gaze, the world is putty in her hands. As Polanski once said, Seigner has the ability to appear "angelic and wicked . . . at the same time." When Corso first speaks with the girl on a night train traveling through Europe, she leans against a window in the hallway. Lights on a passing train flicker against her white skin, strobing, accentuating the good and the bad. One half of her face is light, and the other dark. This is also true with Corso in the hotel room, when her eyes become catlike. Her angelic looks draw him in, and before he knows it, he is enraptured. As impassioned as he may be, Corso is still a man. The girl is nothing like the devil in *Rosemary's Baby*. Delicate and refined, she even goes so far as to wear jeans and sneakers, trying to blend in. As she sits in Corso's hotel lobby holding a copy of the book, "How to Win Friends and Influence People,"[5] she smiles at her own inside joke. After all, the devil doesn't need any help.

The climax of *The Ninth Gate* is drawn out and over the top, but no hellfire and brimstone is too great for this story. Corso meets Balkan in a ruined castle, and Balkan pours gasoline over himself, thinking that he is going home, but only winds up burnt to a crisp (out of kindness, Corso shoots him as he writhes in pain, putting him out of his misery). As flames cast the castle aglow, Corso has sex with the girl, her eyes illuminated in devilish mirth. She wriggles, somewhat awkwardly, as if she is, in fact, only making love to the grass below. She laughs giddily, looking more like a woman practicing a dance routine than having sex. Corso looks as if his soul is being extracted through his sex. When this operatic scene is said and done, the ease of the film up until this moment (following the equally absurd debacle in the château with Liana, her lover, Balkan, and all their fellow Satan worshippers, dressed in shiny black cloaks) is returned to its equilibrium. The waltz-like quality of the entire film, enhanced by the score, is brought back. All along we have danced with Corso and the devil, though rather than sliding to and fro, it has always been forward the deeper we go. As the result of a clue left by the girl in a gas station, the last illustration is found, and Corso is seen on the road to the ninth gate, and as it opens, there is illumination as he is drowned in a white light. In this story, there is no sleep for the wicked. Corso is the ultimate exile, for he chooses his own path, and just like all of Polanski's characters, he is the recreated fugitive on the run. No matter how playful, or how noble, they all have one thing in common—they all wish to live according to their desire. Still, it isn't easy being the odd man out.

11

The Pianist (2002)

In 1939, Wladyslaw Szpilman was a regular on Polish radio. A pianist trained in Warsaw and Germany, Szpilman was known for his interpretations of jazz and classical pieces, especially those written by the Polish-born national treasure, Frederic Chopin. He was also a known composer. One year later, Szpilman was struggling to survive in the ghetto. *The Pianist* is based upon Szpilman's autobiography, originally titled *Death of a City*, and tells his story of survival amid destruction.

In March 2000, when he was already working on *The Pianist*, Polanski was interviewed by Charlie Rose in Paris. He said that he felt he had not yet made *his* perfect film. "I would not put any one of them on my gravestone," he remarked, suggesting that perhaps his next film would prove to satisfy this need. Polanski was prepared to work on a project with a deep social impact, and he had found his subject in Szpilman's story. Here was the opportunity for Polanski to share his experience, without telling his own story. Perhaps this urge to make a different sort of film had something to do with becoming a father and seeing his own childhood in a different light (for through the prism of a child's healthy, happy life, his own seemed more difficult than ever before). Though spry as ever, Polanski was also nearing his 70th birthday, and he may have deemed it time to make a film with a message of depth and meaning unlike his films of the past.

For years Polanski had been encouraged to make a film about the Holocaust, and he had wanted to, though he never found the right approach. Steven Spielberg had asked him to direct his widely successful film, *Schindler's List* (1993), which took place in the Krakow ghetto. Polanski turned the offer down, certain that the story was too close to home. With Szpilman, however, things were different. For one, he was just like Polanski, in that above all things, he remained an artist and a survivor. And, like Polanski, living for his passion had played a key role in his survival.

The Pianist. (Courtesy of Photofest)

Unlike the majority of holocaust memoirists, Szpilman's accounts of his experiences were written in 1945, directly after the war. As a result of this immediacy, there was a matter-of-fact quality to the writing—a lack of sentimentality that appealed to Polanski. Szpilman spoke of the war as it was, without embellishment, just as Polanski did while recounting his own childhood in his autobiography, *Roman by Polanski*. Szpilman treated both the Jews and the Nazis with "astonished and cold objectivity," as was pointed out by Polanski,[1] finding the good and bad in everyone—German, Pole, and Jew alike. This lack of judgment was appealing to Polanski, who didn't wish to vilify anyone more than was required. In Szpilman's memoir, he discovered an account congruous with his own experiences. Through Szpilman's story, Polanski was able to express his own memories without exploiting his pain.

The story of Szpilman was an unusual one, for not only did he survive the war by remaining in Warsaw, hiding among the ruins, but he was saved by a Nazi soldier. Finding him in the broken-down kitchen of a bombed-out building, Captain Wilm Hosenfeld listened to Szpilman play the piano, and he was so moved by his talent that he brought him food in secret and helped find him a better place to hide. Hosenfeld eventually died in a Soviet POW camp, but his memoirs live on (published in part in *The Pianist*), as do those of Szpilman, who made efforts to help get him out of the Soviet camp. Both Hosenfeld's and Szpilman's sons have since worked to commemorate their father's stories (in hopes that the world will bear witness to the nuances of their lives that once challenged the status quo). It was Szpilman's son, Andrzej, who saw to it that his father's memoir, virtually out of print as a result of years of communist suppression, was reprinted in Germany under the title *The Miraculous Survival* (1998), and in English as *The Pianist*. It was to become a bestseller around the world. Fifty years after writing it, Szpilman was still unable to read his own book (he died in 2000 at the age of 88).

Szpilman was saved not once, but many times. The first time, a Jewish policeman who recognized him from local cafés where he played the piano pulled him from the crowd as his family was being loaded onto a train to Treblinka, where they would subsequently be exterminated. He would not allow him to rejoin the crowd. The devastation of being separated from his family, of being forced to live while others died (a sentiment touched upon by Paulina in *Death and The Maiden*, when she remarks to Miranda that she wasn't so "lucky" as to die), was unbearable at times for Szpilman, perhaps forcing him to quarter off these feelings for the rest of his life. Yet he would be one of the few Jewish survivors to remain in Poland and make a life there after the war, connecting him to the renewal as well as the destruction of a city that he still called home. He was quoted in "They Didn't Shoot the Piano Player," an article by Jay Rayner printed in *The Guardian* in March 1999, as saying, "There is racism everywhere. Warsaw is my home." He was spared not only by chance, but because he had a gift. The Eastern European value placed upon art and music (an appreciation that transcends class and creed) was a binding force—bringing him together with nearly 30 Poles who worked to help save his life.

The subject of an artist saved in part by his art was a great inspiration to Polanski as he developed the script with screenwriter Ronald Harwood (*The Browning Version* [1994], *Being Julia* [2004]). Together they laughed and sometimes cried as they brought Szpilman's story to life. The project was to be a French, Polish, German, and British coproduction, and most thrillingly, independent. Robert Benmussa (who had served as executive producer on *Bitter Moon*) would produce the film along with Alain Sarde (David Lynch's *Mulholland Drive* [2001], Mike Leigh's *Vera Drake* [2004] Jean-Luc Godard's *For Ever Mozart* [1996]), who had been a coproducer on *Bitter Moon*. Polanski would also be a producer along with longtime friend and fellow expatriate, Gene Gutowski, who had collaborated on *Repulsion*, *Cul-de-Sac*, and *The Fearless Vampire Killers*. His family had also been wiped out by the Holocaust, and so working with Polanski on *The Pianist* was an especially meaningful project. This sense of personal responsibility and commitment was transmitted throughout cast and crew. Even though the majority of them had not experienced the war, there was a sense of obligation that elevated the production. More than once, you could find crew members weeping while shooting a scene, particularly the one in which Szpilman, shaking with hunger, cold, and perhaps fear, plays for Captain Hosenfeld. He plays his life, and for his life as well.

Finding a project that affected everyone it touched was a new and meaningful experience for Polanski. For a filmmaker in love with the process of filmmaking, concerned with story, but not as the primary draw, the importance found in this story was transformational. He was deeply affected by working on a film with such human, emotional power and a storyline unlike any that he had attempted in the past. In the DVD extra documentary, *A Story of Survival*, Polanski remarks that he would like to have this experience in which cast, crew, story, and personal aspect are unified so beautifully once again.

When, during shooting, a fabricated ghetto wall was erected in Praga, the only remaining prewar section of Warsaw (other than the old town, which only partially consists of original structures), locals, both young and old, came to witness their own history being remade. Though the area is known for its criminal activity, no one interfered with the shoot. Polish set designer Allan Starski (*Schindler's List* [1993]) was given the task of recreating the ghetto, creating a world that had been virtually erased. By rebuilding the wall and adding some buildings, the film was able to have a realistic look. For the bombed-out portion of Warsaw—the ruins through which Szpilman finds himself traveling and hiding to see out the end of the war—old Soviet barracks near Berlin were employed that Polanski's crew was permitted to partially destroy. Remaining segments were filmed at Babelsberg Studios.

Bearing the same weighty obligation of recreating a time in which the director had lived, Polish-born costume designer Anna Sheppard (*Schindler's List* [1993], *Kontrakt* [1980], *The Proposition* [1998]) worked to communicate with Polanski on every detail of the clothing. Polanski clearly recalled the difficulty with which he had tried to draw the Jewish star as a child, the perfection required in its construction. Every aspect of his memory rich in accuracies was available to everyone on the set, a humbling asset for actors and crew alike. For Adrien Brody (*The Thin Red Line* [1998], *Summer of Sam* [1999], *King Kong* [2005]), the young American actor chosen to play Szpilman, the undertaking of this role implied a tremendous responsibility. Understanding that Polanski was not interested in half-hearted devotion, Brody threw himself into the role by giving up many of his stabilizing earthly possessions and cutting contact with many of his friends. He studied piano daily and starved himself to the point of emaciation, doing everything that he could to get inside the role of Szpilman. Just as with *Schindler's List*, the film would be made in English, allowing for a multinational cast and making it more commercially viable.

In *A Story of Survival*, actor Thomas Kretschmann, who plays heroic Captain Hosenfeld, speaks of the extent to which *The Pianist* stems from Polanski's life. He notes how, when the film was completed, Polanski pointed out to him all of the circumstances that he himself had experienced as a child. The reality of working with a director who knew this story of war and degradation as intimately as Polanski did made a deep impact on everyone involved.

Though Polanski had managed to avoid making a film that took place in Krakow and which used straight autobiographical content, he still was able to draw upon his memories of the war. Recalling a day in which his father was smacked by a German officer for walking on the sidewalk instead of in the street, he used this memory in a scene in which Szpilman's father is slapped for the same reason. Remembering how he escaped the Umschlagplatz and certain death with little Stefan, and the young officer who said, "Don't run,"[2] he incorporated this line into the scene in which Szpilman is thrown from the line to Treblinka. Recalling the empty streets littered with furniture thrown from the windows and feathers everywhere, Polanski repeated this imagery in the film as Szpilman walks through the desolate ghetto. Polanski aspired to tell the story in a manner that was true to that time, and he succeeded in doing so.

Wanting to reflect the tone of Szpilman's memoirs, embodying its direct voice both cinematically and in story, Polanski worked with director of photography Pawel Edelman (*Pan Tadeusz* [1999], *Zemsta* [2002], *Katyn* [2007], *The Life Before Her Eyes* [2007]), to exercise restraint with regard to employing visual tricks. The goal was to be simple and direct, which in this case meant using low-key lighting, a scheme that does not create dramatic shadows, such as those commonly seen in film noir. The framing would vary, as usual, according to scene, at times working from a subjective perspective, although more often than not gazing with an objective eye. The soundtrack by Wojciech Kilar (with the inclusion of pieces by Frederic Chopin[3]) is the one exception to permitting overt emotionality within the film. The score soars above the ruins of Warsaw and the broken bodies buried in rubble, to penetrate the heart of the viewer and remind us of the power of art to transcend everything, even death and war, as it does for Szpilman, his flickering light in an era of total darkness. As is pointed out by Kretschmann in *A Story of Survival*, *The Pianist* is "about hope where there shouldn't be any . . . about survival where it's actually impossible to survive."

There is a systematic discoloration evident in the imagery of *The Pianist*. Reflecting a progressively bleak atmosphere, one witnesses the world as it moves from vibrant color to a palette of brown and gray. At first we observe the Poland of the late 1930s, with its strong reds, yellows, and greens, as evident in furniture and in women's clothes. As the war begins, color (as a symbol of life), is slowly drawn out—landscapes become gray, as do the people. As spirits are stripped of independence and pride, the will to shine is also diminished. Mud covers the streets, as do dead bodies, gray/blue in their pallor. Clothes are faded, faces grim. The occasional lamp emanating a golden glow provides the only warmth. These lamps are the last vestiges of home. Light will be the last thing to go.

At times this muted color gives the impression of a black and white film. When Szpilman and his family sit at the dinner table, there is a Nazi raid across the street. We share the family's perspective, as every light goes out in both buildings. Nazi soldiers enter an apartment directly across from theirs, and they turn on the lights to reveal a family not unlike Szpilman's, sitting around the table. Szpilman and his family watch in terror as the soldiers force everyone to rise. When the wheelchair-bound grandfather cannot, they wheel him to the balcony, and lifting his chair, drop him into the street. Wladyslaw's mother's scream is silenced in the dark. His father sits at the table weeping, a delicate, quintessentially Polish lace curtain hanging behind his head, casting his sad frame and his white hair in a bluish light. The deep red bloodstain that forms around the old man's head is the only color in sight. The Nazis and their vehicles are uniformly gray, and as they escort the family out, the prisoners disperse, running in the yellow spotlights cast by the military truck. They are shot one by one, dropping as they run. One figure falls from the wall over which he was trying to escape. The bodies are subsequently run over by the same car. It becomes evident that for Szpilman's family it is only a matter of time before they are on the other side of the lens, the other side of the gun.

The gray palette of the film does highlight the sight of any bloodshed during the war, yet this is not the sole purpose for the lack of color. Though people are shot carelessly, and ad infinitum, *The Pianist* is not an excessively bloody film. It is more likely that when color is seen, as the war progresses and the world darkens, it is in memory of life. When Szpilman works as a laborer and is permitted to exit the ghetto, there is a market stall with flowers and an array of fruit, this rainbow of color bringing to mind the recollection of life. Though blood is life as well, it is only one aspect of this film. Here, music is color as well, for as Szpilman lies in bed, he practices the piano on his chest, drumming his fingers lightly, happily, recalling the sounds that always provided him with comfort.

From the first scene of the film in which Szpilman is playing a Chopin Nocturne on the radio while bombs hit the station, shutting it down, he must fight to keep his music alive. At first, he brushes plaster and soot from his suit, though soon violence takes over. When Szpilman's family gathers round to hear a BBC address declaring war against Germany, they embrace each other with glee knowing that Poland is no longer alone. As the signal is lost, and a speech by Adolf Hitler takes over, a chill runs through characters and audience alike. Darkness permeates light. The manipulation of space adds another dimension to changes brought by the war. As war descends, there is less space and movement is inhibited. Packed into two ghettos, one small and one big, Jews are told exactly where to go and how to do it. The streets on which one could once roam freely are now off limits, and apartments are dirty and small. The streets are crowded with droves of people inhabiting every space. There is no longer the room to breathe or call one's self free. And as Szpilman enters into isolation, finding himself completely alone, though there is more space on the outside, on the inside he is still cornered, still trapped.

Prior to the exodus to Treblinka and other camps, one witnesses various scenes from the ghetto. German soldiers force a crowd of Jews to dance, some of whom are old and ill. Two beggars battle over a small pot of gruel, and when it tumbles to the street, the man kneels down and eats it off the ground. An elegantly dressed woman searches endlessly for her husband, clearly in denial of the fact that he has been killed. A clowning man leads a group of giggling children through a ghetto square, and when they arrive before some German soldiers, he raises his stick and pretends to shoot them with it. He addresses the soldiers in poor German, and they laugh at his playfulness, offering him a cigarette. At the Umschlagplatz, where Jews have been gathered for deportation, Szpilman and his family sit baking in the hot sun, a cruel trick of nature. Behind them a woman cries, "Why did I do it?" over and over. We later discover that she smothered her baby to keep it quiet when a German soldier passed by. A girl stands lost and weeping, dirty and alone. She holds an empty birdcage. Perhaps she is weeping for a lost pet, her parents, us all. A boy, about 12 years old, sells caramel candies for 20 zlotys apiece, and though it is an exorbitant amount, Szpilman's father decides to buy one. Together the family pools their money to buy one caramel, which he cuts into six tiny pieces with a pocketknife. Having spent all that they have on a final pleasure, it is as if they know where they are headed. This is their last sacrament, a morsel of caramel. It is a devastating moment, heightened by the sound of a train as it moves into the station.

When the policeman pulls Szpilman from the crowd, refusing to let him board the train with his family, Szpilman loses a part of himself. He calls out to his father, who waves sweetly, helplessly, and then moves on. When his father is dragged onto the train, he is forced to give up his violin, to which he clings as if it were life. As Szpilman walks away, his legs shake, uncertain of their own ability to withstand the shock. Moments later he weeps while walking through empty streets, past piles of pillows and furniture, feathers falling like snow. Now he is alone. And for the remainder of the film, though he interacts with those who save him, workers with whom he shares his meals, his place of sleep, he will essentially be by himself. Though his wound is internal, it separates him. Like a man with a bleeding arm, he goes inward. His focus is to alleviate the pain, and interactions with others become the means by which to do so. His contacts make it possible for him to survive.

As the war worsens, winter descends. Snow covers the ground, and every night Szpilman marches with his fellow workers along the ghetto wall, throwing guns over to help the resistance. The quiet chill of winter heightens his solitude. German soldiers appear pink and fat, as Jewish workers slip into emaciation and gray hunger. Just like Szpilman, they become broken, shadow people, much older than their years. As the landscape from a world of content and shape descends into one of smoke and dust, Szpilman must do his best to disappear. Like the fugitive Johnny, played by James Mason, in Carol Reed's *Odd Man Out* (1947), he must rely upon the kindness of strangers, willing to risk their own lives to save his. He is a fugitive from the world around him but also from his roots, and ultimately, himself. When he is brought to an apartment on the outside of the ghetto wall, which is to be a hiding place, the resistance worker suggests that it must feel good to be on this side of the wall. Szpilman replies by saying, "Sometimes I'm still not sure which side of the wall I'm on."

As external boundaries become vague, internal ones become diminished. There is only addressing the wound, only survival, and though Szpilman remains good throughout, never succumbing to immoral deeds, the line between right and wrong is blurred. The image of killing, which at first caused him to tremble and weep, is now familiar, so much so that at one point he lies down in the street, pretending to be dead so that passing German soldiers don't shoot him. Death becomes a question, an image so familiar that it merely makes one wonder. When the end of the war is nearing and Szpilman is hiding out in an abandoned hospital, he stands on a toilet to look out of a broken window and watch as German soldiers set fire to a pile of corpses. He simply watches. There is no drama in his expression, only curiosity, and a bearing witness to the events as they pass. There is no judgment and no sentimentality. When the Russians finally liberate Szpilman, he is wearing the coat of Captain Hosenfeld, a Nazi uniform. Nearly shot by the Soviet soldiers he cries out that he is Polish and begs them not to shoot. When one soldier questions why he is wearing the coat, Szpilman responds by saying that he is cold. This small statement sums up much of what has occurred for Szpilman during the war. Here is the lack of judgment, and the irony that survival entails, a starving, frozen Jew wearing a Nazi's woolen coat.

With borders weakened, both literally and figuratively, there is one beacon, one clear line that exists throughout, and that is music. When Szpilman spends the night in the apartment of his former love interest Dorota, and her husband, he awakes to a long forgotten sound. It is the sound of a cello, beautifully gliding through an unaccompanied cello suite by Bach, and it is the sound of pure life. When Szpilman peeks into Dorota's room, he sees her practicing, pregnant and full, and there is the remembrance of possibility and hope. When frozen to the protrusion of bone, Szpilman (who is so starved that he can barely move) is discovered by Hosenfeld as he tries to open a can of pickles. Even though he hasn't played for five years, he sits at the piano to play for the Nazi a Chopin ballade. And as he plays, a fellow German soldier waits outside for Hosenfeld, a gray man in boots and uniform standing beside a car, among the ruins of the Polish capital. But as Szpilman plays, the captain finds himself sitting down. Perhaps he, too, is tired of the war, and he, a novice at the instrument, really listens. A beam of light, bluish-white in color, streams past Szpilman, almost flickering, as does the projection of celluloid. The light touches the floor, and it touches Hosenfeld, for he is moved to help Szpilman.

When the war is over, and Szpilman is free to play the piano once again, an old friend, a fellow musician, walks into his recording session. So moved is Szpilman to find a fellow survivor that he is brought to tears. As he plays the same Chopin Nocturne in C sharp minor that he played on his last day at the station, his feelings come to the surface, and there is finally a connection between heart and sound. Now that he feels safe, the audience senses with him that a new day is born. His colleague brings him to the site of the prisoner of war camp where Hosenfeld had asked for Szpilman, though now there is only grass, trees, and a little mud. The sun sets over the field, and for the first time in years, since the start of the film, there is life and light once again. An orchestra begins to play, and we see Szpilman at the piano, on stage, at the center of a great concert hall.

It is by chance and the sheer will that Szpilman survives the war. He is not a heroic character, though nevertheless, he becomes heroic by his perseverance and his sheer desire to live. The same can be said of Polanski, who has endured great tragedy, emerging as an artist who lives for passion and for the simple pleasures of life. Making *The Pianist* may have been one of the most rewarding experiences of Polanski's career, even of his life. Though he did not pour himself onto the screen, at last he had found a way to translate his experiences to film.

When *The Pianist* was complete, Polanski held a screening of the film for all of his actors. He was surprised to see all of the young men who had played Nazi officers in their plain clothes, to see how normal and kind they appeared without their Nazi costumes. He observed what lovely people they were, and it occurred to him that in another time they could have been those officers, and that "anyone is capable of anything at a given time in history."[4] This calls to mind a speech by Noah Cross, in *Chinatown*, in which he says, "Most people never have to face the fact that, at the right time and in the right place, they are capable of anything." Polanski has revealed the psychology of one of his most despicable characters, and related it to history, exposing a universal connection in his work. Although he may not directly insert himself into his films, there is a thread of far-reaching understanding that delves into his experiences of childhood and the war. This lack of judgment allows him to explore varied subjects and characters without judgment, for there is always an understanding that we are all equally capable of going any which way, just as chance and necessity exist side by side.

Though *The Pianist* is one of Polanski's defining works, it does not define his brand of filmmaking. In an effort to be objective, there is an absence of the distinctive Polanski style which is at once dark and funny, yet always reaching beyond conventional understanding. Here, there is no reaching, only a daily execution of life. Even in the will to survive there is a quiet acceptance, a trembling without reverberation found in the appearance of Adrien Brody's gaunt and effortful expression. There is a distanced quality to the film that gives it a somewhat false impression. Some of these qualities unfamiliar to most Polanski works may stem from the intention of creating an exercise in restraint.

Though *The Pianist* may not be a traditional Polanski film with regard to style and content, it remains the work of a filmmaker who, above all else, loves and believes in the power of film. *The Pianist* bears witness as a quiet observer. Without sentimentality, it murmurs truths of war, buried pain, and the instinct to survive. As *New York Times* critic A. O. Scott wrote in his review of the film, Polanski has a talent for portraying characters as "they are intruded upon by evil forces more powerful than they . . . peeling back their vanity to make them show the face of humanity under duress." This is one common thread that links Polanski's films to one another, reminding us that an auteur need not always shout from the hilltops.

The film was released in 2002, two years after Wladyslaw Szpilman's death at the age of 88. He had lived to experience the international success of his book, though he would not witness the impact that *The Pianist* would have on the world. His son Andrzej and his grandson Daniel (who would be an extra in the film) would. A new century had dawned, and certain pains of the past could be laid to rest. *The Pianist* did not have to experience a period of latency, as had so many of Polanski's films of the past 20 years. It was immediately heralded as a masterpiece.

Longtime friend Adam Holender said in regard to *The Pianist*, "Nothing was gratuitous," and that for him, "It rang true." Being a Polish émigré, he felt content in knowing that as a result, "Many audiences around the world got to know the story of Poland through Polanski."

Some critics accused the film of being too detached, but for most it was an exceptional feat. It would win the Palmes d'Or[5] at the Cannes Film Festival that spring, and would earn Ronald Harwood an Oscar for Best Adapted Screenplay, Adrien Brody an Academy Award for Best Actor in a Leading Role (Pawel Edelman would also be nominated for Best Cinematographer, Hervé de Luze for Best Editor, Anna Sheppard for Best Costume, and Polanski, Benmussa and Sarde for Best Picture). It would also earn Roman Polanski an Academy Award for Best Director. Everyone had thought that this would at last be Scorsese's chance to win an Academy Award for *Gangs of New York*, though when Polanski's name was announced Scorsese clapped as loud as he could. Polanski would not be at the ceremony to accept his award, for his status as an exile had not been affected by an award ceremony in Hollywood. Harrison Ford accepted it on his behalf. Polanski released a speech thanking the academy which said, "I am deeply moved to be rewarded for the work which relates to the events so close to my own life, the events that led me to comprehend that art can transform pain. I believe this still holds true today."[6] Though he could not be at the center of the festivities surrounding the film, he was elated knowing what he had accomplished. A few years earlier he was elected a member of the French society, Académie des Beaux Arts, a privilege awarded to painters, sculptors, architects, musicians, and filmmakers. Now that he had won an Oscar, he was at last recognized as one of the great filmmakers of our time. The great irony of being honored by the American motion picture industry when he was not allowed inside the country was a fact that he could accept. It was an absurdity perfectly congruous with his life thus far.

12

Oliver Twist (2005)

The Pianist was a hard act to follow. For a filmmaker such as Polanski who is in love with the process of the medium above all else, waiting for another project can be frustrating. Now a father of two, to Morgane and Elvis, Polanski wanted to make a film for his children. This, he could be certain, would be a wonderful and worthwhile undertaking. Searching for a new genre to play with the classics of Charles Dickens came to mind. He had always loved *Oliver Twist*, yet knowing that it had already been brought to the screen, first by David Lean in 1948, and second, as Carol Reed's adaptation of the musical "Oliver!" by Lionel Bart in 1968, there was a question as to whether it was worthwhile to make another film. Both of these versions had been successful, but still enough time had passed that the project seemed viable to Polanski and his producers. The fact that David Lean's version was in black and white automatically made it inaccessible to a young, contemporary audience unaccustomed to and generally bored by a lack of color, and a musical was quite obviously different. Making an English classic also meant the possibility of working with an all-British cast, which—because Polanski loves English actors—was a thrilling prospect.

Banding together with the same producers Polanski had worked with on *The Pianist*, Robert Benmussa and Alain Sarde, the film would be made as an independent production. This was a thrill for Polanski. Prior to *The Pianist*, he had been afforded the opportunity to work without an artistic "committee" on his tail only during *Chinatown*. By delving into the story of an orphan, Polanski was again returning to the realm of his childhood. Despite years of making films that on the surface deflected attention away from his own story, late in his career Polanski was choosing to call upon the material of his own life. This is not to say that he was suddenly exposing himself, as have many other great auteurs of the twentieth century in their work,

The Artful Dodger. (Courtesy of Photofest)

yet still there was a deliberate connection now being made, and one might argue whether these choices were as fruitful.

Polanski recruited many of the same people to work on *Oliver Twist* who had participated in *The Pianist*. Ronald Harwood would write the screenplay, and Pawel Edelman would be cinematographer. Production designer Allan Starski and costume designer Anna Sheppard would come back on board, as would makeup artist Didier Lavergne, who had now worked on nearly every Polanski film since *The Tenant*. Sir Ben Kingsley, who had completely embodied the role of Miranda in *Death and the Maiden*, would weave his magic once again to play the role of conjurer Fagin, turning a money-grubbing character into someone lovable and enchanting. For the role of Fagin, Kingsley wore heavy makeup and a prosthetic nose. The moment that he was in costume, Kingsley would be in character, walking the set bent over, cracking endearing, naughty jokes, just as Fagin would. So adept was he at embodying the character of Fagin that even Polanski once remarked that seeing Kingsley off set was somewhat of a surprise. The role of Oliver would go to Barney Clark, and the Artful Dodger to Harry Eden. As always with Polanski, the look of each character was carefully thought out ahead of time, as was the look of the film. As can be seen from the storybook opening in which a black-and-white illustration comes to life, there is an attempt to create something that is altogether different, magical, and made for children.

Making *Oliver Twist* was a treat for many reasons. One was the opportunity to create a bygone world, one that would allow each artisan to build his or her own reality, a pleasure rarely enjoyed in contemporary cinema (often one must go back or forward in time to achieve this good fortune). Another reason was the chance to rework a classic story and enjoy a cast consisting primarily of children. During shooting (in a rebuilt Victorian London erected in Prague), cast and crew marveled at Polanski's ease with the child actors. Capable of entering into their world, he treated them as equals, creating an atmosphere of mutual respect and great fun.

One of the greatest joys for the young actors was to learn card tricks, and the art of pickpocketing from the resident magician on the set. During Victorian times, children were used as pickpockets simply because their hands were so little that they were more adept at this type of robbery than a grown man would be. Fagin is their manager, and they are his minions. Polanski had wished for their perfectly orchestrated robbery scenes to resemble a dance, and they do so perfectly, proving to be some of the most exciting, effortless moments in the film. Picking pockets is all that these children have to offer as they are all orphans, and however imperfect and self-interested he may be, Fagin is essentially father to them all.

Oliver Twist is an orphan who is raised by the system. When he is told that he is an orphan, he asks what an orphan is. He is admonished with the reminder that he has no mother or father and ought to say his prayers every night before he sleeps. He is innocent and good, and though he is brought into one difficult situation after another, he eventually rises to the top. He is expelled from a workhouse, sold for five pounds, taken pity upon so as not to be given to a soot-faced chimney sweeper, but instead sent to a kind, albeit weak, funeral home owner, Mr. Sowerberry. There, he is abused by Sowerberry's apprentice, Noah Claypole, and Sowerberry's rather sour wife. He then walks for seven days, until his shoes nearly fall off, to London where, half starved, he meets the Artful Dodger, who kindly steals him a meal and brings him home to Fagin and his brood. For a little while Oliver becomes a part of their family of misfits. Difficulties continue and even worsen, yet in the end, Oliver, who has fought to emerge triumphant, is taken in by the kind, upstanding, and wealthy Mr. Brownlow and is spared a doomed existence.

Many of the elements of Twist's life relate to Polanski's childhood. Just as Oliver works in the workhouse untying yarn, Polanski also worked in a factory. Having lived the life of an orphan for years during and immediately following the war, Polanski was sure he could relate to Oliver's character. And just as Polanski often depended upon the kindness of strangers (such as the peasants Buchala in Wysoka), Oliver is rescued more than once. First, there is the old woman who takes him into her home after he has fainted on the road. She feeds him and lets him sleep in a stuffed chair by the fire, fretting over how "a little mite" will continue to survive. Then there are the Artful Dodger, Fagin, and finally, Mr. Brownlow, who can offer Oliver a safe life and a real home. Just like Johnny in *Odd Man Out*, who thrives upon the gestures of unknown citizens (often the weak and disenfranchised are more inclined to help), Oliver also finds his way because of others. In delving into the material of his childhood, Polanski has also entered into and embodied the theme of the fugitive—one that has fascinated him since he was a small child.

Though the concept of survival does permeate the film, it is Twist's success in escaping a seemingly doomed destiny that puts all other demons to rest. This is what makes *Oliver Twist* a fairy tale, the fact that at the end of the day everything is okay. There is a fluctuating movement from dark to light, which reigns triumphant in the end. Imagery is transformed from green/gray to color, as Oliver moves from enslavement to freedom.

A Victorian atmosphere is captured in *Oliver Twist*, where back alleys are just as crowded as the main streets, and it is here that much of the action of city life takes place. There is an untouchable quality projected by members of high society, and a layer of grime that covers everyone else. Much of this back alley activity (which includes Fagin's world) is conveyed in what resembles a sepia tone. Clever is the choice to project a greenish brown image rather than a gray one, for it evokes the light of an oil lamp, the browning of an ancient paper, the thick fog of London's pea-soupers (coal-smoke-saturated smog made famous in London). Heightening this atmosphere is the image of Fagin's boys, like little men, who hang around in the pubs and back alleys, smoking pipes and drinking. These boys who have hardened long before their time call to mind the effects of the war on many children who, while still walking around in tiny bodies, were already adults who'd experienced all the horrors of life. Perhaps Polanski is making a statement here, for even though everything works out for Oliver in the end, there is also the heavy conscience of what and whom he leaves behind.

Though Mr. Brownlow is a true figure of comfort and safety (which at times may be just as important to a child as love), it is Fagin who somehow captivates Oliver's heart. Even when Oliver is safe at home, resting in the garden of Mr. Brownlow's house, there is something that gnaws at him, a sense of duty and guilt. In a plot twist not explored by David Lean's film, Oliver implores Mr. Brownlow to bring him to Fagin, who is in prison, waiting to be hanged. It is as a result of his second chance, his purity and goodness, that he absolves Fagin of his wrongdoings.

In a story in which love often misses its mark and winds up disposed of into the gutter, just like Oliver and his fellow orphans, here it does not happen. Though Nancy may feel love for Bill Sykes, he is a man beyond repair, and he winds up killing her as retribution for her betrayal. Though Fagin may love his children, he loves his riches and his security more, and though the Artful Dodger may love Nancy, even if he feels himself a man, he is still a little boy. Yet when it comes to Oliver and Fagin, things are now different. For having succeeded in escaping fate, Oliver has touched Fagin's heart.

It is as if Oliver is the survivor and Fagin is left behind, for he stayed too long in a life of crime and greed, and he has no stroke of luck to set him free. Oliver goes to him out of compassion and the need to offer him comfort. He is aware that with a different turn of events he could have been Fagin himself. Even as a young boy, Oliver feels the weight of responsibility. This is one of the distinguishing marks of a survivor. Even through his madness of fever and regret, Fagin is lucid enough to recognize Oliver, to embrace him with thanks. Oliver, with tears running down his face, prays for Fagin's absolution.

Polanski's version of Oliver Twist holds certain visual similarities to the film by David Lean (such as the orphanage, or the bridge where Nancy meets with Mr. Brownlow—or the look of certain characters), yet it still manages to stand on its own. There is an atmosphere, a vapor that fills these back streets of London, only clearing when in the presence of Mr. Brownlow and his contemporaries. Though locations do conjure up images from David Lean's film, the grime and dark light of Polanski's colors shine through. His personal connection to the character of Twist brings an element of sympathy and delicacy not normally seen in Polanski's films. Perhaps this is a result of the intention of making a film for his children, but here we see a film made with an altogether different touch—one that we might not normally associate with Polanski. Gone is the intense perspective, the perception of being immersed in the story, and in its place is the sensation of a sculptor building a set for display. Still, even if there is not an immediate connection with Polanski's other films, there is a pleasure derived from being in the hands of an expert filmmaker, and watching a story that, though it touches upon difficult subjects, remains light, almost comical at times, as if the father is hesitating to really scare the child.

Dickensian circumstances of comfortable coincidence (such as Mr. Brownlow turning out to be loosely related to Oliver) were presented in the 1948 version and in the musical, yet they were removed by Polanski in order to make the story more believable to a modern audience. Efforts to avoid anti-Semitic stereotypes with regard to Fagin were also made, the result being a complex, sensitive portrayal by Ben Kingsley. The only glaring flaw comes in the soundtrack composed by Rachel Portman, which in its jaunty superficiality pales in comparison to Polanski's customarily evocative film scores. Critical reception to Polanski's *Oliver Twist* was generous in its praise of Polanski's ability to revive this classic, imbuing it with new color and life, rather than casting it further in the past. Though it would not make the same impact as *The Pianist*, Polanski had satisfied his desire to make a film in which his children could both participate (they both had cameo roles).

In examining the story of Oliver Twist, Polanski has revisited his childhood, and in Ben Kingsley's words, "was using his terrible pain to heal other people."[1] Only in his eighth decade, now a father and husband, has he found the professional and internal freedom that allow him to explore these themes in such a transparent light. As *Los Angeles Times* critic Carina Chocano observed, perhaps Polanski made Oliver Twist not only so that his children could watch one of his films, but because he "feels inspired by a need to tell them who he is." Still, one cannot quell the gnawing feeling that Polanski has yet to really place himself on the screen, for commonalities do not necessarily equal revelations. He says that he would rather know the story of the world than to understand the psychology of his own story, yet sometimes we, the audience, request a flickering of exposure in exchange for our total trust. Then again, Polanski is not the sort of director who relies upon the trust of his audience as a means of achieving his desired effect. Perhaps it would do his work harm for us to know him too well.

Polanski is currently working on a new film, *The Ghost*. Based on the novel of the same name by Robert Harris, *The Ghost* is the story of a former British prime minister who hires a ghostwriter to help write his memoirs after his previous helper has died. The story takes place in a secluded refuge by the sea (reminiscent of *Cul-de-Sac* and *Death and the Maiden*), and is to be a sexual-political thriller. Starring Ewan McGregor and Pierce Brosnan, the film is being shot at Studio Babelsberg and on location in Berlin. Robert Benmussa and Alain Sarde are producing once again. It is to be Polanski's 18th feature film.

His is the fast movement of a fugitive in flight, who, even though he has found home, continues to evade. Fully aware that any artist will eventually put himself into his work, he prefers to play with the artifice of the medium than concern himself with any verity. And yet, so much truth has emerged from his lens over the years. His was always the art of expressing longing, terror, and wonderful, comedic absurdity, and now that he has found home, a transition is taking place. As spry as he ever was, Polanski continues to work, drawn to the magic of filmmaking just as he was as a child, dreaming of owning an epidiascope. One can only wish that eventually all of these facets of distance and objectivity will meet with a personal touch, and for a moment, Polanski will pause to examine himself on the screen. It is not his method, though it may happen, for he is a bold and brilliant filmmaker, one who has fought and withstood the test of time.

Epilogue

In 2007 Polanski contributed to a series of 34 shorts titled *To Each His Own Cinema*, a project commissioned for the 60th anniversary of the Cannes Film Festival, which includes contributions from 25 countries. His segment was titled *Cinéma Érotique*. Never ceasing to be thrilled and inspired by the medium of film, Polanski is a persistent light in a business in which many stars shine only briefly. For more than half a century, he has provided his audiences with a wonderfully absurd and at times terrifying humor. Without directly throwing his hidden desires onto the screen or stumbling through a cinematic confession, Polanski has nevertheless revealed himself to be an individual who comprehends displacement and understands the root of longing.

Polanski has given the orphan and the stranger a voice, and if the sound of a scream as distinct as Trelkowski's is too much to handle, he asks that you cover your ears or look the other way. He has no reason to apologize. He gives these characters an opportunity to speak, sometimes inhabiting them from in front of the camera, such as in the case of *The Tenant*, or else from behind, stalking the protagonist, creating a third eye. He gives victims the opportunity to fight back, to persist in their survival. No matter how awkward and shameful their experience may appear, he invites you into the ugliness, exposing more and more until even the most grotesque of characterizations leads to a realization. If anything, everyone is in exile. It is the human condition, and so it is better to laugh and explore life than confine one's self to the shadows. Darkness is a very personal experience amplified by the imaginative mind. So many of Polanski's early works stem from this perception of life, and they are revolutionary in their execution of this theme.

As Polanski continues to bring his career into the twenty-first century, he remains a rare filmmaker with enough experience to have originally worked in black and white and today in color. Though he is a survivor, he is first and foremost an enjoyer of life who has followed his dreams wherever they took him. Looking at his life with the knowledge of the tremendous tragedies he has endured, one cannot help but emerge with a smile. For always he looks for a laugh, an imaginative glance. Watch him direct, and see him change many times. He transforms into an old lady, a laughing boy, a Nazi pulling the trigger on his revolver. He places himself inside the action, directing not only with his acute knowledge and sense of accuracy, but with his sense of play.

Prior to the release of *The Pianist*, Polanski sat for an interview with Charlie Rose, who asked him the question that seems to burn in many American's minds: Why has he not yet made a deal to return to the United States?

"Maybe that's what I am subconsciously looking for," he says. "Exile." Speaking with Rose about *Odd Man Out*, he comments upon the aesthetic and drama of the film, how it captivated his imagination so many years before, and how it still does today. "I always lived out of my country, out of the place," he says. "I always had some kind of nightmares . . . thinking I went where I'm not supposed to be."

Perhaps he has manufactured this idea of himself as an outlaw to feed to a curious public, or as a defense mechanism for what he cannot or does not choose to understand. Yet still it fits perfectly with his persona and his work. Just as he holds onto the Democritus quote, ready to throw it into an interview as an attempt to explain the unexplainable, exile is his crutch but also his point of connection to the outside world.

When asked to speak of his childhood to Rose, Polanski says, "Kids accept life as it is." Perhaps his hesitation to analyze himself stems from this acceptance, learned in childhood, yet carried on into adult life. Speaking of his childhood in *Cahiers du cinéma* in 1992, Polanski said that he "was an adult in a child's body, a hyphenated being, an "adult-child." There was nothing between the two, nothing you would usually associate with childhood, like an education or an upbringing." The flip side to this stunted/accelerated growth is that, even as an older man, Polanski has managed to retain some of the child, an attribute that contributes to the making of a great artist.

"Now when I have children, I relive it," Polanski continues in the interview with Rose. "Very often I think of myself and of my parents. I can somehow imagine them in the same situation. Imagine myself in the skin of my father during those times." In Paris, a place that he can at last call home, perhaps Polanski has begun to move out of exile into communion with his own history. And through his works, he touches eternity.

Afterword

Though this book ends on a positive note, the pervasive element of exile remains. I write this Afterword with the urgency that accompanies the suspense of not knowing. Polanski is once again in jail, in the hospital, behind a new kind of iron curtain, one of individual attack and persecution.

On September 26, 2009, Polanski was en route to a local film festival, where he was to receive a lifetime achievement award. He was arrested by Swiss police at the Zurich airport, in connection with the 1977 statutory rape case that led to his exile from the United States. He has since remained in prison, and is facing possible extradition to the United States.

Polanski is making headlines once again. He is at the mercy of the media and its trickle-down effect into public opinion, evoking outrage and sympathy. On one hand, the world's film community supports him, yet he is simultaneously considered a pedophile who deserves to be punished.

It is a difficult question, this coming to terms with Polanski's 1977 encounter with the adolescent Samantha Geimer and what it really means. It is particularly troubling for me as an admirer of Polanski's work, and as someone with compassion for the man whose childhood trauma and tragic history had a profound impact upon his life. It is impossible for me to assess his actions objectively, knowing that he undoubtedly broke American law by having sexual relations with a minor during a time and in a milieu in which this behavior, although illegal, was tacitly accepted in the prevailing culture of 1970s Hollywood. Were it not for his celebrity status, would Polanski even be in this position of public scrutiny?

The fact that Polanski's crime is a sexual one raises a myriad of questions and controversy because of the charged nature of taboo and titillation associated with his encounter with an adolescent. Though the question may be a moral one, this is not the only issue. Aside from legal discrepancies within the case, it becomes extremely challenging to disentangle facts from mythology.

In 2008 Polanski and his lawyers made an attempt to have the 1977 statutory rape charges dismissed by the state of California, though after some discussion and speculation, the request was denied because of his status as a fugitive, under the Fugitive Disentitlement Doctrine, which discourages a court from adjudicating a claim made by a fugitive. There is no knowing what is to come, but many believe that Polanski will be extradited to the United States and be forced to face a U.S. courtroom once again. Perhaps he isn't finished doing his time . . . perhaps there is a price he has yet to pay. What is it about this man that inspires such passionate feelings in a distant, unfamiliar public? Why does he shake people's sense of morality and inspire witch hunts over and over again? He is not a victim, as he uses his talent and life force to continue to make artistic contributions to the cinema, and thus to the world's perspective, yet it always comes back to this exile.

This is an afterthought that transforms into a labyrinth of questions from which the exit point, the light of day, is yet to be discovered. Borges advised always bearing to the left to find your way out of a labyrinth. Dear Polanski, if only it were that simple.

Filmography

Bicycle (**1955**). Written by: Roman Polanski; Director of Photography: Nikola Todoroff; Cast: Adam Fiut, Roman Polanski.

A Murder (**1957**). Running Time: 1 min; Written by: Roman Polanski; Director of Photography: Nikola Todoroff.

Teeth Smile (**1957**). Running Time: 2 min; Written by: Roman Polanski; Director of Photography: Henryk Kucharski; Cast: Nikola Todoroff.

Break Up the Dance (**1957**). Running Time: 8 min; Written by: Roman Polanski.

Two Men and a Wardrobe (**1958**). Running Time: 15 min; Studio: Panstwowa Wyzsza Szkola Filmowa; Written by: Roman Polanski; Director of Photography: Maciej Kijowski; Production Manager: Ryszard Barski; Original Music by: Krzysztof Komeda; Cast: Jakub Goldberg, Henryk Kluba.

The Lamp (**1959**). Running Time: 8 min; Studio: Panstwowa Wyzsza Szkola Filmowa; Written by: Roman Polanski; Director of Photography: Krzysztof Romanowski; Production Team: Adam Holender, Andrzej Kostenko, Vasil Mirchev;

When Angels Fall (**1959**). Running Time: 21 min; Studio: Panstwowa Wyzsza Szkola Filmowa; Director of Photography: Henryk Kucharski; Production Designer: Kazimierz Wisniak; Original Music by: Krzysztof Komeda; Cast: Barbara Lass, Roman Polanski, Henryk Kluba, Andrzej Kondratiuk.

The Fat and the Lean (**1961**). Running Time: 15 min; Studio: A. P. E. C.; Produced by: Roman Polanski, Jean-Pierre Rousseau; Directed by: Roman Polanski, Jean-Pierre Rousseau; Written by: Roman Polanski; Director of Photography: Jean-Michel Boussaguet; Production Management: Claude Joudioux; Original Music by: Krzysztof Komeda; Cast: Andrzej Katelbach, Roman Polanski.

Knife in the Water (**1962**). Running Time: 94 min; Studio: Zespol Filmowy "Kamera"; Produced by: Stanislaw Zylewicz; Written by: Jakub Goldberg, Roman Polanski, Jerzy Skolimowski; Original Music by: Krzysztof Komeda; Director of Photography: Jerzy Lipman; Film Editor: Halina Prugar-Ketling; Production Designer: Boleslaw Kamykowski; Cast: Leon Niemczyk, Jolanta Umecka, Zygmunt Malanowicz; Krystyna's voice: Anna Ciepielewska; Young Man's voice: Roman Polanski.

Mammals (**1962**). Running Time: 10 minutes; Producer: Wojtek Frykowski; Written by: Andrzej Kondratiuk, Roman Polanski; Original Music by: Krzysztof Komeda; Assistant to the Director: Andrzej Kostenko; Editors: Janina Niedzwiecka, Halina Prugar-Ketling; Cast: Henryk Kluba, Michal Zolnierkiewicz, Wojtek Frykowski (uncredited).

The Beautiful Swindlers (**1964**). Running Time: 108 minutes; Studio: Cesar Film Productie, Primex Films, Ulysse Productions; Produced by: Pierre Roustang; Written by: Gérard Brach, Roman Polanski; Director of Photography: Jerzy Lipman; Edited by: Hervé de Luze; Original Music by: Krzysztof Komeda; Cast: Nicole Hilartain aka Nicole Karen.

Repulsion (**1965**). Running Time: 105 min; Studio: Compton Films; Produced by: Michael Klinger, Tony Tenser, Gene Gutowski; Written by: Gérard Brach, Roman Polanski; Director of Photography: Gilbert Taylor; Editor: Alastair McIntyre; Art Direction By: Seamus Flannery; Sound Supervisor: Stephen Dalby; Original Music by: Chico Hamilton; Cast: Catherine Deneuve, Ian Hendry, John Fraser, Patrick Wymark, Yvonne Furneaux.

Cul-de-Sac (**1966**). Running Time: 113 min; Studio: Compton Films; Produced by: Gene Gutowski, Michael Klinger, Tony Tenser, Sam Waynberg; Written by: Gérard Brach, Roman Polanski; Director of Photography: Gilbert Taylor; Editor: Alastair McIntyre; Art Director: George Lack; Original Music by: Krzysztof Komeda; Cast: Donald Pleasence, Françoise Dorléac, Lionel Stander, Jack MacGowran, Ian Quarrier, Jacqueline Bisset.

The Fearless Vampire Killers (**1967**). Running Time: 108 min; Studio: Cadre Films; Produced by: Gene Gutowski, Martin Ransohoff; Written by: Gérard Brach, Roman Polanski; Director of Photography: Douglas Slocombe; Editor: Alastair McIntyre; Production Designer: Wilfred Shingleton; Sound: Lionel Selwyn, Len Shilton, George Stephenson; Original Music by: Krzysztof Komeda; Cast: Roman Polanski, Jack MacGowran, Alfie Bass, Jessie Robins, Sharon Tate, Ian Quarrier, Terry Downes.

Rosemary's Baby (**1968**). Running Time: 136 min; Studio: William Castle Productions; Produced by: William Castle, Dona Holloway; Written by: Ira Levin (book), Roman Polanski; Director of Photography: William A. Fraker; Editor: Sam O'Steen, Bob Wyman; Production Designer: Richard Sylbert; Music by: Krzysztof Komeda; Cast: Mia Farrow, John Cassavetes, Ruth

Gordon, Sidney Blackmer, Maurice Evans, Ralph Bellamy, Patsy Kelly, Elisha Cook.

The Tragedy of Macbeth (1971). Running Time: 140 min; Studio: Caliban Films; Produced by: Hugh M. Hefner, Andrew Braunsberg, Timothy Burrill, Victor Lownes; Screen Adaptation by: Roman Polanski, Kenneth Tynan; Director of Photography: Gilbert Taylor; Editor: Alastair McIntyre; Production Designer: Wilfred Shingleton; Sound Mixer: Simon Kaye; Original Music by: The Third Ear Band; Cast: Jon Finch, Francesca Annis, Martin Shaw, Nicholas Selby, John Stride, Stephan Chase, Paul Shelley, Terence Bayler.

Che? (1972). Running Time: 114 min; Studio: Compagnia Cinematografica Champion; Produced by: Carlo Ponti; Written by: Gérard Brach, Roman Polanski; Director of Photography: Marcello Gatti, Giuseppe Ruzzolini; Editor: Alastair McIntyre; Production Designer: Aurelio Crugnola; Sound: Fausto Ancillai, Bernard Bats; Original Music by: Claudio Gizzi; Cast: Marcello Mastroianni, Sydne Rome, Hugh Griffith, Henning Schluter, Roman Polanski.

Chinatown (1974). Running Time: 131 min; Studio: Paramount Pictures; Produced by: C. O. Erickson, Robert Evans; Written by: Robert Towne, Roman Polanski; Director of Photography: John A. Alonzo; Editor: Sam O'Steen; Production Designer: Richard Sylbert; Sound: Bob Cornett, Larry Jost; Original Music by: Jerry Goldsmith; Cast: Jack Nicholson, Faye Dunaway, John Huston, Perry Lopez, John Hillerman, Diane Ladd, Roman Polanski, Joe Mantell, Bruce Glover, James Hong.

The Tenant (1976). Running Time: 126 min; Studio: Marianne Productions; Produced by: Hercules Bellville, Andrew Braunsberg, Alain Sarde; Written by: Gérard Brach, Roman Polanski, Roland Topor (novel); Production Designer: Pierre Guffroy; Director of Photography: Sven Nykvist; Editor: Françoise Bonnot; Sound: Michèle Boëhm, Jean-Pierre Ruh; Original Music by: Philippe Sarde; Cast: Roman Polanski, Isabelle Adjani, Melvyn Douglas, Jo Van Fleet, Shelley Winters.

Tess (1979). Running Time: 190 min; Studio: Renn Productions; Produced by: Claude Berri, Timothy Burrill, Pierre Grunstein, Jean-Pierre Rassam; Written by: Gérard Brach, Roman Polanski, John Brownjohn; Director of Photography: Ghislain Cloquet, Geoffrey Unsworth; Production Designer: Pierre Guffroy; Editor: Alastair McIntyre, Tom Priestley; Sound: Hervé de Luze; Original Music by: Philippe Sarde; Cast: Nastassja Kinski, Leigh Lawson, Peter Firth, John Collin.

Pirates (1986). Running Time: 121 min; Studio: Accent Films; Produced by: Tarak Ben Ammar, Mark Lombardo, Thom Mount, Umberto Sambuco; Written by: Gérard Brach, John Brownjohn, Roman Polanski;

Director of Photography: Witold Sobocinski; Editor: Hervé de Luze, William Reynolds; Production Designer: Pierre Guffroy; Costume Designer: Anna Sheppard; Sound: Jean-Pierre Ruh; Original Music by: Philippe Sarde; Cast: Walter Matthau, Damien Thomas, Richard Pearson, Cris Campion, Charlotte Lewis.

Frantic (1988). Running Time: 120 min; Studio: Warner Bros. Pictures; Produced by: Tim Hampton, Thom Mount; Written by: Roman Polanski, Gérard Brach; Director of Photography: Witold Sobocinski; Editor: Sam O'Steen; Production Designer: Pierre Guffroy; Sound: Laurent Quaglio, Jean-Pierre Ruh, Jean Gouldier; Original Music by: Ennio Morricone; Cast: Harrison Ford, Emmanuelle Seigner, Betty Buckley, John Mahoney.

Bitter Moon (1992). Running Time: 139 min; Studio: Canal+; Producers: Robert Benmussa, Roman Polanski, Alain Sarde, Timothy Burrill; Written by: Gérard Brach, John Brownjohn, Jeff Gross, Roman Polanski; Director of Photography: Tonino Delli Colli; Editor: Hervé de Luze; Production Designer: Willy Holt, Gérard Viard; Sound: Daniel Brisseau, Laurent Quaglio, Roberto Garzelli, Bill Rowe, Ray Merrin; Original Music by: Vangelis; Cast: Peter Coyote, Emmanuelle Seigner, Hugh Grant, Kristin Scott Thomas, Victor Banerjee.

Death and the Maiden (1994). Running Time: 103 min; Studio: Canal+; Produced by: Jane Barclay, Ariel Dorfman, Sharon Harel, Josh Kramer, Thom Mount, Gladys Nederlander, Bonnie Timmermann; Written by: Rafael Yglesias, Ariel Dorfman; Director of Photography: Tonino Delli Colli; Editor: Hervé de Luze; Production Designer: Pierre Guffroy; Sound: Laurent Quaglio; Original Music by: Wojciech Kilar; Cast: Sigourney Weaver, Ben Kingsley, Stuart Wilson.

The Ninth Gate (1999). Running Time: 133 min; Studio: Araba Films; Produced by: Michel Cheyko, Wolfgang Glattes, Adam Kempton, Roman Polanski, Mark Allan, Antonio Cardenal, Inaki Nunez, Alain Vannier; Written by: John Brownjohn, Enrique Urbizu, Roman Polanski; Director of Photography: Darius Khondji; Editor: Hervé de Luze; Production Designer: Dean Tavoularis; Sound: Laurent Quaglio; Original Music by: Wojciech Kilar; Cast: Johnny Depp, Frank Langella, Lena Olin, Emmanuelle Seigner, Barbara Jefford.

The Pianist (2002). Running Time: 150 min; Studio: R.P. Productions; Produced by: Robert Benmussa, Alain Sarde, Roman Polanski, Timothy Burrill, Gene Gutowski, Henning Molfenter; Written by: Ronald Harwood; Director of Photography: Pawel Edelman; Editor: Hervé de Luze; Production Designer: Allan Starski; Sound: Jean-Marie Blondel, Alexandre Widmer; Original Music by: Wojciech Kilar; Cast: Adrien Brody, Thomas Kretschmann, Frank Finlay, Maureen Lipman, Emilia Fox, Ed Stoppard.

Oliver Twist **(2005).** Running Time: 130 min; Studio: R.P. Productions; Produced by: Robert Benmussa, Timothy Burrill, Petr Moravec, Roman Polanski, Alain Sarde, Michael Schwarz; Written by: Ronald Harwood; Director of Photography: Pawel Edelman; Editor: Hervé de Luze; Production Designer: Allan Starski; Sound: Jean Goudier; Original Music by: Rachel Portman; Cast: Ben Kingsley, Barney Clark, Jamie Foreman, Harry Eden, Leanne Rowe, Edward Hardwicke.

Cinéma Érotique **(2007).** Running Time: 3 min; Studio: Cannes Film Festival; Produced by: Robert Benmussa, Roman Polanski, Alain Sarde.

Notes

INTRODUCTION

1. Ronald Harwood is a South African playwright and screenwriter.
2. A quote taken from the article "Waiting to Come in from the Cold" by Vanessa Thorpe printed in *The Observer*, December 7, 2008.
3. Sir Carol Reed (1906–1976) was a British filmmaker responsible for *Odd Man Out* (1947), *The Third Man* (1949) and *Oliver!* For which he won an Academy Award for Best Director in 1968.
4. James Mason was an Academy Award-nominated actor who played in films such as *A Star is Born* (1954), *North by Northwest* (1959) and *Lolita* (1962).
5. Fritz Lang was an Austrian Film Director known for his mastery of German Expressionism, best known for films *Metropolis* (1927) and *M* (1931).
6. Otto Preminger was an Academy Award-nominated, Austrian-born film director, best known for *Laura* (1944), *Fallen Angel* (1945) and *The Man with the Golden Arm* (1955).
7. Douglas Sirk was a German filmmaker known for making colorful melodramas specific to the confines of American Life in the 1950's, such as *All that Heaven Allows* (1955) and *Imitation of Life* (1959).
8. *Cahiers du cinéma* is a seminal film magazine, which was created in part by film theoretician André Bazin and which acted as a springboard for the careers of Jean-Luc Godard , François Truffaut and many others.
9. Charlie Rose is an Emmy Award-winning television journalist and host of "The Charlie Rose show."

CHAPTER 1

1. The Treaty of Versailles was a peace treaty signed on June 28, 1919, at the end of World War I intended to establish peace within Europe. It required Germany to make territorial concessions, and some believe its terms contributed to the start of World War II.
2. *A Story of Survival: Behind the Scenes of* The Pianist (2003), a DVD extra documentary about Roman Polanski's life and the making of *The Pianist*.
3. Ibid.

4. Kapo were prisoners who worked within Nazi concentration camps and were subsequently awarded privileges that other prisoners were not.

5. Stalinism refers to the politics of the Soviet Union under Joseph Stalin, who used oppressive methods (including spying, propaganda, limited rights, and virtual dictatorship) to achieve control during his years of leadership, from 1928 to 1953.

6. Vladimir Lenin (1870–1924) was an intellectual, a revolutionary, a powerful activist, and leader of the Soviet Union. He was also a contributor to Marxist theory, his theories known as Leninism.

7. Marxist principles relate to Marxism, a concept of social revolution developed by Karl Marx and Friedrich Engels, who cowrote *The Communist Manifesto* in 1848, which in its purest form attacks capitalism and calls for equality of the working class (or proletariat) and mobilization.

8. Wladyslaw Gomulka was the Polish Communist Party secretary from 1956 to 1970. Under his power, political confines weakened, although he was overthrown following shipyard strikes.

9. Cannes Film Festival, founded in 1946, is one of the most prestigious film festivals in the world.

10. Brigitte Bardot is a French film star who reached the peak of her success in the 1950s and 1960s, starring in films such as *And God Created Woman* (1956) and *Contempt* (1963). She also collaborated with French musician Serge Gainsbourg. She was worshiped for her beauty and sex appeal, which was referenced in songs and immortalized in sculpture.

11. David Lynch is an American director of surreal films such as *Blue Velvet* (1986) and *Mulholland Drive* (2001).

12. Zbigniew Cybulski was the star of Andrzej Wajda's film *Ashes and Diamonds* (1958), which inspired a generation of Poles. Handsome and captivating, often compared to James Dean, he died at the age of 39 while trying to catch a moving train. The confusion caused by his death was dealt with in Wajda's 1968 film, *Everything for Sale*, which starred Andrzej Lapicki and Elzbieta Czyzewska.

CHAPTER 2

1. Jerzy Skolimowski is a graduate of the Polish film school Lodz, a writer, actor, and film director of *Hands Up!* (1967), *The Menacing Eye* (1960), and *Success Is the Best Revenge* (1984). His father was a member of the Polish resistance and killed by the Nazis, and his mother helped a Jewish family by hiding them in her home. He has also been a boxer and poet.

2. "The Method" is a style of acting derived from Constantin Stanislavski's system, which sought truth in performance and placed emphasis on emotional and sense memory. Lee Strasberg and Stella Adler developed this technique in the United States, and it was most famously taught at the Actors Studio in New York City, which boasted students Marlon Brando, James Dean, Paul Newman, and countless other talented actors.

CHAPTER 3

1. Gillo Pontecorvo was an Italian filmmaker who made *The Battle of Algiers* (1965), which was nominated for three Academy Awards; *Kapò* (1959); and *Burn!* (1969).

2. Max Ernst was an artist who engaged in the surrealist and Dada movements. He lived and worked in Germany, France, and the U.S. He died in 1976.

3. Federico Fellini was an Italian director who is considered to be one of the greatest of his time. He was the creator of groundbreaking works like *8 ½* (1963), *Juliet of the Spirits* (1965) and *Satyricon* (1969), and heartbreaking films such as *Nights of Cabiria* (1957) and *I Vitelloni* (1953). His films received multiple awards and he won an honorary Oscar for lifetime achievement in 1992.

4. Giulietta Masina was the wife of Federico Fellini and the star of many of his films (*La Strada* [1954], *Nights of Cabiria* [1957], and *Juliet of the Spirits* [1965], among others). She was a character actress with a tremendous capacity to convey humor and emotion.

5. Catherine Deneuve is an Academy Award–nominated French actress who became a star after *The Umbrellas of Cherbourg* (1964) and *Belle de Jour* (1967). She has continued to work consistently, starring in films by François Truffaut, Lars Von Trier, and many others. She is also known for her beauty and sense of style.

6. François Dorléac was the beautiful older sister of Catherine Deneuve, who costarred in *The Young Girls of Rochefort* (1967). She died in a car accident at the age of 25.

7. Donald Pleasence was an English actor revered for his talent. He performed in *The Great Escape* (1963), *You Only Live Twice* (1967), and countless other films.

8. Lionel Stander was an actor from the Bronx, known for his gravelly voice and rough exterior. He was in *Mr. Deeds Goes to Town* (1936), *Meet Nero Wolfe* (1936), and *A Star Is Born* (1937). He was also known for his work in television and radio. Accused by the U.S. House Un-American Activities Committee of having communist sympathies, he was blacklisted. He left America to work in Europe before eventually returning to the United States.

9. Jack MacGowran was an Irish actor who worked in both theater and film, and he was beloved by Beckett. He played in films such as *The Quiet Man* (1952), *Tom Jones* (1963) and *Doctor Zhivago* (1965). He died in New York at the age of 54.

10. *The Kid Stays in the Picture* (2002) is a documentary about Robert Evans, directed by Nanette Burstein and Brett Morgen.

CHAPTER 4

1. Gloria Steinem is an American journalist and feminist who is famous for her social activism.

2. John Cassavetes was an American method actor and filmmaker. He is considered by some to be the first independent filmmaker. He is best known for his collaborations with his wife, actress Gena Rowlands, on films such as *Faces* (1968) and *A Woman under the Influence* (1974).

3. Sam O'Steen was an American film editor known for his work on *Who's Afraid of Virginia Woolf?* (1966), *The Graduate* (1967), *Chinatown* (1974), and *Postcards from the Edge* (1990).

CHAPTER 5

1. Peter Sellers was an Academy Award–nominated British actor and comedian, famous for his work in *The Pink Panther* (1963), *Dr. Strangelove* (1964), *Lolita* (1962), and *Being There* (1979).
2. Bruce Lee was a martial artist, philosopher, instructor, martial arts actor, film director, and screenwriter. Lee played in many films in Hong Kong, eventually achieving stardom in the United States with *Enter the Dragon* (1973). Lee died just weeks before the film's release. He founded the Jeet Kune Do combat form.
3. Quote extracted from a British publicity video.
4. Milos Foreman is a Czech filmmaker who, since the 1970s has worked primarily in the U.S. He is best known for his films *One Flew over the Cuckoo's Nest* (1975), *Hair* (1979), and *Amadeus* (1984).
5. Sandro Botticelli was an Italian painter of the Renaissance period, known for his works *Primavera* (1482) and *The Birth of Venus* (1486).
6. The Manson Family was a hippie cult led by Charles Manson, who instigated a killing spree in California in the late 1960s.
7. Susan Atkins is a convicted murderer. She was a member of the Manson family, and was involved in multiple murders, including those of Sharon Tate, Jay Sebring, Wojtek Frykowski, Abigail Folger, and Steve Parent on Cielo Drive.
8. Reuters, 2005.
9. Marcello Mastroianni was an Italian actor and leading man known for his good looks and casual charm. He starred in films such as *Divorce, Italian Style* (1961) and *8½* (1962). His film career extended from 1939 to 1997. He died on September 24, 2009

CHAPTER 6

1. This quote is taken from the *Chinatown* DVD extra, *Chinatown: The Beginning and the End* (2007) by Laurent Bouzereau.
2. Raymond Chandler was an American writer of stylish crime novels who created the detective character, Philip Marlowe. In 1939, he published *The Big Sleep*, and in 1946, he wrote the screenplay for *The Blue Dahlia*. He also cowrote the scripts for *Strangers on a Train* (1951) and *Double Indemnity* (1944). He wrote *The Long Goodbye* (1954).
3. Anthea Sylbert was a costume designer known for such films as *The Last Tycoon* (1976), *Shampoo* (1975), and *Carnal Knowledge* (1971).
4. *Bonnie and Clyde* (1967) is a film by Arthur Penn starring Faye Dunaway, Warren Beatty, Gene Hackman, and Estelle Parsons. It follows the adventures of notorious bank robbers during the Depression.
5. This quote is taken from "On Refining Story: A Conversation with Robert Towne" from the American Film Institute.

CHAPTER 7

1. Ingmar Bergman was a celebrated Swedish film director, revered by many filmmakers today. He is best known for his films *The Seventh Seal* (1957),

Wild Strawberries (1957), *The Virgin Spring* (1960), and *Cries and Whispers* (1972).

2. *Light Keeps Me Company* is a documentary about cinematographer Sven Nykvist that was made by his son, Carl-Gustav Nykvist, in 2000.

3. Isabelle Adjani is a French actress of German and Algerian descent. She is known for her extraordinary beauty and talent, having starred in François Truffaut's *The Story of Adèle H* (1975), *Camille Claudel* (1988), and *Queen Margot* (1994). She has been nominated for two Academy Awards and has won several prestigious acting awards in France.

4. Melvyn Douglas was an American actor who performed in many American Classics, including *Ninotchka* (1939), *Mr. Blandings Builds His Dream House* (1948), and *Being There* (1979). He won two Academy Awards and was nominated for three.

5. Shelley Winters was an American actress known for her work in *The Night of the Hunter* (1955), *The Diary of Anne Frank* (1959), *Lolita* (1962) and *Alfie* (1966). She won two Academy Awards and was nominated for four.

6. Julia Kristeva is a Bulgarian born philosopher, critic, psychoanalyst, feminist, novelist and professor of linguistics. She lives and works in France.

7. Klaus Kinski was a German actor who performed in numerous films, yet he is most famous for his work with director Werner Herzog in films such as *Aguirre: The Wrath of God* (1972) and *Fitzcarraldo* (1982).

CHAPTER 8

1. *Apocalypse Now* (1979) is a film about the Vietnam War, based on the Joseph Conrad novella *Heart of Darkness*. Directed by Francis Ford Coppola and starring Martin Sheen and Marlon Brando, it is an intense investigation of the disintegration of self, experienced during war. It won two Academy Awards, three Golden Globe awards, and the Cannes Palme d'Or.

CHAPTER 9

1. Lech Walesa was a Polish politician and activist who cofounded Solidarity, Poland's first independent trade union, which began a great political movement in Poland in 1980. He won a Nobel Peace Prize in 1983 and was Polish president from 1990 to 1995.

2. Walter Matthau was an Academy Award–winning actor and comedian who starred in *The Odd Couple* (1968), *Hello, Dolly!* (1969), *The Bad News Bears* (1976), and countless other films.

3. Vladimir Nabokov was a Russian-American writer famous for writing exquisitely in English and Russian, and who immortalized his character Humbert Humbert in *Lolita* in 1955.

4. Gérard Brach was an integral part of Polanski's creative process for many years, and at times he seemed to appear as an alter ego of sorts. Brach was a writer in his own right, working with directors other than Polanski (in particular, Claude Berri and Jean-Jacques Annaud), even directing his own film, *Le bateau sur l'herbe*, in 1971. Late in his life, Brach became a recluse, and he died in 2006 from cancer.

CHAPTER 10

1. Franz Schubert was an Austrian composer who lived from 1797 to 1828. He wrote nine symphonies, opera and chamber music, and is regarded as one of the great Western composers of his time.
2. Friedrich Nietzsche was a German philosopher and writer of *Human, All Too Human*, which was published in 1878, and *The Gay Science*, published in 1882, among many other groundbreaking works. He suffered a mental breakdown and died at the age of 55.
3. A MacGuffin is a term made popular by filmmaker Alfred Hitchcock to describe an element of the plot that initially drives the story, yet often proves to be secondary or even meaningless to the story's development and outcome.
4. Cary Grant was a British actor who got his start in the Bob Pender stage troupe in England, with whom he traveled to the states. He became a film star in Hollywood and was known for his charm and good looks. He starred in *Blonde Venus* (1932), *The Philadelphia Story* (1940), *Notorious* (1946), and many other films ranging from screwball comedy to Hitchcock mystery.
5. *How to Win Friends and Influence People* (published by Simon & Schuster) was a best-selling book written by Dale Carnegie in 1936; it gives helpful tips for interpersonal relationships. It was one of the first best-selling self-help books written, and it continues to sell today.

CHAPTER 11

1. This quote is taken from the *The Pianist* DVD Extra, *A Story of Survival*.
2. Ibid.
3. Frederic Chopin was a Polish-born composer who lived and worked in France, and he was known for his romantic compositions, mostly written for the solo piano. He had a love affair with French writer George Sand and died in 1849, at the age of 39. Though his adult life was spent in Paris, his work is treasured in Poland. His heart is preserved within a pillar of the Holy Cross Church in Warsaw.
4. This quote is taken from the *The Pianist* DVD Extra, *A Story of Survival*.
5. The Palme d'Or is the most coveted award for high achievement in cinema at the Cannes Film Festival in France.
6. Excerpt from article "Polanski's Belated Acceptance Speech" by Josh Grossberg, E! Online.

CHAPTER 12

1. This quote is taken from the *Oliver Twist* DVD Extra, *Twist by Polanski* (2006), by Laurent Bouzereau.

Bibliography

BOOKS

Borde, Raymond. Chaumeton, Étienne. *Panorama du Film Noir Américain*. Paris: Éditions de Minuit. 1955

Cronin. Paul. *Roman Polanski: Interviews*. Jackson, Mississippi. 2005. Includes: *Incest Is Interesting*. Der Spiegel, December 16,1974; *Interview with Roman Polanski*. Baecque, Antoine, and Jousse, Thierry. Cahiers du cinéma, May 1992; *Ben-Hur's Riding Crop*. Vachaud, Laurent. Positif, April 1995.

Kristeva, Julia. *Strangers to Ourselves*. New York: Columbia University Press, 1991.

Leaming, Barbara. *Polanski: The Filmmaker as Voyeur*. New York: Simon & Schuster, 1981.

Polanski, Roman. *Roman by Polanski*. New York: William Morrow and Company, Inc., 1984.

Naremore, James: *More Than Night: Film Noir in Its Contexts*. Berkeley and Los Angeles: University of California Press, 1998.

Salvato, Larry. Schaefer, Dennis: *Masters of Light: Conversations with Contemporary Cinematographers*. Berkeley, Los Angeles, London. University of California Press, 1984. Includes: Interview with William Fraker.

PERIODICALS

Canby, Vincent. "The Screen: Roman Polanski's 'The Tenant' Arrives," *The New York Times*. June 21, 1976. www.nytimes.com

Chocano, Carina. "Oliver Twist," *The Los Angeles Times*. September 23, 2005. www.losangelestimes.com

Ebert, Robert. "Bitter Moon," *Chicago Sun Times*. April 8, 1994. www.chicagosuntimes .com

Rayner, Jay. "They Didn't Shoot the Piano Player," March 21, 1999. guardian.co.uk.

Scott, A. O. "Film Review; Surviving the Warsaw Ghetto against Steep Odds" *The New York Times*. December 27, 2002. www.nytimes.com

Thorpe, Vanessa. "Waiting to Come in from the Cold," *The Observer*. December 7, 2005. www.observer.guardian.co.uk

Time Magazine. "Nothing but Bodies," August, 15 1969.

INTERNET

www.eonline.com. *Polanski's Belated Acceptance Speech.* Josh Grossberg. March 24, 2003.

www.youtube.com. *British Publicity Video for Polanski and Tate Wedding.* January 20, 1968.

www.fathom.com. *On Refining Story: A Conversation with Robert Towne.* Interview with the American Film Institute. 2002.

www.szpilman.net. *The Official Website for Wladyslaw Szpilman.*

TELEVISION

Charlie Rose interviews Roman Polanski. March 9, 2000.

Charlie Rose interviews Johnny Depp. May 11, 1998.

DVD

Chinatown: Filming by Laurent Bouzereau (2004). Paramount Home Entertainment.

Chinatown: The Beginning and The End by Laurent Bouzereau (2007). Paramount Home Entertainment.

Filming Tess by Laurent Bouzereau (2004). Columbia TriStar Home Entertainment.

Light Keeps Me Company by Carl-Gustaf Nykvist (2000). Beluga Film AB.

A Story of Survival: Behind the Scenes of "The Pianist" (2003).

The Kid Stays in the Picture by Nanette Burstein and Brett Morgen (2002). Highway Films.

The Ninth Gate: Commentary with Director Roman Polanski (1999).

Twist by Polanski by Laurent Bouzereau (2006). Sony Pictures.

Wanted and Desired by Marina Zenovich (2008). Antidote Films.

Index

About the Author

Julia Ain-Krupa was born to theatrical artists in Poland and was raised in New York City, where art played a great role in her life. She attended The School of Visual Arts and Columbia University, studying with film critics Andrew Sarris and David Sterritt. Ms. Ain-Krupa has worked in fashion, film, and television and recently held an Artist-in-Residence position at the Alexander W. Dreyfoos School of the Arts. She has made several short films, one of which was screened at the Angelica in 2005, and at a black-and-white festival at the Metropolitan Museum of Art in New York City. She has contributed to the quarterly magazine *Cinema Editor* and has recently adapted the Colette novel *Le blé en herbe* into a feature-length script.